WHAT OTHER PEOPLE THINK OF YOU

(IS NONE OF YOUR BUSINESS)

A guide to overcoming
bullying, depression, and lack of self-worth.

By J.D Moórea / Dan Shearin

jdmoorea.com

© Copyright 2023. All rights reserved. No part of this book may be reproduced or used in any manner without the prior written permission of the copyright owner, except for the use of brief quotations in a book review.

IBSN: 978-0-9872439-7-3

"There's not much difference between an auditorium full of cheering fans and a pack of angry haters screaming abuse at you.

They're both just making a lot of noise.

*How you take that noise is up to you.
Convince yourself that they're cheering for you.
If you can do that, then someday they will".*

– Jane Lynch (as Sue Silvester in Glee, Season 1, Episode 4)

TABLE OF CONTENTS

DEDICATION 1
PROLOGUE 2
ACKNOWLEDGMENTS 6
PREFACE 8
INTRODUCTION 11
Why write another book on this topic/story?..................... 11
CHAPTER ONE 22
Let's start at the very beginning.. 22
1973; A different world from today................................... 34
Sometimes, it's not always good that comes from my mouth........... 48
Back to 1990 and the Hello Dolly rehearsals 50
Life is what you make of it... 57
Viva Las Vegas... 60
What comes out of you when you're squeezed? 61
So this is what failure feels like?...................................... 63
CHAPTER TWO 69
The elephant in every room 69
Five-hundred, twenty-five-thousand, six-hundred minutes 73
You're not the first and you won't be the last 75
Why the fuck would you destroy a perfectly good bike? ... 76
I am not a fan of fake breasts! 79
My first brush with suicide... 82
Insecurities; If you disown them – they will own you....... 85
F.A.A.F.I.A.S.S (Funny As A Fart In A Space Suit) 89
"The Mile-High Club".. 91
Uncomplicate' shit 94
K.I.S.S (Keep it simple stupid) 96
I am perfect. We are all perfect; just the way we are 97

CHAPTER THREE 99
What other people think of you; is none of your business. 99
Negative versus positive 109
Is there a "P.R Anonymous"? 111
When you change how you look at things; the things that you look at change 114
Being right versus being happy 115

CHAPTER FOUR 120
From the Penthouse to the jailhouse 120
The deeper you go; the more juice you find in the fruit 128
Frank's way, Michael's way, and My Way. 131
The "M-word" 133
We are all human and we all make mistakes 135
The "rise and fall" of me? 141
A real sign from above 144

CHAPTER FIVE 148
The real law of attraction and how to use it 148
The most important "What if's" in life 148
The real secret 152
The real issue with domestic violence 155
My gift to you – the answer to stopping domestic violence 159
A different approach to Domestic Violence 163
Not all gifts can be taken back 166
The world and all of us are in perfect balance 168
Finding both sides of everything; leads to peace in anything. 172
For a season or a reason 176
Feed the mind, nourish the soul 182

CHAPTER SIX 185
The "Hero's Journey" 185
Sunday Night interview 196
Never trust the mainstream media 203
My real message; that you never saw 205
Who is the real stalker? 208

More about "The list" 209
Does God laugh at you too? 215
The bigger the opponent, the greater the hero 220
The greatest of lessons are found in the simplest of places 221
Being chosen is a gift 222

CONCLUSION 226

Don't stop believing 226
Loving thyself 230
Lessons from Ed Shearin (not Sheeran) 234
The path to forgiveness starts with you 236
I'm sorry! | Please forgive me! | Thank you! | I love you! 240
A million dreams 241
Life is always happening for you; not to you 245
A new reason why 246
Breeana's legacy 249
The final word 251
Recommended reading 255
Recommended authors 255

DEDICATION

This book is dedicated to any young girl or boy / man or woman who has felt unworthy. Any person of any race, gender, sexual orientation or religious belief who has been discriminated against. Anyone with a physical or mental disability who has been teased and finally, anyone who suffered at the hands of a bully just because you were "different".

"No matter what you have done or not done, you are worthy of love"
– Dr John Demartini

"The more critics you have, the closer you are to your true purpose"
– J.D Moórea

PROLOGUE

When trying to fit everything that I wanted to say into this book, I faced the dilemma of how to have two prefaces. I had two different things that I wanted to convey, but how to squeeze them both into one preface didn't make sense.

Even though I've written six books and three feature-length screenplays, I am aware enough to realize that I still know very little about writing compared to what is known. That said, while writing this book, I discovered that a preface and a prologue are two different things. A preface is how an author conceived and wrote a book, while a prologue sets the scene for the story to come.

When learning this, I was instantly taken back to the prologue of the musical Westside Story where I played the character of "Action". The prologue sets the musical up by illustrating the conflict between the jets and the sharks in the upper West side of Manhattan in the 1950s.

Without the prologue, the audience may not understand certain elements of the drama that unfolds for the rest of the musical. In this prologue, even though it may seem abstract, I hope that it will assist in helping you to understand the overall story that I am wishing to convey in this book; so here goes.

We've all played that hypothetical game where we ask each other who we would invite to a dinner party if we could invite anyone; dead or alive. Over the years I've had various ideas regarding my dinner guests. These include my mentor Tony Robbins, Mother Teresa, Oprah, Nelson Mandela, Jesus Christ, Jennifer Love Hewitt (Don't judge me), and Don Bradman.

It was only recently that I settled on three women who I have been inexplicably drawn to at various stages of my life. Now. Before anyone thinks I'm cold-hearted for not wanting to invite my mother who passed away in 1999, I'd prefer to be with her one on one, to not miss a moment of my time with her, talking to anyone else.

PROLOGUE

While my first dinner guest would be easy for anyone to guess; Breeana Robinson, I would bet my life on no one guessing who the other two were. The other two women share something that I too have experienced and while our individual circumstances are all different, we all share a common "enemy" and a unique feeling that very few people in the world have been through.

Even though I have never met these two ladies, by way of six degrees of separation and our biggest challenges in each of our lives, these women feel closer to me than one would expect.

One is a lady whose story caught my attention as a six-year-old and the other has captivated me as an adult. Both of these women have had their lives turned upside down and scrutinized within an inch of their lives as their stories played out in the public eye.

While the media, the courts, and every Tom, Dick, and Harry have voiced their opinions on these two ladies' innocence or guilt, I have never had an opinion on them either way.

For me, their cases were manipulated by the media and conducted in a way that the real truth may never truly be known by anyone; other than them. This is what fascinated me long before my own similar story played out in the public eye.

Despite extensive court cases and so much evidence being sifted through, no one can say one hundred percent what the truth is in these cases; except for these two ladies.

This is why I would invite these two ladies to my hypothetical dinner party because I can empathise with them and truly know what they have been through. I also know that they too can understand what I have been through; unlike anyone else in the world.

I don't care if they are innocent or guilty and I wouldn't even ask. I'd just love to say that I understand them both and I have great admiration for them and what they have endured during their lives.

You see, just like them in their situations, I am the only person in the world who knows one hundred percent what happened to Breeana Robinson. The media can speculate, so-called witnesses can say what they want and anyone else can have their opinion. Even the courts can rule on my case, but at the end of the day, I am the only one who truly knows. That in itself is an incredibly heavy burden to bear.

The reason I would want Breeana to be at my hypothetical dinner party is that I would love for her to see how two incredible women have risen above some seemingly insurmountable odds and come out the other side. I think that this is the main reason why Breeana is not here today.

She was not able to find a role model who could show her that no matter what life threw at her, she could get through it. Her mother was hardly a role model in this way, or in the way she lived, how she treated herself and her health, or how she treated other people.

On the other hand, these two women I am about to mention are an inspiration to women when it comes to how you should never give up. They don't claim to be victims and no matter what, they have stayed true to their beliefs.

If you haven't guessed who my other two dinner guests would be, I am talking about Lindy Chamberlain and Schapelle Corby. Everyone has an opinion on their cases and even though both were convicted (and Lindy later acquitted), I honestly don't believe anyone can judge them beyond any doubt.

These ladies have shown that while it is not always easy, as long as you know in your heart what the truth is, that is all that truly matters.

If you're wondering how I am even remotely connected to these two women; here's how. In 2004, my brief acting career began with the role of a 1980's Northern Territory Cop in "Through my eyes" the Lindy Chamberlain story. You probably didn't see me as we sat around in the background eating donuts and I had a hairstyle that was for the era and not my usual style.

As for Schapelle; my ex-sister-in-law who has lived in Bali since 2003 was apparently at one time Mercedes Corby's publicist when the shit hit the fan for Schapelle. I no longer have contact with my ex-sister-in-law but in 2010 when I visited Bali with my sister, the topic came up.

Even before my story was manipulated by the media, the stories of these ladies never sat comfortably with me. I had always suspended my judgement due to neither case really passing the "sniff test".

It has always been the case with humans that we make a decision and then search for confirmation bias to back our judgements up. Most people who thought Lindy and Schapelle were guilty could always find evidence to back up their argument, but so could those who believed that these women were innocent.

For me, too many things just didn't make sense. Thankfully for Lindy, we live in a country where if there is reasonable doubt then you can't be convicted. Unfortunately for Schapelle, Indonesia runs its judicial system very differently from Australia.

PROLOGUE

This is not to say that I think she is innocent. It is simply my thoughts that despite her conviction, only Schapelle knows the absolute truth. It is not my place to judge either of them, because at the end of the day, I can't say one hundred percent either way; only they can.

I have never felt the need to judge either of these ladies, whereas most people have. Far too often, people jump to judgements based on their own issues and insecurities, rather than the facts.

I'm sure many have judged me in the same way, but as per the Hebrew meaning of my birth name Daniel, "God is my judge", and no one else. As far as I am concerned, that is the only judgement I am at all concerned with.

To get to the crux of this little ditty, while I have never met these two ladies, I have no doubt that regardless of what they had read or heard about me, I am certain that neither of them would judge me.

Lindy and Schapelle know firsthand what it is like to see your life misrepresented by the media and by uneducated people in general. They have seen the truth manipulated for the sake of a story and they have risen above it, despite countless obstacles.

People often say, "There is always someone worse off than you". This may be the case when you compare what Lindy and Schapelle went through compared to me, but I would rather put a different spin on it.

For me, they have forged a path and shown me that if they can somehow find the light at the end of the ever-darkening tunnel, then so can I.

Oh, and for the record, Schapelle's homecoming where she taught the entire media of Australia how stupid they all were by switching flights and running decoy cars was fucking brilliant. Well done Schapelle.

The thing I admire and have learnt most from these two women is the "me against the rest of the world" mentality that they both have. For all intents and purposes, they fought their battles on their own, against corrupt authorities and manipulative media.

They were both extremely brave in standing tall against the system, regardless of the toll it might have taken on them physically, emotionally, and mentally. It is this kind of strength that I have drawn on many times throughout my own battle against the system.

ACKNOWLEDGMENTS

Firstly, to those members of my family who have stood behind me throughout some of the toughest times that anyone could experience. You may not have always agreed with me or my actions, but your support never waned; especially when it really mattered.

To the group of people who I proudly call friends these days. While many of my so-called friends turned their back on me and showed their true colours and intentions, it was when I was down and out that my true friends stood up.

I don't need to name you here, because you know who you are, and let's be honest, naming you would expose you to many ill-informed haters who need to attack others to make themselves feel better.

I may not have thousands of "Facebook friends" anymore, but the friends that I have are the most incredible rock that anyone could wish for. You picked me up and dusted me off when I felt like I couldn't get up off the canvas. For this, I am forever grateful.

Speaking of haters. As funny as it may sound, I want to thank you too. This includes internet trolls, misinformed people in the street, Breeana's family, and the misleading media, all of which have attacked, belittled, defamed, and harassed me to the point that would have broken most humans. If it wasn't for you, I would not have realised how strong I could be and how far I could be stretched on my journey to becoming the person I am today.

While you were certainly misguided, you have been worthy adversaries and have forced me to lift my game so far as becoming stronger, wiser, and better in knowing who I am and what I am worth.

To God; It goes without saying that there were many occasions when you came good on your promise (As per the poem "Footprints in the sand") where I was unable to walk through life and at which point you carried me until I was able to resume the journey myself.

ACKNOWLEDGMENTS

I no longer walk alone, and while it hasn't always felt pleasant, it has been my pleasure to serve you in bringing your message to the world through me.

Finally, to my legal team over the last decade. Chris Hannay, Mark Donnelly, Angus Edwards, Bob Butler, and Chris' team at Hannay Lawyers. Not only have you been the best legal representation I could ask for, but each one of you has become close personal friends.

You have worked your butts off both in and out of court and have rescued me legally and emotionally on more occasions than I care to admit.

Chris, while your legal advice has been second to none, it has been your emotional support at any time of the day or night and even on weekends that have been most valuable as I dealt with this unsavoury issue. For that, I am eternally grateful.

PREFACE

In late June 2019, I had been on bail for murder for almost five months and by this stage, my sixth book was beginning to take shape. Like any author, songwriter, entrepreneur, or businessman, I had moments where I questioned if this project was something I truly wanted to do.

I had no doubt that I should do this, and I never questioned my role as a messenger for the good Lord, however, as is the case when any mammoth task is begun, I wondered if it was worth all the effort.

Besides the fact that books were no longer a cash cow for authors since anyone can self-publish, I also faced several adversaries in getting the wider public to even see this book.

I had no doubt that the media and so-called armchair critics would attempt to discredit the content and myself, but I also faced an army of ex-girlfriends, unknown disgruntled women, and anyone who was simply looking for a reason to be offended or outraged so they could justify their outward anger; with me being the random target.

By this stage, my life had returned to some sort of normality, despite me wearing a GPS tracker, having to report to the Police daily and the Police visiting my house randomly pretending to be checking on my welfare and feigning concern for my state of mind.

I had grown accustomed to the quiet life and wasn't sure I wanted to willingly thrust myself back into the public firing line more than the desperate media searching for some sort of a story would eventually do.

The fact that I was one man facing many, was only a minor deterrent as I knew that some of the greatest battles in history were where smaller contingents overcame insurmountable odds to become victorious. I mean, that's the premise of all great movies, where the hero battles against the darkest of forces.

More about that in a later chapter. I knew that attempting to take on the ever-increasing army of haters head-on was akin to literary and personal suicide, so I drew on stories of victories where smarts outweighed bravery.

Even contemplating such a battle required bravery, but I figured that if I was going to achieve my ultimate goal of making sure that the truth about Breeana Robinson's death was finally revealed and to help anyone facing similar online bullying, then I needed to be more cunning than the Rats of Tobruk and bolder than William Wallace's men.

This meant that just like the Rats of Tobruk I had to make the enemy think that one thing was going on, while quietly conducting a counterattack unbeknownst to them.

Let me get this out of the way as early on as possible.

A lot of what I am going to write in this book is going to piss a lot of people off and for that, I must sincerely apologise for NOT GIVING A FUCK! Three of my literary/personal development heroes have similar outlooks in relation to their non-mainstream messages that they want the public to hear and I am no different.

Well before it was a best-seller, Mark Manson's book "The subtle art of not giving a fuck" was one of my top ten reads in a list of over fifteen hundred books that I have read in the past eight years.

Don Tolman, who exposed the misleading practices of the pharmaceutical industry famously comes on stage for his presentations and makes sure that the audience is under no illusion that he is about to piss them off by breaking all of the paradigms when it comes to how to live a healthy life and how drugs that are supposed to heal us, are actually making us sicker.

Finally, a man I have had many personal conversations with and who has read two of my books, Dr. John Demartini, who most notedly was a part of the movie "The Secret" is quoted as saying, "The more people you piss off, the closer you are to discovering your true self."

In all of these cases, these men have challenged what many believe to be true. They have faced criticism and backlash. Not because what they are saying is incorrect, but because most people believe what they are told and are too gullible to think logically about something, or God forbid; do some research on the topic. They think that if it isn't sprouted by the media, or a so-called expert (who incidentally often has a hidden agenda) then it can't be true.

Throughout this book, I will be posing some tough questions and putting forward some alternative thoughts on how things should be. I want this book to make you uncomfortable and even pissed off because most people don't have a clue when it comes to making their own decisions about things that are important to their lives. They would rather make excuses, blame someone else, and live in their comfort zone than take full responsibility for the quality of their lives.

I've long let go of my hatred of the media and the haters from Breeana's family. These days I see it as part of my growth and somewhat of a game. Not a game in the sense that I flippantly discard people's emotions or feelings, but in that, I don't put too much weight on the outcome or get too invested in the situation.

At the end of the day, it's all a matter of perception. Life and everything that happens is neither good nor bad, but rather it is only how we perceive it to be.

I truly believe this to be the case. So much so that the tagline for one of my feature-length screenplays is, "How we see life, depends on the type of lens we look through". I'll leave that for you to think about; both in the context of your own life and which screenplay it is a part of.

On that, as this story unfolds, perhaps there is more to this than meets the eye; or maybe there isn't. Is this book a decoy, or a prelude to something even bigger? Is the book a vile book by "The Devil" as Bree's Aunty calls me, or is it a piece of work that can help people overcome similar situations to what Breeana and myself have encountered and help to open people's eyes through an honest assessment of their own lives, which will in turn, lead to happiness?

Perhaps it is simply a prelude to something much bigger than any of us ever imagined. Remember; it is the space between the lines and the silence between the musical notes that makes a true work of art.

INTRODUCTION

WHY WRITE ANOTHER BOOK ON THIS TOPIC/STORY?

That is the question I am sure many people will ask when realising that I have written yet another tell-all book about Breeana Robinson's suicide, along with my protracted battle to clear my name. So let's address the first and most important reason.

Breeana Elaine Stewart Robinson killed herself!

That's it! She wasn't murdered. She didn't "die at the hands of a convicted text pest". She killed herself by throwing herself off the eleventh-floor balcony of the H^2O building in Southport, Australia. I know this may be incredibly hard to read for some people, but it has to be stated accurately for a reason.

Why am I being so brutally upfront and blunt about this? Because that is precisely what happened. For more than a decade everyone has either alleged something different or danced around the facts to avoid the brutal truth about Breeana's struggle and the struggle that tens of thousands of people face every day.

She didn't slip, fall, or get thrown. She climbed over the railing and jumped to her death to escape the pain that was inside of her.

Since Breeana killed herself in 2013, the suicide rate has been increasing; with slight exceptions in 2016 and following the COVID-19 pandemic.

AUSTRALIAN SUICIDE RATES (From A.B.S)

Year	Deaths
2012:	2,580
2013:	2,610
2014:	2,922
2015:	3,065
2016:	2,866
2017:	3,128
2018:	3,138
2019:	3,318
2020:	3,139
2021:	3,144

To make matters worse, for every death by suicide, it is estimated that as many as thirty people attempt to take their lives. That is close to 65,300 suicide attempts every year.

As a society, we have sugar-coated suicide or made it taboo to talk about, just like we did with domestic violence or an individual's sexual orientation for many years.

Thankfully where the latter are concerned we have embraced both and are working to remove the stigma of talking about or accepting either. As for Suicide, we're not there yet.

The only way to do this is to confront it and see it for what it is. A person who commits suicide kills themself. Plain and simple. It has taken me more than a decade to accept the harsh reality of this myself, so I understand that it is going to take time as a society to follow suit, but we have to start now if we hope to overcome this tragic loss of life.

I don't blame Breeana's family for not believing her death was suicide. No family wants to think that their spouse, child, or sibling is mentally ill or not strong enough to move beyond some form of depression. The mental stigma attached to suicide or depression is horrible. I have several friends who have lost a husband or wife to suicide and it took them forever to accept these facts.

This is one of the difficulties with diagnosing someone with depression or the possibility of committing suicide. Most suicidal people are very good at hiding it from their loved ones.

INTRODUCTION

Even the professionals tasked with diagnosing it have no clue (I mean that respectfully). Scanning for depression is nothing more than a questionnaire or a series of back-and-forth questions between practitioner and patient.

Therefore, I would hardly put faith in a professional to deem whether or not someone other than the patient themselves is "depressed". The only person who can categorically state if they are depressed is the patient.

Breeana never went to a doctor or psychologist about her battles and she was very good at putting on a happy face in front of her family and friends. I'm not sure why she trusted in me to disclose that she believed she was depressed to, but she did.

So why didn't I do more to help her? Well, just like her family, I did not believe she was depressed. She was a bubbly and happy young woman and I couldn't see it in her.

In hindsight, this is one of my few regrets in life; not taking her comments more seriously. I wish that I took more proactive steps to help her and to support her while arranging for her to seek professional help.

Why does someone commit suicide?

If I had the definitive answer to that, I'd be awarded some sort of genius prize and a bucket-load of money, but I don't. Having said that, there are many clues that I believe can help and several ideas that I wish to share in this book with the sole motivation of helping those suffering from mental illness overcome their demons, their adversaries, and their doubts so that they can be a survivor and not another statistic.

I don't need money. I don't want more fame. I've got money and had fame throughout my career and life; whether it be through my career successes, or via my infamy from being Breeana Robinson's much older boyfriend. The E-Book version of this book will be free and all profits from the paperback will be donated to charity.

My focus is to get this message to as many people as possible to save lives. Everything happens for a reason. The purpose of my life is to impact people positively, through the heartache of my past. I was handed this blessing to save other people's lives and thanks to the media, I now have the platform to do so.

In 2016 when I published "The Blame Game" under my original name; Dan Shearin, I thought that everything that needed to be told had been said and that no one was really interested in my story, or the story of my beautiful Breeanna.

As it turns out, I was completely wrong. Since publishing The Blame Game, the media, and Breeana's family have continued their relentless assault on me, and like my dogs with a bone; they won't let it go until there is nothing left to devour. The only difference between my dogs and the media / Breeana's family is that my dogs are relentless with both sides of the bone.

Despite my trying to bring the truth about Breeana's suicide to the public's attention, every attempt by myself to do so has been met with the same misleading information and blatant lies. I understand that the family doesn't want the truth to be published for fear of them looking as bad as they have portrayed me to be. I also know (as do most smart people) that the media never tell the whole story. They always manipulate the facts and rarely report the truth.

Why? Because the truth doesn't sell papers or advertising spots on primetime television during the news. Only bad news sells; not good news. For this to occur, we as a society need to be as stupid as we have been by inadvertently supporting the media in their misleading behaviour. If society was smarter they would stop buying papers and watching the news until the media learnt that they are harming people.

The biggest threat to life as we know it these days is not climate change. It is the media. They cause more harm to people's mental health than anything else we are subjected to in the world. The good news is that there is a way that all of us can combat this, and it's not that hard to do.

So why does Breeana's family not want the truth?

Just like the line in A Few Good Men, "They can't handle the truth." If they accepted the truth, they would no longer have someone to blame. God knows they would never blame themselves because that would mean taking a look in the mirror, and if they did that, I am certain that they would not like what they saw. They would also have to let go of the anger, resentment, and hatred that they have and which their family has leveled at each other for several years before they focussed on me. We all want an excuse for why we act the way we act, and this is their excuse for holding such anger in their souls.

Throughout the past decade, since the media first misled the public by publishing the first of many lies in the "Gold Coast Bullshittin" … (Did I misspell that), I keep getting told by the media that this is a "public interest story" and that is why they continually want to talk to me about it and air it regularly.

This claim by the media is interesting because now that the media claim that it is a public interest story, it allows me to tell my story without ramifications regarding the proceeds of crime laws.

You see, if I was to commit a crime, write a book, and sell copies, this would be considered proceeds of crime. However, because the media and Breeana's family have been so relentless and made it a "public interest story" I am simply telling that story, which is in the interest of the public.

When Breeana committed suicide at 21.50, on the 29th of January 2013, the last thing I wanted to do was write a book about it; let alone two. Both the media and Breeana's family have refused to accept the truth and let Breeana rest in peace so unfortunately for them, they have created this "loophole" themselves.

Having said that, it must be stated that there was no crime committed concerning this story, so the topic of proceeds of crime is inconsequential. The only crime that could be tied to any part of this was when I foolishly pleaded guilty to sending an offensive text message to Breeana before her death.

Other than that, I have of course been fully acquitted and can finally tell the truth about her death with the complete justification of the judicial system.

The interesting thing about that last sentence is that when a person is acquitted of a crime, they are never found "innocent". They are merely found "not guilty". While it may seem to be a distinction without a difference, this means that despite the person being wrongly dragged through the courts, and in some cases the public spotlight, they can never claim to be truly "innocent".

When I was first charged with murder I was fucking furious. While sitting in the watch house cell my mind was compiling all the things that I wanted to put into a book and not too many of them were useful or constructive.

As my life once again resembled some sort of normality after I was released on bail and began rebuilding my life emotionally, it dawned on me that these horrific circumstances that I had been thrust into were precisely what I needed to bring my message to so many more people than could have been imagined before the media shit storm that accompanied my arrest and charge.

This book, my previous book, or any subsequent interviews have never been about me clearing my name or telling my side of the story. All I have ever wanted to do was to give Breeana's family, her friends, my family and friends, and the public the facts relating to Breeana's death.

As it turned out, I now have a much bigger platform than I could ever have imagined at the time of her suicide. I have always believed that her death was the opportunity to bring the topic of suicide to light and to start a conversation on how to eliminate some of the ugliest parts of society today.

From the night Breeana killed herself, I felt that there was a much bigger reason for these circumstances happening. Bigger than me or Breeana and this has been my challenge over the last decade to discover what it was and to bring it forward so others could benefit from our story.

My aim in writing this book is to share my journey in the hope that you can draw some parallels to your own life, and hopefully benefit from my mistakes and triumphs. As I delve deeper than I have in any of my other books, I hope that you can relate and find the inspiration to overcome your challenges, online bullies, or lack of self-worth/depression.

As it has been pointed out in many media stories, online comments, and reviews of my past work, I am not a trained journalist, a "straight-A English student", or a brilliant wordsmith.

This is precisely why I have written eight books. The reason why so many people in the world are illiterate is that most people don't relate to the author. Far too many authors try to sound intelligent and that doesn't sit well with the average person. Sure, if you're writing a thesis then your audience (your professor) will get you. If you want people to relate to you, then you need to write completely differently.

I base my writing style on a conversation I had with the late, great Australian cricketer; Max Walker. I met Max when he was staying in the hotel I worked in and we shared a half-hour conversation about everything from cricket to life.

At the end of my chat with Max, he gave me a copy of one of his books. What I found when I read the book was that I could hear Max's voice in every sentence. The way he wrote was the way he spoke.

Max was a great storyteller and that storytelling shone through the pages of his books. This made reading his book so much more joyful.

INTRODUCTION

He wasn't trying to be fancy or impress his readers. There were no airs or graces. It was just Max telling stories. That is how I've tried to write my books.

I want anyone who reads them to feel like they are listening to me telling an animated story. My books are more conversational than correctly written or precisely punctuated. I swear, use slang and badly structured sentences, but that is what makes me just like you. Besides, I would not want to be referred to as a journalist.

I am an author; not a journalist!

The difference between an author and a journalist is that an author will never let their ego get in the way of the story. An author will sacrifice everything to ensure the story is as authentic as possible. The author puts the story before their own self-preservation. Most importantly though, a journalist tells someone else's story to make that person look bad, but an author dares to tell their own story regardless of how bad they may look.

In short, authors are self-effacing, while journalists are self-serving. Unlike a journalist, my goal is not to bring people down, scare them, or mislead them. My goal is to lift them up, empower them, and open their eyes to the truth and their own possibilities.

I think Kevin Bloody Wilson summed up journalists in his crass but correct song "That's what he really said" by singing, "Half of what you read is bull and the other half's all shit."

This book is a culmination of a decade of growth, learning, and thoughts all thrown into a book format. Life doesn't travel in a straight line and neither do our thoughts. This book is the same. I jump around from thought to thought. I detour and then swing back around to topics I touched on previously and occasionally repeat myself or seem to in order to make an important point.

A trait I learned while studying screenwriting was to foreshadow later events and drop little nuggets of information that may not make sense to the audience at the time, but later on create the "ah-ha" moment.

The book was largely written on my new iPhone that I had to buy when the police stole mine (Yes, they stole it, because it was illegal how they acquired it and they had no need to have it). Most of the paragraphs were written while walking my dogs, having a coffee, or driving; of course, I pulled over first Mr. Police Officer.

WHAT OTHER PEOPLE THINK OF YOU IS NONE OF YOUR BUSINESS

I'm a regular guy with a passion for life and a love of sharing stories, along with a desire to help people overcome their greatest challenges in life. I have achieved so many great things in life through persistence and determination. I have been to hell and back (Forgive me lord – that comment will make sense later), but to the displeasure of Breeana's family; I am still alive – and getting stronger by the day.

This story is not about me. It is about two things. The truth about Breeana's death and a journey that I feel compelled to share to save other people's lives. How can I save others' lives? Simple. We all go through tough times and on occasions, we've all felt like there was no way out.

It is through knowing that someone else has experienced similar challenges to ourselves and that they have overcome them that we can gain the strength to carry on.

I have no idea what challenges you face, or what heartaches you've been through, but my hallucination is that in most cases it's not as bad as watching the woman you love jump from an eleventh-story balcony, having your name disgraced around the world, and then being charged with her murder.

If it is, then I apologise, but I say this to make a point. We all experience tough times and at the time we go through them we think the world is going to end, but once the haze has cleared and we have the chance to put it into perspective, it may not be so bad after all.

I had a female friend who was moaning on social media a few days after Breeana died about her own life. Now, this person was a dear friend and I am by no means belittling her by mentioning this, but her post read, "Broke a nail getting ready, had a flat tyre, and spilled coffee on my top on the way to work. FML." (I'm sure you can work out what the "FML" stands for).

Upon reading this I smiled and posted the following comment, "Hey Bec. How about we swap lives?" I didn't mean this comment to be nasty in any way and she knew that. She also knew what I was going through and replied to my comment, "Hey Dan. Thank you so much for the massive dose of reality xx."

I mention this in conjunction with my earlier comment because we often get so caught up in our own world that we forget not only how good we have it, but that there is always someone worse off than us.

I want you to know that if I can overcome what I have, then you can overcome whatever challenges you are currently facing or will face in the future. Over the last eight years, I have read more than fifteen hundred books on human behaviour, finance, religion, and personal development; all since publishing The Blame Game.

When embarking on such a quest you can't help but have some of these thoughts and lessons rub off on you. I figured that if I learned one thing from each book then that's fifteen hundred things I now know, that I didn't previously.

As it turned out, it wasn't just the things that I learned from each book, but also the lessons in discipline and many areas of life that I have discovered that have brought me to a far different place physically, emotionally, and spiritually than I was in 2013 when Breeana died, or in 2016 when I published The Blame Game.

This is not to say I was wrong in what I wrote in The Blame Game. It is simply the case that I now have different information at my disposal which has allowed me to form a different opinion.

Only a fool would hold onto the same opinion for many years if different information is presented to them. There is nothing wrong with thinking a certain thing one day, and then knowing something different the next. It's called growth.

In many of the books that I read; I found the answers to various problems that I had in an area of my life. The answers came in the form of the discoveries of the author as they had encountered a similar problem and found a solution.

By them sharing their solution, I didn't have to go through the same trial and error or make the same mistakes they did. That is essentially why I am sharing my story with you.

I've always been one to bare my soul, sacrifice my dignity, and overshare for the benefit of others. That's what entertainers do. A dear Aussie friend, Anita, who is a huge star in London's Westend called me from London after reading "The Blame Game" and said, "Dan, why are you making yourself look so bad?"

I explained to Anita that while as entertainers, we are used to portraying ourselves in a certain light, there comes a time when the "stage mask" must come off and we need to put our own self-preservation and reputation second to the needs of the greater good. I told her that it was about the truth, not about me looking good.

Anyone who has read my other books knows a lot about me but even so, this book is going to shock even my most attentive readers and friends. I have no intention of holding back whatsoever because it is only through complete honesty and brutal analysis of our own actions that we find the deepest answers to the problems we face in life.

I do this in the hope that it will help people realise that we all have insecurities and by seeing what I have gone through, perhaps you too can step beyond your limiting beliefs, insecurities, and personal issues to stand tall and live your best life without fear or trepidation.

Besides, as a result of the media, any dignity or privacy that I may have had has been taken away, so why not just expose the rest of my flaws before they do? Just like Eminem's character in "8 Mile" did in his final rap battle, I am going to beat the media and my haters to the punch.

It's kind of also like Rebel Wilson's character (Fat Amy) in the movie Pitch Perfect when she says "I do it so twig bitches like you don't do it behind my back". I will get into that previous comment later in the book, but that is part of the answer to my own self-discovery and that which will also lead you to true happiness. I'll leave it there for now.

The above paragraphs are the long-winded answer as to why I wanted to write this book but really it comes down to a much shorter answer; to help others. If I can help just one person overcome their own depression or help someone to be strong enough to not cave into bullies, then my journey has been worthwhile, and Breeana's death was not in vain.

The original title of this book was "What other people think of me is none of my business", but as the book evolved the story became less about me and more about how my journey can help you.

As the original title suggests, I don't care what you think of me. I don't give a fuck what the media write or say about me and I honestly don't think about how anyone perceives me to be - and neither should you.

There is only one person, one voice, and one opinion that I am in any way concerned about; MINE! That is my lesson. Now flip that around and apply it to you and you have the new (current) title and the most important philosophy to help you live a happy, and purposeful life.

Once this book is published, I will pay no attention to what people think of it (whether good or bad), and even as I write it, I give no thought to contemplating whether or not the contents of this book will offend or upset anyone.

If you want to live a life that is bound by others' opinions then you may as well stop reading now. If, on the other hand, you want to free yourself from mainstream conformity that breeds insecurities in your life, then perhaps there are some nuggets of wisdom dipped in sweet and sour sauce throughout the following pages.

I have little idea how I got to this point in my life where I am happier than ever, despite the horrific challenges I have faced in recent

INTRODUCTION

years, but perhaps the answer lies in that sentence itself. Now I want to share what I believe made a difference in my life so that I can fulfill my lifelong dream of helping other people.

I will be touching on many topics that need more explanation than the pages in this book allow, so I ask you to suspend your judgement for now. Just because you don't understand something now, doesn't mean it is untrue, or that you won't see it as fact in the future.

I mean, even though the ancient Greeks suggested that the earth was round over 2,000 years ago, it wasn't until relatively recently that most of the human race believed it as fact. As Oliver Wendell Holmes stated, "A mind that is stretched by a new experience can never go back to its old dimensions." By suspending your judgement and opening your mind, you may just discover something new that I too have recently learnt.

I'd love to share all the things that I've discovered in the 1,500+ books that I have read in the last eight years but that's not possible. I do hope that if something gets your attention or raises a reaction (either a positive or negative one) you look further into it for your own happiness.

I will list as many resources as I can throughout, or at the end of the book to aid in your journey, so please investigate these resources if they are of interest to you.

So now that I've rabbited on quite a bit already, I think it's time to get into the crutch of what this book is all about. To quote the most incredible choreographer/director I have worked with; Mr. William A Forsythe, right before our "full runs" of the shows during rehearsals –

"LET'S ROOT THIS PIG".

WHAT OTHER PEOPLE THINK OF YOU IS NONE OF YOUR BUSINESS

CHAPTER ONE

LET'S START AT THE VERY BEGINNING

"When the voice and the vision on the inside are louder than the opinions on the outside, that is when you're living a masterful life"
- Dr. John Demartini

As Julie Andrews famously sang in The Sound of Music; Let's start at the very beginning, a very good place to start. When you read you begin with A.B.C. When you sing you begin with Do-Rei-Mi. The first little chapter is about Dan Shearin and me.

Okay, so I added the last bit, but you get what I mean.

I'm not sure how many authors have written a book under two different names at the same time, or if it is clever, weird, confusing, or all of the above but hey, I think we all know that I'm not your average author; so why not?

The reason I do this is simple. Not because I am bipolar like my Canadian ex (her words via her doctor; not mine). Not because I am schizophrenic, but because I changed my name in 2016 after much unwanted media attention.

I had a lack of employment opportunities as a result of said media attention, so to save people from getting confused about who is writing this book; I used both. I'm sure that makes sense; kind of.

At no point was deception or future criminal activity my motivation for changing my name. It was a simple case of me wanting to move on with my life in a peaceful way.

According to the good Lord though, this was only a temporary reprieve from attention, as he had bigger plans for me and wanted my situation and my story to be shared to benefit others. After much reluctance and God continually pushing my life in the direction that they had intended for me, I succumbed and here I am.

Why Jayden Daniel Moórea for the new name? Well. After attending Tony Robbins' "Date with Destiny" seminar in early 2016, I had some coaching sessions with one of his awesome trainers and the topic of my situation arose.

I mentioned that I wasn't able to get on with my life due to factors beyond my control, at which point he reminded me that this was a limiting belief and that I needed to take action, instead of making excuses.

As I contemplated various options, many ideas came to mind. If I was going to go to such lengths to change my name, I wanted it to be one that I was happy with, as I had no intention of ever changing it again.

Can I just say that having changed my name legally and adhering to all the rigmarole that this entails, I empathise with women who get married and must go through it all after their wedding. The easy part was the name change. The hard part was all the other shit (banks, licence) that goes with it.

Throughout my career as an entertainer and in particular at sea and after, friends and colleagues had called me Dan Cruise. This originally came about when we were the support act for Vanilla Ice in 1991. Our crew was called "Streets Ahead". There was The Judge, Kid Kruze (Me), Kid Wiz, and DJ Andre (Peter's brother).

This name then morphed to Dan Kruze when we toured as the Australian tribute to the Backstreet Boys and then "Dan Cruise" when I was on cruise ships...... Wow. There are a few nuggets to unpack in that paragraph that we have to come back to.

So this was my first thought, but given that there was already a famous "Cruise" (and a very good-looking one) I didn't want to seem egotistical by using that name; plus, it was a little obvious.

I have always loved cruising and the ocean so the next option was Dan Ocean or Danny Ocean, but for obvious reasons, if you have seen the movie Ocean's Eleven, you can see why I let that idea slip through to the keeper.

The issue I had was that it wasn't just me who had to deal with the name change, but also my friends. I also didn't want it to be just a surname change. This would make me far too easy to discover by

CHAPTER 1

Breeana's aunty who had made it her purpose in life to stalk, defame, and harass me, my family, my friends, and several employers.

Her calling my girlfriend's Aunty in Melbourne claiming I was on murder charges way back in 2013 was just the beginning of Breeana's aunt's unhinged behaviour.

So, this is what I finally came up with.

Jayden was the name that my daughter would have been called if she had been born a boy. Only one other person in the world knew that tidbit of information; I told you I would bare all.

I moved Daniel to the middle, so my friends didn't get confused. However one of my brothers still gets himself in a knot when he addresses me because he can't remember which one to call me.

Moórea is the name that my Canadian (bipolar) ex and I said we wanted to call a daughter that we were planning when we were engaged because we met on the beautiful island of Moórea in Tahiti in 2003. On my mother's side of the family, there was also Polynesian blood, so this wasn't too far-fetched; even though I am pale, covered in freckles, and don't look remotely Polynesian.

Why would I want to have a name that reminds me of two ex-partners? Well, to be honest, part of me doesn't give two hoots about either of them, plus a small part of me laughs when I think about it. No doubt, it would piss both of them off to know that I used the names.

Let me say though that I am far from someone who intentionally goes out of my way to piss people off these days, but it is funny. My father also travelled to Tahiti when I was a child and he loved the place as much as I did in the six months I spent there, so part of the idea was to honour both Mum and Dad as they have now passed on.

I mention the name change and use it as a "co-author" thingy because to understand where I am now and where I am headed in the future, you need to know where I came from. I must be clear though that I am not making any excuses or blaming my past. As Oprah says in her book "What Happened to You", "Your past is not an excuse, but it is an explanation."

This is what many people do to justify their actions; but not me. I want to give you the rawest account of who I am, in the hope that you can relate and hopefully realise that whatever you are currently going through or have been through, it is all part of who you are meant to be.

It is not a noose or a burden, but rather a blessing that you have or are experiencing certain things.

As I shared in my most recent book "The No B.S Approach to Create the Life You Want" my hero Tony Robbins asks the question, "What if life is happening for you; not to you?" The line I quote is from his promo video on YouTube for his 2016 Date with Destiny seminar that I attended. He goes on to ask, "What if everything in life is a gift? What if everything is divine timing; even the pain?"

For some, this may be difficult to accept, but since that moment, I have come to ask that question when things happen in life that are seemingly not nice; like being wrongly charged with murder.

Everything from our time of birth happens for a reason. It may be a much-overused cliché, but it is true. Nothing happens by chance and if you can untangle the real reasons for each moment occurring, you can discover your destiny.

You can learn a lot about someone by knowing about their childhood. From birth to the age of seven we are like sponges. This is known as the imprint period. During that time we absorb everything around us and develop most of our beliefs and habits that stay with us throughout life.

Having said that, I am not a fan of people who say, "That's just who I am" or "I can't change" or "That is because of my childhood." To me, those are just excuses. I am not someone who blames my past or my circumstances for my decisions.

I accept full responsibility for where I am in life, the decisions I have made, and the missteps and successes that I have encountered along the way.

Now that I have taken far longer to set up this chapter, let's move on.

In 1973, Australia was a very different place than it is today; so far as women were concerned. The rights, freedoms, and equality that women enjoy and in some cases take for granted these days were far from being realised back then.

My biological mother was a smart, beautiful eighteen-year-old just finding her way in the world when she fell pregnant to a man who she thought was committed to her; even though she barely saw him.

I have often joked with my mother as to how naïve she must have been, but in all seriousness from all accounts, I think most women would have fallen for the same trap.

You see, my mother believed that the reason that my biological father was only able to see her one or two nights a week, was because he was an interstate truck driver and was away from home most of the time. As it turned out, he was married to another woman, with whom he had four children; unbeknownst to my mother.

Like most eighteen-year-old girls dating an older man back then, she believed everything he said and didn't think for a second that he would be married with four kids. By all accounts, he was not the nicest person. Now, I don't want to pass judgement on a man with whom I have only spent a couple of hours when I was twenty-three.

I have always been someone who judges people purely by how they treat me. Maybe I am wrong for not listening to other opinions about people, but the way I see it, I honestly could not give a shit how someone is with anyone else. I only judge a person by how they treat me.

In "The Blame Game" I spoke about how I met the so-called notorious conman Peter Foster and while he has a reputation (as do I) I could not speak highly enough about Peter because he was kind and thoughtful as well as a genuine guy when I met him so that is what I go by.

Funnily enough, when I went into my lawyer's office before originally writing this paragraph, Peter was there. Even though more than four years had passed since Peter and I shared the police wagon up to Brisbane Correctional Centre in 2014, Peter not only remembered me, but he was as friendly and caring as I mentioned in "The Blame Game."

I know my biological mother more than likely dislikes that I choose to judge my biological father solely by how he was with me and not by how badly he treated her or what my grandparents said about him, but at the end of the day, if we live our lives based on other people's feelings or emotions, we never really develop our own set of beliefs.

That's why racism is rife in society. We are not born racist. We learn those beliefs from in most cases our parents. We end up spending our lives being driven by others' beliefs and having seen my best mate of forty years be dictated by his father's beliefs, I would rather live by my own set of rules and judgements; even if they are wrong.

My biological father probably was all the bad things that I was told, but by the time I met him, my family had not seen or heard from him in twenty-three years, so perhaps he had changed. Some people say "A leopard never changed its spots" which I disagree with in some situations and that is when the leopard wants to change its spots. We can all change, and this book is proof of that.

It's now been more than twenty-five years since I spent an afternoon with my biological father, introducing him to his baby granddaughter.

Since then, I have not had an urge to keep in contact or form a relationship and he had not made contact during that time either. I'm not sure why I didn't pursue contact with him; I just didn't.

There have been a few occasions over the years where I have thought about it and I even looked up "Arthur Squire" on Facebook and in the white pages with the idea of perhaps reconnecting.

Even though my biological mother and I have had some verbal stoushes over the years as a result of me blaming her for my insecurities or lack of whatever in my life, I guess my morals of respect that I was raised on deterred me from making contact with a man whose mere name would undoubtedly upset or offend both her and her parents.

Her parents both despised Arthur Squire and even though I knew only a few details of the situation, this was enough at the time for me to quell any urges to make contact with the man who was 50% responsible for me being on earth.

It is with some regret that while writing this chapter in 2019, my biological mother called to inform me that Arthur had died. After a brief stunned pause to establish how I felt about this news, my first comment was "When is the funeral?" to which she replied, "Today".

I chuckled as I looked at my watch which showed that it was one in the afternoon. "The funeral was at twelve," she said. While a part of me was a little disappointed that she didn't tell me beforehand, I completely understood her dilemma and how torn she must have been in calling me at all regarding his death.

Here was a woman who has since been married for over thirty years and who had barely given my biological father a thought for forty-six years having to put her own feelings aside to inform her son of his father's death so that it didn't come from anyone else down the track.

The likelihood of me ever knowing he had died was a million to one, but she knew how much of a curious fucker I am, and no doubt the question would have come up sooner or later, at which point she would have had to confess that she knew about his death all along.

Even though the guy had no influence on my life and had no contact in almost half a century, a part of me wanted to find out more about him and perhaps unearth some information about myself in doing so. I knew how emotional my biological mother was about the whole situation and I didn't want to add to that for my own selfish purposes, so I went to someone who might be able to give me clarity on what to do.

CHAPTER 1

I called my adopted mother's best friend of twenty years. Kerry knew my adopted mother better than anyone and no doubt knew the ins and outs of how she and my adopted dad felt about this Arthur Squire guy.

FYI: For those living on the Gold Coast who drive past the pink FX Holden perched in the wall of the Reedy Creek wreckers on the Pacific Highway; Kerry's late husband Warren restored it and owned it before it was destroyed. Okay, now I have diverted, I have to finish the story.

Many people see the old car which has been there since around 1983, but very few people know the story behind how it got there. Warren was a mechanic for the Gold Coast council and spent many years in his spare time doing the old FX up. The car was green and had won Warren many awards at car shows. Myself and his son who I knew from kindergarten had ridden in the car on several occasions.

Warren was approached one day by a guy who offered him a ridiculously high price for the car, so Warren sold it. Unfortunately for Warren, the buyer didn't tell him that he was the owner of a 1970's style "Malt Shop" opening in Surfers Paradise a few weeks later and the car was going to be the centrepiece of the restaurant.

A month later, my adopted Dad and I went to "Olivia's Malt Shop" on the Gold Coast Highway in the middle of Surfers Paradise for dinner. We were greeted by waitresses on roller skates and an atmosphere like a typical American dinner as portrayed in the movie "Xanadu".

As we waited for our meals, I looked up at a beautiful pink car that had been cut in half and placed on the wall. I said to Dad, "That looks a lot like Warren's old car." Dad curiously looked at the car and upon arriving home, he called Warren to inform him of the possible demise of his beloved FX Holden.

The car did turn out to be Warren's and the malt shop went bust a few weeks later. One of Dad's client's "Will the Wrecker" acquired the car and it has become an iconic image of the Gold Coast's history with tens of thousands of cars driving past it every day.

People might say, "Why would Warren care when he got paid well for it?" Well, as it turns out, the buyers had approached several FX owners and told them their plans for their cars, and subsequently, all of them refused to sell.

When they approached Warren, they did not disclose their intentions, and Warren was adamant that if they had done so, he would never have sold it as it was a labour of love restoring it.

Okay. Back to the original story.

I spoke to Kerry about my thoughts about my biological father's death and asked her if I should make any enquiries or contact with his surviving family which I met in 1996 and who were my half brothers and sisters.

Kerry is a straight shooter and as blunt as a sledgehammer. This is precisely why I called her. I knew she would be straight and not bullshit me.

Kerry explained how much my adopted mother and father despised this guy. This was all I needed to hear. My adopted father was a gentle, easy-going man. There were only two people he hated in his ninety-one years on earth. One was the man who was M.C. at my best mate's wedding, whom Dad punched out decades earlier. The other was Arthur Squire; my biological father.

I know it sounds contradictory to say Dad punched the guy out, but my point is that for a peaceful guy like Dad to do so, shows his level of distaste for the guy. The fact that my adopted father held Arthur in the same regard was all I needed to hear in deciding that I should simply close this chapter of my life.

1973; A DIFFERENT WORLD FROM TODAY

By the time I was born, my mother was eighteen, a single mum, and by all accounts on the skin of her ass financially. Remember, in 1973 child support in Australia was still fifteen years away and no government agency was going to chase my biological father for money back then.

I mean shit, even today the Child Support Agency is unable to accurately bring suitable resolution to estranged couples so far as ensuring that it is fair financially, so my mother had no hope in 1973.

Given her circumstances, my mother had two (soon to be four) options. 1. Struggle as a single mum with no money and a newborn baby to raise, or 2. Adopt me out to strangers and never see me again.

While the first option would more than likely have led to a less-than-ideal life for both her and me, the second option was only leading to one outcome; heartbreak for both of us.

From all accounts, when my biological father got wind of my mother's thoughts of giving me up for adoption, he suggested that he could adopt me, and I live with his existing wife and four children.

CHAPTER 1

Enter my softly spoken and strict grandfather who hates very few people, but detested my biological father with the words "Over my dead body."

By this stage, my Grandparents were well past the child-raising age with their youngest child being nine years old. My grandfather who was a prominent accountant on the Gold Coast was nearing retirement and looking forward to kicking back, not raising another baby; so this was a huge call for him to make.

Long story short, I was adopted by my grandparents and was saved from being another child never to know who their biological parents were. By the time all the paperwork was finalised, I was still a baby so psychologically this wasn't going to affect me at all; or so I thought.

I was baptised in the local Anglican church and my Godparents lived right next door to us. My Godparents were very religious and founded the city's community Christian radio station (Radio 4CRB) that is still going today.

They started their test broadcasts in their garage in 1977 and I am proud to say that while the music on their station isn't my cup of tea, the community is a much better place for their contribution over the past forty-plus years.

Growing up, I was your usual cheeky child. I loved sports and participated in scouts, Little Athletics, soccer, AFL, and cricket. I was a very curious child and was always asking questions. I know all kids ask a lot of questions, but I took it to a new level. So much so that my adopted mum's best friend, Kerry (who I mentioned a moment ago) nicknamed me "The Professor". I would often look at something like a chair or the steel that holds something up and think, "How did that come about."

There are so many things that we see but take for granted without even a second thought about how they came to be. As a kid, these were the questions I was constantly asking myself. I now know that the steel and the chair are all energy fields vibrating at extremely fast rates, but that is a completely different book and not worth getting into now.

My point is that I have always questioned what is and even though it has only been recently that I have discovered how beneficial this is in achieving an exceptional life, it has always been a part of me, as it is with most people; even if it's undeveloped.

Another quick detour. In order to save confusion, from now on, when I refer to mum and dad, I am talking about my "legal" mum and dad; my grandparents.

For as long as I can remember, they were mum and dad and it was only when I was about three years old that I learnt that the woman who I thought was my older sister, was actually my real mum.

Even at fifty, I still haven't found an easy way of explaining that so that people don't look at me like a dog would when you tell them a joke or when they smelt a fart. So, from here on, when I mention the name "Sue" she is my biological mother (now my sister-by-law).

I always thought I was the only person in the world in this situation, but I recently discovered that the woman who Sir Isaac Newton thought was his sister and who was only twelve years older than him, turned out to be his mother. Isaac didn't discover this until just before he received his Nobel Prize. His grandparents were so ashamed of their twelve-year-old daughter for falling pregnant that they adopted Isaac.

If you want to achieve something great with your life then start praying for a huge challenge because as Dr. John Demartini says, "Your greatest challenges may just be your greatest opportunities." Or "It's not what happens to you; it's what you decide to do with what happens to you," that counts.

I am by no means suggesting that my life will be punctuated by the invention of the lightbulb, the theory of relativity, or the flushing toilet like some of history's greatest minds.

I am simply suggesting that the greater the challenges we face, the greater the prospect of greatness we can achieve. There are only three things that we have control over. Our perceptions. Our decisions and our actions. (A quote by John Demartini).

So, while Kerry called me the professor because according to me; I knew everything, my scout leader nicknamed me "Motormouth". In short, I was a smartass who never shut up. According to my childhood mates, the doctor smacked me on the ass I haven't shut up since.

From a young age, I developed a reputation as the class clown at school. I was the kid that when someone said "Hey wouldn't it be cool if someone did..." who went and did it. I always got the laughs and respect of my schoolmates, but I was no teacher's pet.

I got my mouth washed out with soap in grade two, I had a girl show me her vagina in the same grade and I ended up doing detention for a week in grade two with my best friend for convincing him to piss in the middle of the school ground at lunch by saying no teachers were around; even though one was watching.

Incidentally, looking back, I had already developed both sides of my personality. My best mate had to sit outside the principal's office every lunch hour for a week as his punishment. So what did I do? I sat there with him every day to keep him company.

CHAPTER 1

Perhaps my motivation was that if he was there and I wasn't then I didn't have a friend to play with. Either way, in hindsight, this was my first example of how we all have both good and bad sides to our personalities.

In grade nine science class when Miss Boyett asked the class to give an example of "A-sexual reproduction" I blurted out at the top of my voice, like someone suffering from turrets "doggy style" which brought thunderous laughter from the rest of the class.

In my defence, I thought her question was in relation to sexual intercourse and not related to plants being pollinated. At the time I couldn't see how sex related to science, but hey, hindsight is a wonderful thing.

While in Sport's Science class two years later when asked to give an example of a soft muscle contraction, I told my teacher that it was "cracking a stiffy". The funny thing was that this answer was actually correct so subsequently, the entire class of boys used this answer when it came up on the test and the teacher had to mark us all right.

My earliest memory of my desire to be a singer was at the age of three. My older brother had his Kiss album playing most days and for Christmas, I got a Paul Stanley guitar and Kiss makeup set. Instead of running around the street dressed as Batman, (that was my night gig - wearing my underpants over my cape or head) I slapped on the white face paint and coloured a black star over my eye.

Looking like an extra from a horror movie, I went out terrorising the neighbours as the lead singer from Kiss, armed with a guitar that blasted out "Shandy" when you pushed certain buttons.

After boring the neighbours and freaking their cats and dogs out, I'd prop myself in front of the mirror and sing those lyrics over and over. "Shandy, tonight must last us forever". Thankfully for my mother's sanity, my hours of "rehearsing" took place in our large rumpus room downstairs in an area furthest away from the lounge or kitchen.

I could have been Gene Simmons or Ace Freely, but no. I had to be the singer. Even though Gene Simmons has over five thousand notches in his bedhead, it was Paul Stanley who I idolised, but little did I know at the tender age of six that singers really do get the girls.

Somehow from there, my musical taste progressed and after winning a Rank Arena stereo in McDonald's Monopoly at the age of six, I bought my very first cassette; The Beach Boys' greatest hits. I know. What is a six-year-old doing buying a Beach Boys cassette?

Who knows, but I do know that my Muppets cassette that mum bought me had worn out and I'd used her Barry Manilow record as

WHAT OTHER PEOPLE THINK OF YOU IS NONE OF YOUR BUSINESS

a discus off our second-story balcony; watching it fly off the hilltop railing and into the thick bush lining Skyline Terrace below. My last sighting of it was as it soared towards the Palm Beach sporting fields several kilometres away.

People often ask where my talent came from; my Mum or Dad's side, to which I say "Neither". That's not to say my parents were talentless schmucks, they simply had no musical abilities.

My abilities did develop from my formative years, or the years that experts call the "imprint period" from ages 3-11. During this time, I was subjected to the right types of influences at which time my sponge-like behaviour took over.

I got my musical taste from listening to my mother's eclectic music collection which consisted of Glen Campbell, John Denver, Barry Manilow, and Neil Diamond, with some classical artists thrown in. I developed my comedic timing by watching Ronnie Barker and Ronnie Corbett.

With only one TV in the house, I had to watch what Mum and Dad watched but that proved to be a good thing so far as my career. My love of performing came from watching Young Talent Time on Saturday nights, which I particularly loved when they stayed and performed at what is now the Paradise Resort in Surfers Paradise.

Finally, as a child of the 1970s, my obsession with cruising grew from watching the idyllic and romantic episodes of The Love Boat every Thursday night. I remember saying to Mum one night while watching the show, "I want to be like Julie McCoy." Funnily enough, twenty-something years later I was a Cruise Director, minus the short skirt; on most occasions.

Well, there wasn't a skirt, but there were tiny lime-green hot pants, a matching frilled crop top, and knee-high purple lace-up 'come fuck me' boots with three-inch high platforms as part of my character as a cross-dressing blonde from ABBA in a 70's disco show. Sigh. So much of that last sentence should have been omitted from this book.

With my eclectic taste in music, I had no idea how I ended up with a singing voice that earned me a lot of money, but somehow, I did. With music playing in the house that ranged from Barry Manilow, John Denver, and Glen Campbell to Pink Floyd, The Village People, and Kiss, I'm surprised that I didn't form a kind of "schizophrenic singing voice".

I guess such a diverse selection of music in the 1970s and 1980s subconsciously taught me about good melody and proper pitch. Look at most singers on reality TV shows and to a trained ear, most are

CHAPTER 1

off-key. Don't believe me? Trust me, the runner-up's album from the original series of Aussie Idol had as much auto-tune on his voice as on Cher's single "Believe". The big difference being that Cher used it as an effect, not as a means to sing in key.

On a side note, I very nearly came up against Guy, Shannon, my mate Stu, and the rest of the contestants on the first season of Australian Idol. At the time I had sent demo CDs off to a few record companies and Mark Holden called me and wanted to meet for lunch.

We met at a swish restaurant in Milton in Brisbane and Mark advised me that while he wanted to sign me alongside Vanessa Amorosi to his management label, he had recently committed to a new talent show that was about to start.

I had just returned from a cruise ship contract in the U.K. and saw the final few weeks of "Pop Idol" there, so I knew the concept. Unfortunately, I had just signed a contract as a production show singer with Princess Cruises on their flagship and was due to leave in a few days.

Mark mentioned that the only way record companies were signing artists at that stage was on the back of talent shows because of marketing constraints in the industry. Mark asked me to reconsider my contract with Princess Cruises.

I asked Mark why he was so keen to have me on the show and his reply left me speechless for the first time in my life. "Because there is no one in the country of the same calibre as you" was his reply. "Fuck me", I thought to myself. That's some high praise from a man in his position in the industry.

Now let me say that while his comment was extremely flattering, I have always been self-deprecating and never one to boast about my talent. Having said that I really would have loved to have gone head-to-head with Anthony Callea (from the following season) as I rate his voice as one of the richest and most incredible male voices I have heard.

With all that aside, upon enquiry, it turned out that the maximum age for the show was thirty and I had just turned thirty so it was inconsequential.

BACK TO THE 70'S.....

Music in the '70s and '80s had wicked melodies. I mean come on. We all laugh, but if anyone plays "YMCA", "Dancing Queen", or "Wake Me Up" I'll bet your leg starts bopping involuntarily and you suddenly turn into the world's greatest karaoke king or queen.

By the time I was in grade three, Mum had heard from several of

WHAT OTHER PEOPLE THINK OF YOU IS NONE OF YOUR BUSINESS

my teachers that I had a beautiful singing voice. This meant nothing to me at the time, but Mum had exquisite taste in music and was willing to encourage me to explore this more.

Hearing that I had a beautiful voice was no big deal to me. I loved to sing and other people's opinions of that back then meant as little to me as their opinions of me do now.

Ask any of my music teachers, directors, or choreographers and they will all tell you that my biggest flaw was that I doubted myself on stage. I worked hard and knew my lines and moves, but right up until opening night, I'd be questioning if I was right.

I've always felt like I had some talent and I loved what I was doing singing or dancing, but I never saw myself as anyone special. I was always my own worst enemy, doubting myself and being unsure of my ability. In hindsight, it was this doubt that drove me to be better and eventually allowed me the success that I achieved.

The funny thing is that it wasn't until a fellow entertainer put it in a way that made me stop and think (while laughing) that I truly grasped that I had a God-given gift that I was sharing. One of the male dancers on the Tahitian Princess said to me while having a drink one night that his nickname for me was "Vermin".

Sheldon was a funny gay dancer and had an interesting sense of humour, so I didn't think much of it until he explained. He said, "I call you Vermin because you have the voice of an angel and the mind of a two-dollar whore".

Now, the whore part was funny because I had a dirty mind, but somehow in the context of the slight insult, he said one of the nicest things I had heard about my voice. Sheldon wasn't one to say things he didn't mean and as an exceptional entertainer himself, I was flattered by his comment. (The voice of an angel part - not the whore bit).

As it turned out, the nickname of Vermin stuck for the next six months. The name even followed me to a stint at Dracula's restaurant where we named one of my characters "Vermin" as part of one of my two fill-in gigs in 2004 and 2006.

I was never a really bad student; just a ratbag, or scallywag. In grade eight I told my teacher Mr. Howard to "Sit on it Howey" (A line from Happy Days) when he yelled at me and in grade nine I asked Mrs. Howard (Not Mr. Howard's wife) when being sent outside the class for talking "What about the others you fucking bitch."

Oh, and in grade ten I swallowed my breath so many times when Mr. Madge left the room, that by the time he returned, I let out a belch that rivalled the roar of an alpha-male lion wanting to eat you.

In all examples my behaviour was met with raucous laughter by the students and then a teacher frog-marching me out of the room. Hey. At least my teacher didn't put my head through a plate-glass window as one did to my mate John in grade nine.

Probably the worst thing we did as teenagers was being caught stealing skateboard bearings worth $5 (Even though we had the cash on us) or riding our motorbikes along the Pacific Motorway and asking an undercover police car for a drag race when they pulled alongside (I know; very stupid).

Okay, so that wasn't the worst thing I ever did in my teenage years, but I'll be fucked if I am confessing everything I did when I know how much the police and the media love reading my books and taking every word I write as gospel.

Hasn't anyone in the police force or the media ever heard of poetic licence? Needless to say, I laugh when I see teenagers have blown up people's letterboxes with gunpowder, or wrapped a front lawn in toilet paper before setting the paper alight.

If I am completely honest, I was part of the country's top graffiti crew. How did I know we were the best? Because artists from Melbourne and Sydney used to come to the Gold Coast to watch us work and learn from us. I must say though, that I wasn't the best. My crew was, but I was just okay.

I was okay at spraying, but they were brilliant artists. We were also paid by many businesses on the Gold Coast to decorate their business with graffiti. The world-famous Playroom at Tallebudgera, La Cucaracha at Mermaid, and many more had our pieces on their buildings, and we got paid for it.

Our favourite was doing a "Tone Loc" piece at The Playroom, then meeting Tone himself after his show and getting a photo in front of the piece with him.

I won't name the name of our crew here because I'm pretty sure once, Matt, Rory, George, and I left the crew, a new generation took up the name and did more illegal shit than we did. Almost all of our work was legal and paid in cash so we didn't have time for illegal pieces and hey, we had fame without fear of getting busted.

I know none of these things are too outlandish by today's standards but in hindsight, I can now see why I did those things. It was to feel significant. One of the primary human needs is the need for significance.

Even though I didn't know it at the time, I guess I was crying out for attention as a result of an underlying, but yet-to-be-discovered fear of abandonment or lack of feeling significant. This isn't something that I even contemplated until I was in my late thirties, but it does explain a few things so far as my behaviour as a child and even a young/old adult.

Once again, I am not making excuses for my behaviour, or anyone else's. It is merely an observation and more importantly a realisation because until you realise something, you can't fix it or change it. As Charles Kettering said, "A problem well stated, is a problem half solved." The reason I mention these traits is that in most cases they stem from limiting beliefs.

A limiting belief is a belief that a person develops as a result of a situation, circumstance, or perhaps a comment that then becomes imprinted in their subconscious and dictates their behaviour. For example. In grade four, my teacher Mrs. Fletcher told me that I would never be a good reader. Clearly, at that age, I wasn't great at reading and she thought that it was her duty to tell me.

Thankfully these days, teachers would never say such a thing to a child, because as a society we understand the effect it can have. In my case, I took Mrs. Fletcher's words and subconsciously created my own limiting belief. As a result, from the age of ten, until I was in my late twenties, I only read one book. I'll get back to this limiting belief in a later chapter because it is important as part of my message in this book.

In another example though, in grade eight, my speech and drama teacher Miss Flannery told me that I would never be a good singer. Clearly, she got that one very wrong. In her defence, to put her comment into context, she had never heard me sing and was referring to the fact that my voice was resonant and more like a radio disc-jockey voice than that of a tenor.

Thankfully throughout my primary school years, all my teachers had told my mother that I had the voice of an angel. I also had one of my all-time favourite teachers Miss Zlatic tell me the following year in speech and drama that (I quote) "You have such a lot going for you and a lot of talent."

The reason I can accurately quote Miss Zlatic's line is because she wrote it on a small square pink piece of paper that I have kept to this day. I used to carry it in my first-aid kit that I took to my shows and I would often read it when I doubted my ability.

On opening night of my first professional show, I placed the small

CHAPTER 1

piece of paper in my back pocket of my jeans as I went on stage. I had bought two tickets for her and her boyfriend and after the show when we went to greet the audience in the foyer, I pulled the piece of paper from my pocket and showed it to her. She welled up when she recognised her own handwriting. She was surprised that I had not only remembered her words but that I was carrying the note ten years later.

I mention these things because as humans we hold onto limiting beliefs either consciously or subconsciously and they dictate our lives. They stop us from reaching our dreams and quite often we don't have a clue why or how. It's interesting how we let others' actions or comments dictate decades of our lives. Sometimes in a good way, but mostly in bad ways.

The reason that is the case is simple. If someone says we're rubbish at a sport for example, yet we know we're not, then their comment will more than likely have no effect on us. On the flip side, if someone says we're fat and we have the slightest doubt or insecurity about our weight, we take that on board, and this becomes a limiting belief.

What I am trying to say is that it is our own insecurities that allow us to take on these limiting beliefs. If you know in your mind that you are a certain way, or good at a particular thing and someone tries to tell you otherwise, it won't affect you.

On the flip side, if there is any doubt in your mind, a simple comment like "you will never be a good reader" could control the rest of your life. We need to be careful what we say to ourselves and others because even though this book is all about caring less about what other people think, it's not always as easy to put this into practice.

Even though as a child I was a bit of a ratbag, I always knew what was right and wrong. One of my mother's favourite sayings was from Jesus' Sermon on the Mount, which was "Do unto others as you would have them do unto you." Although I have not always lived precisely by the golden rule, I do try to act in accordance with it as much as possible.

Even though it wasn't obvious until after my mother passed away in 1999, she was quite a religious person. My Godparents were heavily involved with the local church and one of my mother's favourite books was the Bible. When I was in grade six, my parents enrolled me at a brand-new Christian school called "Somerset College" in the hope that I would adopt some of the principles taught there.

The school was in its second year so most of the classes were in demountable buildings and the school only went to grade nine. There were only two classes in each grade and the student body was very small. Therefore, everyone knew everyone.

To be honest, I hated how (as I felt) they rammed the Bible down my throat daily. It is only now, nearly forty years later, and having read both the Old and New Testaments of the Bible, that I realise the benefit of the daily lessons on the subject. I guess my point at the time was that I felt that it should be a person's choice; not forced upon them, if they wanted to learn about and pursue a relationship with God.

Back then the school was in its infancy, but now it is considered one of the top schools in the city. Having come from a public school, Somerset College was a huge shock to my system, and to some extent, I rebelled even more at the very expensive private school.

Most of the kids at the school lived the principles of the school so that tended to rub off on even the worst among us. As I said, my mother always taught me to treat other people well so when I saw someone treating another person badly, I felt that someone needed to step in.

Despite what some people may like to allege, I've never been a violent person. Most people who think they know me know, that the only weapon I've used is my wit and my words. In the grade below me at Somerset College, there was a mentally disabled child by the name of Margaret.

I can't recall what her exact disability was but she had a learning disability. Margaret was plain-looking and very awkward around other students, but nonetheless, almost everyone was as understanding and considerate as grade five and six students could be.

This was except for a grade six kid named Tom. Margaret, Tom, and I all caught the bus from Somerset College in Mudgeeraba to Burleigh Heads, which was about a thirty-minute ride with stops. For a couple of days in a row, Tom was teasing Margaret and calling her horrible names like "Spastic". Back in 1984, there was not the same tolerance and acceptance of disabilities so Margaret had no other option but to suck it up.

Tom was an ugly git of a kid with the world's biggest ears. While I don't condone discriminating against someone based on their physical appearance, I make mention of this because looking back, I believe that Tom's motivation to pick on Margaret, was not because of Margaret's disability, but rather from his own insecurities.

The first day Tom began teasing Margaret I warned him that if he didn't stop it, I would "smash him". This curbed his nastiness for the rest of the bus ride, but the following day he launched another horrible barrage of insults Margaret's way. It's one thing for kids to call each other names, but he was attacking her based on her disability, which in my eyes is the worst type of insult.

As it turned out the next day, I was getting off the bus in the heart of Burleigh Heads so I could go to my Dad's accounting office. This was also Tom's stop, so when the two of us got off the bus, I punched Tom as hard as I could in the face three or four times. I watched as Tom dropped to the ground crying.

I looked across the street to see his mother watching on; horrified. I looked up to see all the students on the bus leaning out the window cheering, as I casually walked across the main road to Dad's office.

The following morning upon arriving at class, I was swiftly dragged down to the principal's office. When I arrived at the office, I saw the two grade nine school captains seated across from the principal. I thought I was screwed, but when the school captains who both caught the same bus explained to the principal that I only hit Tom because he was tormenting Margaret, the principal took a far dimmer view of Tom's behaviour than my reaction to it. It turned out that as the only student with a mental disability at the school, Margaret was much loved by all the teachers and many students.

While this situation elevated me to 'legend status' and saw me promoted to the back seat of the bus with the 'grade niners', the principal cautioned me from repeating this in the future. The principal advised that any bullying is to be reported to a teacher so that they can deal with it. Tom on the other hand was threatened with suspension if he teased Margaret again.

From that day on I was the cool kid and enjoyed mixing with the seniors on the back seat of the bus. My mother would be horrified to find this out, but I learnt more about girls, kissing, foreplay, and other 'boy/girl stuff' for the rest of that year on the back seat than any book she ever gave me about 'where I came from' etc.

This leads me to my next "growing pain" in life; girls. Like most boys, girls weren't a real focus until the girls began to grow breasts and my singing voice went from sounding like Michael Jackson to Barry White. Apart from a kiss with Angela Graham (Remember that name) in grade seven and a regular "oral encounter" each afternoon for a few months with a friend Leesa from another school in highschool, I had hardly any experience even speaking with girls, let alone engaging in sex or intimacy with them until my final year of school.

WHAT OTHER PEOPLE THINK OF YOU IS NONE OF YOUR BUSINESS

It was over the Christmas school holidays when I was staying with Sue and her husband in Brisbane when we rented the movie Grease. On most school holidays I would stay with Sue and this was our time to bond. We spoke on the phone regularly but didn't see each other as much as we probably should have, but that was all part of the situation. Dad had made it very clear when he and Mum adopted me that Sue would have absolutely no say in my upbringing. It must have been so hard for Sue to have to sit back and not have an opinion on crucial decisions in my life.

As I was growing up and spending time with Sue, I did notice though that there was still a special bond there. If Mum yelled at me, it was just part of life and no matter how cranky she got with me, it usually had very little effect.

If Sue even slightly raised her voice at me though, I would burst out crying; and that was in high school. I always knew who Sue was in the overall picture growing up and even though we have had some real issues over the years, we're now in a place that a mother and son should be as we move into the second half of our lives.

So, there we were on a Saturday night in January 1990, and apart from the night Breeana died and the night my daughter was born, I don't think there has been a night that has influenced my life more than that one.

At the time I didn't realise it but watching Grease, I had discovered my first real crush, which was Olivia Newton-John, but more importantly, I discovered that I wanted to be a professional singer. This might not be too farfetched if I had trained from a young age, but up until then, I was more interested in sports, graffiti, and rapping; than singing.

Even though I didn't realise it consciously, I also discovered that singers get the chicks. Whether you're John Travolta or the ugliest singer in the world (I'm struggling to think of a really ugly singer), if you sing, the girls will find you sexy. It goes both ways. To me, talent is the sexiest thing a woman can have.

Apart from Cindy Crawford, all of my celebrity crushes in my life have been singers. Olivia Newton-John, Vanessa Williams, and Jennifer Love Hewitt are all a hell of a lot sexier when they sing.

Later that year, I fell into the lead role of the school musical. I say "fell" because no one in the entire school saw it coming; except for me. I won't bore you with the exact details as I talk about it in my book "C.R.U.I.S.E", but can you guess what the school musical was that year? Yepp. "Grease". Up until that point, I was an aspiring rapper and worked as a D.J. in clubs so the prospect of singing in front of people was quite daunting.

So, there I was. Previously the captain of the cricket team and the A-Grade rugby league hooker and I was on stage playing Danny Zuko. As I said earlier, I had very little intimate interaction with girls, and as a matter of fact; I was still a virgin.

I finished the three shows and as I walked off stage, I was greeted by a hot blonde from Nerang High who had played "Sandy" in their school's production of Grease that year too. Long story short, we spent most of the night making out in a nightclub in Surfers and agreed to see each other again.

I have withheld her name because she is a well-known entertainer on the Gold Coast and I don't want to drag her into what I have endured. I will be vague with some names throughout the book. It is not because I am name-dropping or lying. I just don't want innocent people to be caught up in my situation or harassed by the media or Breeana's unhinged aunt.

The next Monday, all the grade twelve students went off to school camp for a week. Three days into camp, my mate Kirk told me that two girls (Tracey and Tania – a brunette and a blonde) had made a bet to see who could take my virginity.

WTF I thought to myself (before WTF was cool or meant What The Fuck!) No wonder Barry Manilow became a singer. Even he could get laid. There you go. There's my ugly singer. I do love Barry. In fact, he was one of Mum's favourite singers and I love his songs. Yepp. I'm a "Fanilow". Shit. Did I just admit that?

So, clearly, I had a big decision to make, and given that both girls were hot, I was a winner either way. In case you're wondering who won; Tracey the brunette did. Why did I choose her, or either of them? Quite simply. It's like when you call your travel agent to book flights and they tell you that there are only two seats at that price. This is what is called "creating urgency" and in most cases, it's a lie.

I know because after travelling the world, I became a travel consultant. The idea is to create a sense of missing out if you don't act. When I was presented with the first opportunity to date a girl and potentially get laid, I didn't want to miss it. That's right; F.O.M.O (Fear Of Missing Out) was a thing back in 1990.

For whatever reason my mind thought that this might be my only shot at getting a girlfriend and given that we were approaching Schoolies Week in a few months, I didn't want to throw it away like 30% of virgins back then. So instead, I jumped in bed with the first girl who offered herself to me. That makes complete sense; right?

But why exactly did I do this? If you asked the horny sixteen-year-old me, my answer would be vastly different, but in hindsight, now aged fifty, the answer is pretty clear. It all comes down to insecurities.

On some level, I believed that I was not worthy. I somehow believed that I was not good enough, smart enough, good-looking enough etc, etc. The funny thing is that no one told me these things. Like most people, I developed them all by myself. It all comes down to the questions we ask ourselves. Our brain is designed to give us answers, but just like Google; we need to ask the right questions.

Google is nearly as amazing as our brains, but as my daughter will tell you, ask the wrong question and you get a really bad answer. When she was fourteen, she was staying at her grandmother's and was sitting at her grandmother's computer in the lounge room.

As her grandmother walked past, my daughter jumped up, shut the computer down, and gave her grandmother a huge fake hug; as if she had something to hide.

Later that night her grandmother looked through the history on the computer and was mortified to see dozens of pages of porn sites and videos. Her grandmother asked my daughter why she was looking at so much porn. My daughter burst into tears and said, "I only asked Google – How to have sex."

Any red-blooded adult knows that what my daughter asked was certainly going to give you plenty of visual examples, but not so many lessons on the act itself. Well, that's not completely true because most young adults these days gained their bedroom skills from "Pornhub tutorials". According to Breeana; that's where she learnt to be a "Freak in the sheets." Sorry Elaine, but your daughter had a wicked sense of humour.

What my daughter was actually trying to achieve was to know how the act of sex was done. All her friends were discussing sex and you can imagine how embarrassing it could be for a teenager if they knew less than their friends. What my daughter didn't count on, was the hundreds of pop-ups that opened up back in those days when you clicked on porn sites.

My point is that if you ask a stupid question, you get a stupid answer. If you ask yourself, "Why do I always attract arseholes" your brain will say, "Because you're an idiot." We are wired by default to question ourselves, to look for danger, and to avoid potential risks. That's what our thousand-year-old brains are designed for.

When we were young, we all thought we could fly. We jumped off the garden shed and broke bones, so then any time after that when we thought that we could fly, our brains chimed in and said, "No you can't, you idiot." Our brain is programmed to answer in the negative. That's because, for thousands of years, we needed to protect ourselves from real danger.

As we grow up, we hear comments from parents and adults like, "Life isn't meant to be easy", "You need to get a real job" or "Money doesn't fall from the sky". Although as Charlie Harper says in Two and a Half Men, "It does if you're sitting ringside when a pole dancer turns upside down." My point is that we start retaining these comments in our early years and develop them into limiting beliefs. Whenever something good comes up, our subconscious tells us we can't do it before our conscious mind can say "I've got this."

I mentioned in my book "The No B.S Approach to Create the life you want" a lesson I learnt in my first personal development book that I read when I was in my mid-twenties. The book was called "You Can Do It" by Australian author, Paul Hanna. I've since heard the analogy from several mentors, but Paul was where I heard it first. Paul explains that our subconscious is like the autopilot on a plane. If a plane flies off course, or dips below the set altitude, the autopilot corrects the plane.

Our subconscious works in the same way. When something bad happens in our lives, our instincts (autopilot) kick in and save us from crashing. Unfortunately, the opposite also occurs. When something great happens, we self-sabotage. Why do we do this?

It's because our brains like to live in what most people refer to as our comfort zone. The place where things are not too hectic, or too blissful. Just like Goldilocks when she likes things that are "not too heavy – not too light" (come to think of it, that's from a cereal commercial) but anyway, my point is that just like Goldilocks, we like things to be "just right."

Our subconsciouses don't like things to move outside our comfort zone so when they do, it corrects things, so we feel "normal". The problem with this is that we reinforce this behaviour over and over and before we know it, it's like the groove in a record, and we find it very hard to get out of it.

WHAT OTHER PEOPLE THINK OF YOU IS NONE OF YOUR BUSINESS

This is one of the main reasons why people stay in violent relationships. It's not that they want to, or believe they deserve it on a conscious level, but on a subconscious level, they have set their autopilot and it does the job they set it to do. Most people have a deep limiting belief that they deserve what is happening, or that they can't get any better.

I have no doubt that the previous line will get much attention and violent denial by many people. The fact of the matter though is that this is precisely why so many people attract and stay in violent relationships. Most of us (me included until recently) have very little idea of how our subconscious mind controls our day-to-day behaviour.

I really don't have time here to delve deeply into this right now, but I will say that if there is anything in your life that you are unhappy with, you are in some way responsible for it being in your life.

This is not to say that it is your fault, but it is your responsibility. We will unpack that in detail later in the book, but for now, let that percolate because if you can accept the facts in that sentence and use it, your life will change for the good, no matter how fucked up it is.

So, with the subconscious limiting beliefs that I had already developed by age sixteen, it made perfect sense why I jumped at the first opportunity to have a girlfriend. This may not seem like a big deal at age sixteen, but like most of us, this wasn't the last time that I made this mistake.

I am by no means saying that Tracey was a bad person or wrong for me. What I am saying is that I was training myself for later fuck ups by developing that groove; like in the record, that would be harder to break, the more I played the same old song.

Tracey and I dated for a while and as my first love/shag/girlfriend, she will always have a special place in my heart. Unfortunately, at the time I was not thinking with my heart or my head. Well, I was thinking with my head, but it wasn't the big head I was thinking with.

Seeing as I am being honest, I must admit that even though it has been over thirty years, I often think about Tracey and hope that she is healthy, happy, and receiving the love she deserves. Perhaps she will read this and understand that I was nothing more than a horny idiot and a knob for letting her go.

As a footnote, the last time I saw Tracey when we were in our twenties, she was heavily addicted to Heroin and wasn't in a great place. She missed our fifteen-year school reunion in 2005 and if I am completely honest, I often wonder if she is still alive. I sincerely hope

CHAPTER 1

she is and is healthier because she was such a beautiful person when we were together.

While still in grade twelve, I ended up stumbling into my first show outside of school and soon realised that in a cast of twenty guys, less than three were usually straight. To me, it didn't matter if someone was straight or gay. I looked more at their ability as a dancer than their sexual preference.

To be honest, I loved the fact that most entertainers were gay because as I soon discovered, being one of only two or three guys in the cast who were straight meant that all the single girls in the cast focused their attention on me.

As I mentioned before, after starring in Grease, I began dating a girl who played Sandy in another high school's production of the same musical. She had landed one of the lead roles in the musical Hello Dolly at the Gold Coast Arts Centre. Unbeknownst that I wasn't supposed to be there, I went to sneak a look at her rehearsals one day.

As I watched the ensemble warming up, I stood by the coffee station set up outside the large rehearsal space for the best view. Helping himself to a cup of coffee was a tall, slim man in his late forties wearing tight shiny black leggings and white leg warmers.

The man wore glasses and a tight t-shirt and had a different type of poise than I was accustomed to. The man offered me a coffee (which I declined) as he watched the warm-ups taking place. I thought that he was perhaps a "gay coffee lady" which I presumed big productions employed to make the cast feel at home.

After a moment the man walked inside the rehearsal auditorium and began calling out orders to the cast. "Whoops!" I thought to myself. He's the director, not the coffee lady. As I cast my eye over the cast, I noticed the gender balance was largely tilted towards females.

As I scanned the room, I heard the same male voice from the coffee station ask me, "Can you dance"? I turned to see the tall man standing right in the doorway looking at me. "Ahh. Actually, yeah I can." I replied. "Great. We're short of boys. Would you like to be a part of the show?" he asked. I nodded my head. "I'm Robert, the director. Welcome." he continued. Robert led me into the room and continued with the rehearsal.

Fast forward eight years and I was about to audition for my third musical with Robert. Sadly, shows of this calibre no longer exist on the Gold Coast, but for those who have seen a show at the Art Centre, (now called HOTA) you will know that I am talking about the late, legendary New Zealand and Australian director/choreographer; Robert Young.

Anyone who worked with Robert knows that even though his shows on the coast were largely amateur in theory, they were among the most professional shows in the country.

Robert gave his all and expected the same from his young cast members. I know I speak for the thousands of entertainers that Robert mentored and directed over twenty years on the Gold Coast when I say that we are all better performers and better people for having worked with him.

Robert instilled the discipline in me that allowed me to travel the world, but one thing I will never forget was how hard he was on us about fidgeting during rehearsals. He would say that if we fidgeted during rehearsals, we'd fidget during the show and that would pull focus from where the audience was meant to be watching. If you had an itchy nose or needed to sneeze, you did everything you could not act on it. As silly as it seems, it really did get me through many occasions on stage.

During rehearsals for Westside Story in 1998, there were two occasions where even Robert knew I took his commands too far. As the character of "Action" and one of the leading roles in the show, I tried to set an example for the younger cast members. On the first occasion, while being thrown in the air for a chuck-sault, I misjudged the landing and landed on my right knee from six feet in the air; landing heavily on the solid timber floor. The scene we were running at the time was the "dance at the gym" and the entire case was involved, so stopping wasn't an option in my opinion.

Even though my fellow cast member "Riff" played by Brad Hayes stood in shock that he may have badly injured me with his throw, I immediately (but gingerly) stood and continued to dance, even though everyone around me could see that I was in serious pain as I hobbled through the next eight bars. Thankfully Robert saw what happened and stopped the rehearsal so I could be looked at by support staff.

During the same show and in almost the same position in the rehearsal room a few weeks later, Robert once again stopped rehearsals as I displayed a reluctance to fidget no matter what happened.

We were doing a full run of the show with the entire orchestra so it was a big deal. At the time I was wearing track pants with easy-release clips down both sides. These pants were designed so you could easily rip them off without having to remove your shoes; if you were wearing shorts underneath.

CHAPTER 1

Thankfully, because I was a major character, I was wearing a microphone with an elastic mic-pack belt around my waist; on the outside of my pants. As we ran the routine, my thumb got caught in the gap between the clips on one side of my pants, and in a flash, my pants were almost completely dragging on the ground with me dancing in my jocks. Despite this, I was not going to fidget or fiddle with them until the number was complete.

As I looked up at Robert standing at the front of the room, I saw him shaking his head; laughing. He quickly motioned to the Musical Director to stop the orchestra and signalled the cast to stop. Robert then turned his attention to me and asked me to do my pants back up, at which time the entire room was laughing.

As I did my pants up, I simply smiled and said, "Well, you did say not to fidget; no matter what." We all laughed and shortly afterward, continued the technical run, with me being ever so cautious not to disrobe a second time.

SOMETIMES, IT'S NOT ALWAYS GOOD THAT COMES FROM MY MOUTH

While we're on the topic of embarrassing moments in shows, it was during a promotional photoshoot for Westside Story that I made a name for myself as someone who speaks first and thinks later.

The main cast members were all in costume for a photoshoot. The photos taken that night were for the posters and programs for the show. This all occurred before rehearsals had commenced so I only knew a few of my fellow cast members.

The five main "Jets" had just done our signature jump for a photo. This became one of the main images that were used in promoting the show. Shortly afterward, I was standing side stage with Anthony Holt who played "A-Rab". On the stage was Diana, (who was to play Anita), getting her promo shots done, when I said to Anthony, "Geez, she's hot. I'd love to give her one." Anthony looked at me, smiled and nothing more was said.

Shortly after, I was standing in a different wing with Trent, with whom I had done many shows, including at Dracula's and Crazies comedy restaurants. I told Trent what I had said to Anthony. Trent said, "My fucking God! You didn't?" I looked completely puzzled at Trent, as he explained. "That's Diana Holt. Anthony Holt's wife, you numb nuts." "Whoops," I replied.

A week later, Robert gathered all the male cast members together; two weeks before bringing the girls in. Robert needed to turn us boys into classically trained dancers before he unleashed us on the rest of the cast. To start the evening, Robert had us all sit on stage in a huge circle and introduce ourselves.

As it turned out, I was the one to go first. I said, "Hi. I'm Dan and if any of you have wives or girlfriends in the cast, please tell me now so I don't make a complete idiot out of myself as I did with Anthony. The group cracked up and that was the perfect ice-breaker for what became one of my fondest experiences of any show I had ever done.

Even though I have performed in over thirty different professional shows, that show is still at the top of the list. Part of that was thanks to Robert bringing Carole Lawrence in to chat with the entire case before the curtain went up on opening night.

Carol Lawrence is the legendary American actress who played Maria in the original Broadway production of Westside Story. To meet Carol and hear her inspiring words was incredible.

As for Diana Holt. My admiration for her grew well beyond her looks. Along with Carmel Parente, who played Maria in the show, Diana is one of a small handful of female vocalists who have given me Goosebumps. Diana's rendition of "Memory" from Cats at a local event rivalled even the great Elaine Paige's version.

Beyond that, Diana also put me in touch with her singing teacher, who took my voice from that of a rapper who sang a little, to a tenor with a range only surpassed by my singing hero John Farnham.

I say the previous sentence, not to boast of my talent, but rather of the incredible ability of my teacher Ann to enhance my God-given gift so much that I was able to travel the world doing what I loved.

When I started with Ann, my top note was a G; like most male singers. When she had finished with me, I was easily hitting D-sharps above top C. In my humble opinion, my regular voice was nothing spectacular, but as a few of my directors have said, it's when I get to the top of my range that my voice really comes alive.

Ann, Diana, and Robert, along with so many others from Westside Story are a constant source of joy when I look at the large framed photos from that photoshoot that hang on my wall at home.

The Arts Centre used to hang all the framed photos from all the shows that Robert directed on the walls of the foyer, but when a new General Manager took over around 2009, they were all taken down and stored in a dark room hidden away from the public.

Thankfully in 2012, the week before Breeana and I moved into our apartment, the assistant director from Westside Story called me and offered the two large framed photos that were previously on the foyer wall to me as a gift. These photos are each one of a kind and I have been so honoured to have them in my possession.

One day I will donate them to the historical archives of the City of Gold Coast, but for now, they hang proudly on my wall. This ends one very long-winded detour off topic…..

BACK TO 1990 AND THE HELLO DOLLY REHEARSALS

During rehearsals, I quickly fell in love (well it felt like love) with a hot little blonde dancer who was three years older than me. Like me, Nicky also had a partner, but I guess she was training to be a cougar, so we dropped both our partners and were suddenly a couple. A shit move on my behalf I know.

And let me state for the record in case my first girlfriend Tracey reads this. There was nothing wrong with Tracey at all. Tracey was funny, sweet, naughty, and just awesome, but unfortunately for her, I was not coping with having so many options for the first time in my life and I somehow thought that if I didn't capitalise on them that I might miss out.

I recently saw an early episode of Glee; yeah, I know, lame for a forty-year-old to be watching, but I'm an entertainer. In the episode, Finn; played by the late Cory Monteith, who was still a virgin, was exploring his options with girls as a result of his newfound fame from being the quarterback and lead male of the Glee club.

While his heart was saying he should settle into a relationship with Rachel, his head (in particular his little head) was telling him to say yes to any girl who offered "her honour" to him.

You know; If a girl offers her honour, you must honour her offer, then all night you're on her and off her, on her and offer. "Honour an offer" (Read it out loud with a lazy Aussie twang and it makes sense)

At this point in my life, I was no different from Finn in that this was all so new to me and my partially developed pubescent brain rationalised that if I didn't say yes to them all now, I might never get another girl for the rest of my life.

As it turned out I got my comeuppance six months later when Nicky dumped me on Valentine's Day. Yes; Valentine's Day. She even let me go to the trouble of cooking the most romantic dinner that included watermelon carved into the words "I Love You" with tiny rockmelon balls all around it before she dumped my ass.

To her credit, Nicky gave me one last taste of why I was so infatuated with her by taking me to my Dad's bed on his forty-foot boat and leaving me with a lasting memory of her hotness. FYI: Dad was away at the time and his bed was a double bed and not a bunk bed.

Nicky also told me fifteen years later when we had one of our regular coffee meets that she had been carrying the guilt of breaking up with me right through her ten years of marriage. I laughed and told her that I got over it a week later at which point she reminded me that she remembered that I had shagged my best mate's cousin on that same bed on the boat, not a week after she dumped me. Nothing like getting right back on the horse, right?

After finishing high school I had very little direction but I knew that I wanted to be an entertainer. I was bumming around and not working so only two months after graduating, and a few weeks after catching me shagging Nicky on his bed on the boat, Dad kicked me out of home.

Even back then I knew that he did it for all the right reasons. If he had not done that, I would have bummed around for probably a year or so and leached off him instead of creating a life for myself. In hindsight, it taught me many life lessons that have since allowed me to have many successes in several endeavours throughout my life.

Apart from getting a job as an apprentice cabinet maker with my mate's father, I had put the whole singing thing as a career to one side and was focussing again on being Australia's first white rapper.

At the time rap music was not widely accepted in Australia and it was only successful artists such as N.W.A, Public Enemy, M.C Hamer, and Vanilla Ice who sold records here. Australia was not ready to embrace a home-grown rapper; especially not a white one.

While doing my apprenticeship I spent every spare moment practising my dance moves. On many occasions, the cabinet makers would laugh while having lunch on a building site as I would breakdance on flattened cardboard boxes in someone's brand-new half-built kitchen.

After a few months, my mate's father decided to let me go because he knew that my heart was elsewhere, and he didn't want to stifle my dreams by letting me become a cabinet maker.

It was also at this time that I was caught between wanting to be a professional cricketer and an entertainer. I was captain of the cricket team at high school and part of the South East Queensland rep side,

CHAPTER 1

and I intended to finish school and hopefully play for Queensland and Australia. I will never know if I would have made it, but my state rep captain went on to play for Queensland and at the time of writing this book has been the coach of the Australian women's world champion cricket team for several years and is now coaching England's men's one-day side.

It was in 1991 that I landed my first professional dancing gig and was part of the first studio in the country to teach or perform what was called American funk. (You know; the running man etc.) I landed the job because I did my first funk class with a broken leg (I didn't know it was broken at the time) and then spent the next six weeks watching every single class and rehearsal, despite not being able to participate in either.

The manager of the studio said that if I was that dedicated, then he knew I would be a great performer. As it turned out, by the time I started learning the routines, it all fell into place very quickly.

There is countless research proving that the mind is not able to decipher between what is real and what we vividly imagine. For decades, professional athletes have used visualisation as an integral part of their training. As a professional entertainer, I always visualised my shows both during rehearsals and before going on stage. Once my mind knew what to do, my body and voice just followed without much conscious thought.

Having spent six weeks watching the dancers learn routines back in the studio as a seventeen-year-old, by the time I could physically dance again, it was like I had always been practising them physically all along. My mind had vividly processed the routines, so when it came time to do them; they just happened.

This auto-pilot type of recollection helped over the following months because consciously I was distracted by more female attention. Over the following year, I ended up dating four of the thirty female dancers that we were working with as we prepared for the opening ceremony of the first-ever Indy car race outside of North America.

I say this not to boast or as some sort of achievement, but truth be known, the fact that the four of them didn't team up and kill me is in some ways an accomplishment in itself.

Performing on the grid of the first Indy car race on the Gold Coast in 1991 was very exciting, but that was just the beginning of what turned out to be a big year. A group of us from the studio landed the support act gig for Vanilla Ice, Snap, and Two in A Room when they all toured the country in late 1991.

Working closely with these artists taught me early on that no matter how successful or famous people are, they are still just human beings. At the time Vanilla Ice was the most recognisable and famous artist in the world. His music was at the top of every chart worldwide and his unique look made him instantly recognisable anywhere he went.

Like most famous recording artists, Vanilla Ice wore sunglasses almost everywhere he went in an attempt to live a semi-normal existence so when he appeared via satellite link on the Steve Vizard show wearing sunglasses straight after our concert at Brisbane's Festival Hall, no one batted an eyelid.

Most people watching the interview would have thought that Vanilla Ice was just being a pretentious prat by wearing sunglasses, but what only a few of us knew was that the reason he was wearing glasses was that he was sporting the beginnings of a huge black eye.

Earlier in the night, he came running off stage at the end of the show and headed for his dressing room. At Festival Hall most of the dressing rooms were downstairs under the stage. His dressing room was directly below the stage and when he came down the stairs, he flung himself around the bottom of the staircase but failed to see the low roof and clocked himself right in the eye.

With only a short time before his interview was being beamed to Melbourne live, and his eye already looking like he had been hit with a Mike Tyson right hook, he had no other option but to cover it up with sunglasses.

As much as Robert Van Winkle (Vanilla Ice) appeared on the surface to be an arrogant knob, in person he was a warm and genuine guy who loved a laugh and to take the piss out of himself. His dancers and DJ were all awesome too. In particular, his choreographer John who called himself "Hi-Tech" was a hoot.

John took a shine to one of our female dancers, so we showed him around town. John invited me to hang with him and Rob in Miami, Florida if I was ever in town and when they left, Rob left me with a raw unedited demo of his new album that as it turned out never got released. In my opinion, this tape was Ice's best work so it's a shame the world never got to hear it.

The reason I mention these things is to illustrate that people's perception of other people is usually quite distorted. I mean, I am certain that anyone who was asked what sort of a guy I am would say that I am a complete fucktard who treats women worse than any man alive. This would be purely based on the voice of a loud minority and manipulative media pushing an agenda of hate and negativity to produce revenue.

The truth is that I adore women and treat them like a princess when we're together, but that said, in the past, I would not tolerate crap and told them so in no uncertain terms; which none of them liked.

My point is that it doesn't matter how people perceive you. What matters is how you are and how you perceive yourself. On the flip side, before perceiving someone to be a certain way, ask yourself, "Is this who they really are, and is my perception based on fact, or someone else's opinion?"

Whenever I tell people that I was Vanilla Ice's support act, it always gets a giggle, and so does the next line. One of our female dancers (Actually the same one who dated Vanilla Ice's choreographer) was Peter Andre's girlfriend and Peter's brother Michael was our DJ (DJ Andre I mentioned earlier) for one or two of the previously mentioned concerts. (I actually can't remember which ones as it was thirty years ago)

I worked out at Pindara gym with Peter several times a week, but while he was doing three hundred sit-ups, I was more focussed on bench press (I hated sit-ups). It was cool hanging out with someone who was about to reach the level of their goals that I was aspiring to.

Peter had only just signed his record deal and had not yet released his first single. We would often hang with him and his brother and jam or share ideas for new songs. Some people get jealous or intimidated by someone having achieved the goals that they want, but I was looking at it from a different angle.

Peter was at the level that I wanted to be, so it made sense that if I learned from his successes and what he had done, then surely I would achieve similar success. One of the biggest things that I learnt from Peter was that he had taught himself to sing for the most part.

This inspired me that even though I was not headed to N.I.D.A, ED5, or Brent Street to learn my craft, it was still possible to achieve my dreams if I was focused enough. Even though the elusive record deal didn't eventuate, I was blessed to have a lucrative and successful career as a professional singer travelling to over four hundred beautiful destinations around the world.

Peter Andre was a friend but more importantly an idol and inspiration. As Peter's songwriting career took off, we were jamming with his DJ brother Michael and I was like a sponge soaking up as many lessons and tips as I could from Peter. At the time I was a rapper and an aspiring singer. I used Peter's journey as a sign that if I showed as much dedication to my craft as he did, I too could be successful.

As it turned out, it wasn't a recording contract that led to that success but rather a prolonged professional career performing in shows on land and at sea, many credits as a session singer for various artists, and a long list of radio jingles that I still hear on the radio from time to time.

Just like Peter, this all came with no formal training and just six months of singing lessons. What it did take though was a shit load of dedication, and discipline to spend endless hours going over single notes until they sat perfectly where I wanted them to in my voice.

Over the next three years, I worked as a session rapper for some famous international pop stars and came oh so close to being signed to record labels on several occasions, but by the age of twenty-two, I had begun looking for a "real job". This goal was expedited when my girlfriend at the time fell pregnant.

Although I don't want to give too much attention to internet trolls, or disgruntled ex-girlfriends, Sonia is one of the ones who have for some reason got the biggest bugbear after twenty years and has felt the need to air old lies on any current affairs program that would listen to her crap.

At the time she fell pregnant, I thought that I had better get a stable job and look to be a responsible father and partner. Even though the situation was not ideal, I felt that it was the right thing to do to try to make it work. Given the way things turned out and the way she in particular turned out, that was a lesson learned and a mistake that I will ensure I never make again.

The big mistake was not that she was crazy, treated me badly, was insecure, and was just one of these women who you see in horror movies boiling rabbits (although she was all of these things). My mistake was that I put someone else's needs and wants before my own. Sure, it's a noble thing for a man to do, but in reality, if I wasn't going to look after myself, then who would? You are the most important person in the world and while I am not suggesting anyone should be selfish or self-centred, you need to take care of number one first.

Society wants us to conform to the way of life that it believes is best for us. Society dictates that you must get a good education, get a stable full-time job, get married, stay married, have children, pay as much in

CHAPTER 1

taxes as the government needs, buy a home, get a mortgage, don't take risks, and live an 'average' life.

While I am not saying that any of these things are bad, it doesn't mean you're a bad person if you take different paths to these either. For example, in the finance section of my book "The No B.S Approach to Create the Life You Want," I explain how far wealthier you would be if you invested the money you spent in better investments, rather than on a mortgage over thirty years.

Again, this isn't the best option for everyone, but it is a far better alternative for many than the mere 0.5% return per year over thirty years that you're looking at with a mortgage in many cases.

Similarly, while society says that if you're a good person you will get married, start a family, etc. If this is what you want, then great. But as it turned out for me, I am far happier having never been married.

So far as the security of a full-time job, well that myth was blown out of the water when Covid-19 hit the world. I go into more detail later, but for most people, that "secure job" wasn't so secure.

The big problem was that those who thought their job was secure failed to have six months' worth of savings to tide them over when the pandemic hit because they thought their job was safe; no matter what.

My point in all of this is that you don't have to live a "conventional" life to be happy, or successful. There is nothing wrong with not getting married, having your own small business, or renting. This is on the provisor that you make the alternative work for you.

The biggest thing I have discovered since being thrust into my current situation is that if it didn't happen, then I'd still be trying to conform to society in those ways and I'd be extremely unhappy.

I was seriously unhappy trying to make things work with Sonia back in my early twenties. I had allowed her to trap me in the relationship, and this made me resentful. I was desperate to escape but subconsciously, I wondered if I could handle being alone until I met someone else.

These days I would be grateful for the time alone to enjoy my own company, but back then I was so insecure that I would rather be in an unhappy relationship than be alone. Sound familiar?

I know this is how many people feel, and this is why so many relationships take a turn for the worse. Like anyone else, I wanted to be loved, but couldn't see beyond the mess I was in to take the leap.

This level of insanity is like trying to climb a ladder without letting go. You can't get to the next rung until you let go of the one you are holding onto first. I wasn't happy, but I was holding on until something else came along. I don't think I was doing this on purpose, and it wasn't that I set out to wait until I got a better offer, but subconsciously this is precisely what happened.

LIFE IS WHAT YOU MAKE OF IT

On many occasions throughout my adult life, people have said, "You have lived such an exciting life." The subtext behind that is that many of them are either envious, or they thought that I was full of shit about half my antics. If only that were true. I myself look back and think, how on earth did I manage to fit so much into such a short amount of time?

I guess I unknowingly trained myself while still at school. My parents were far from poor, but because they were approaching retirement, they were preserving capital while trying to educate me about being smart with money. I never went without; however, I certainly did not get spoilt.

In my final year of high school, I was more focussed on co-curricular activities such as the cricket team, rugby league, snow camp, Rock Eisteddfod, school musical, drama week, and anything other than schoolwork. With all that going on during school hours, who had time for schoolwork?

With an unhealthy disregard for my formal education, I spent my weekends and some weeknights working two jobs. At sixteen I ran the kitchen at Sizzler on Friday nights, then went to the local nightclub that my brother's best mate ran to work as a glassy and bartender until five in the morning. I slept all day, worked at the club again Saturday night, then went back to Sizzler on Sunday night.

The fact that I was ignoring all my school subjects meant nothing because I was fucking loaded! I was the only kid in school who was earning $300-$400 per week (in 1989) and the only one cool enough to be working in a nightclub, while everyone else was begging the bouncers to get in.

Back then the laws were far more lenient and the fines for underage drinking were $50, so who cared? Plus, two of the bouncers at this club were police cadets so the venue never got raided and I was well protected.

Fast forward to 1993 and I realised that the music industry was tougher than I had expected, so I ended up back working in the clubs

CHAPTER 1

to avoid starvation. By this stage, I had a lot more experience than most twenty-year-olds, so I ended up managing the bar at Melbas.

Man did that place open my eyes. Anyone who has lived on the Gold Coast has a story of a night at Melbas nightclub, but to work there for six months is on a whole new level.

As previously stated, I sucked at saying no to beautiful women so my "on-again / off-again" girlfriend (Who ended up being on and off again several more times over the next few years) was off again as I started dating one of the hot waitresses at Melba's.

Megan worked on the floor a few nights a week and after we had dated a few times I found out that her other job was as a high-class escort. I wasn't sure what to make of this, but to be honest, I didn't really care.

Megan was hot and threw money around like it was birdseed at Currumbin Wildlife Sanctuary. Apart from my final year at high school, I had never had lots of money so this whole concept was very new to me. Megan knew that I was chasing a record contract as a rapper and knew that Los Angeles was the heart of the rap scene, so she suggested that we go to L.A together. She said that if I buy my ticket, she will pay for everything else.

At that stage, I had never been out of the country, so I was super excited to be heading over to L.A. As our travel dates drew closer, Megan and I fell out but remained friends. She said that she wanted me to go and that she would still take care of hotels etc. for me. "Okay", I thought. In hindsight, a little naïve, but hey, I was rolling with it. I went to the bank and got a credit card with a $1,000 limit on it. The day before I was due to leave, Megan said she would transfer money into my account once I was there.

I headed off on my own and was pumped for what lay ahead. When I arrived in L.A, I grabbed a sporty little rental car and headed into the city to find a hotel. I checked into Sheraton near Santa Monica pier and as was the case with the hire car, I put it on my new credit card.

For the next few days, I drove around L.A, booked a recording studio to lay down some tracks, and did some sightseeing. I felt like a frickin' king. Twenty years old and living the dream; or so I thought.

It was the morning after Halloween 1993 and as I hoped in the car, I knew it wasn't going to be a normal day. The first two news reports (Yeah, I listened to the news back then) were about River Phoenix overdosing only a block away from where I was staying, and then a story about some gangsters doing a drive-by shooting on a group of young kids in South Central L.A.

Living in Australia back then, we rarely heard of those kinds of things. Maybe I was just naïve or was oblivious to it. Either way, I was shocked. I wanted to lift my mood so I drove into the only place in L.A that could turn anyone's frown upside down; Rodeo Drive.

I strolled into a shop that had some awesome hip-hop apparel and saw what at the time was a very cool red, white, and blue "stars and stripes" leather jacket. This jacket was exactly what Bobby Brown would have been seen in, so I had to have it.

I went to the counter and presented my credit card to pay for it. Back then transactions were done with the "clicky-click" imprinter merchant machine using triplicate paper. I guess they are just called merchant machines, but for the life of me I can't remember, or find any reference to them on Google so let's call them clicky-click machines.

If you're under thirty years of age, ask your parents what I am talking about. Because the jacket was over USD$500 the clerk had to call it through for authorisation. She went to the backroom to do so, but on her return, she had bad news; my card was declined. How could my car be declined? With a depressed look on my face, I put the jacket on the rack and disappeared out of the store with my head down in embarrassment.

When I got back to my hotel, I called the bank at which point they advised me that I was already at $6,000 and my hotel and car had not yet been added to that amount. "Holy Fuck"! I thought.

Back in 1993 international credit card transactions took days or weeks to filter through to your bank, so this situation was only going to get worse.

As it turned out, once I left the country Megan had become very hard to contact and the money that was promised never showed up in my account. In hindsight, I know it was both naïve and unreasonable to presume any girl would fund my lavish holiday; especially when we were no longer together.

At the time though I felt betrayed. I can hear you laughing from my laptop as I write that. As it turned out, Megan and I remained close for several years but lost contact once she married somewhere around the time I went away to work on ships.

I arrived home from my L.A trip a few days later having survived on Southern Comfort and ice and one-dollar 7/11 hotdogs to make my last few dollars last. FYI: I bought the Southern duty-free on the

CHAPTER 1

way over, so I wasn't that stupid to buy it after I was totally broke.

By the time all of the transactions had piled up, I had racked up $10,000 in ten days. That is a fuckload of money in 1993; especially for a broke twenty-year-old. I mean shit! I spent $5,000 on a five-day holiday in the Maldives in 2018 but that was for an overwater bungalow, business class flights, and all meals and alcohol. Even my twenty-one-day trip to the Caribbean, a White Christmas, and Las Vegas in 2017 was only ten thousand dollars.

Subsequently, I spent the next five years paying the L.A trip off and had a bad credit rating for five years too. At the time I hated the fact that all of my money went to that bill and I couldn't borrow anything either, but looking back there were so many positive lessons that I gained from the experience.

So often we do stupid things and look back with regret. I no longer have regrets. Sure, there are things I might not do again, but everything that has happened in my life has been divine timing. No matter what you do in life, see it as a valuable experience and an example of life happening for you; not to you.

You may not always see the blessing or silver lining while you're up to your neck in it, but there will always come a time when you realise just how valuable that experience was.

VIVA LAS VEGAS

Twenty-five years later I found myself in a similar but vastly different situation. I was in Las Vegas alone, but I had my own money. I still had the same cheeky curiosity with no fear of where my adventures led me. I headed to the old part of Vegas (Freemont Street) where all the old casinos were. I watched the incredible light show that plays every night then went looking for a place to have dinner.

I wandered into a hotel/casino and took an escalator upstairs. At the top of the escalator, I noticed a narrow hallway leading to a bar. Lining the walls were black-velvet-lined walls with approximately thirty-centimetre holes in them at about shoulder height.

The best way to describe the holes is to call them "Glory-holes". You know, like the ones in porn movies where…. well, do I really need to go into detail? Regardless, instead of penises sticking through the holes, there were women's arms wearing black velvet gloves holding champagne flutes full to the brim.

Along the hallway, there were at least five or six arms poking through on either side of the walkway. There was no one else in the hallway so I thought I'd grab a glass of champagne and see where the hallway led. As I got to the end of the hallway, I noticed a stunning array of fresh peeled prawns, lobster, smoked salmon, and crab. A young lady handed me a serviette and I helped myself to a few prawns before continuing into the main bar area.

As I looked around the room, I noticed that most of the people there were wearing cocktail dresses and suits. In contrast, I was wearing a pair of jeans and a black leather jacket. By this stage, I wasn't really sure where I was, why I was there, or if I was meant to be there. All I knew was that the prawns were delicious and the champagne kept coming. I chatted with a few people, but mostly just meandered from the bar to the seafood table.

After about thirty minutes, I thought the chances of me getting discovered and possibly having to fork out for what I had ingested were increasing, so I decided to cut and run. By the time I left, I had devoured more than a dozen large king prawns, five lobster tails, and a handful of smoked salmon; plus, who knows how many glasses of champagne. I was as full as a fat lady's sock and happier than a breastfeeding baby.

As I stumbled back to the bus stop to catch the shuttle back to the MGM Grand where I was staying, I felt satisfied that while the USA had gotten the better of me decades earlier, in a small way I did what most people fail to do; beat Vegas.

WHAT COMES OUT OF YOU WHEN YOU'RE SQUEEZED?

It was an awesome summer in 1995 and I was managing the pool bar at a 5-star hotel on the Gold Coast when things changed for me. My now ex-girlfriend (the one who was on again, off again) was only two months away from giving birth, yet we had not spoken for her entire pregnancy. I was trying to move on with my life, yet the impending fatherhood was hanging over my head.

The weather all summer was awesome, and we had some big-name actors staying in the hotel for several months while they filmed the movie "The Phantom". Hanging with the likes of Billy Zane, Treat Williams, and Catherine Zetta Jones was exciting, but meeting one of my teenage crushes, Kristy Swanson was super cool.

Kristy was super hot and her accent when she kept saying "Thanks Danny" while I took my time performing first-aid on her cut toe, was enough to make any young guy dribble with excitement.

CHAPTER 1

I was prowling the perimeter of the pool deck one day when a hot little blonde who looked like Camera Diaz ordered a drink. She gave me her room number to put the drink on, but when I rang the drink up in the system, the name on the room was an older gentleman.

I questioned the girl who was eighteen and definitely not the guest's partner. She told me that it was her stepdad's room and that she was staying there while he was working on the movie.

As it turned out, her step-dad was one of the most important crew on the movie and I found out later that her biological father was a man who was responsible for several opening and closing Olympic ceremonies.

If I am being shady about the girl's identity, that is out of respect for her and her family. Needless to say, she and I spent the next few weeks hooking up all over the hotel.

She was one hot-blooded young woman. She jumped me in the corridors, the elevator, and even the fire escape. Wherever I turned, she seemed to show up, willing and able. The fact that she had a boyfriend back in Sydney made no difference to her.

At the end of the few weeks, the eighteen-year-old went back to her northern beaches mansion in Sydney and I went back to being insecure and struggling to be happy. Sure, I had heaps of fun, but I was unfulfilled.

That summer I also slept with the married daughter of one of Australia's state's Premiers. I had sex with a female police officer in the bathroom of her hotel room and broke an outdoor chair having sex on the balcony of the hotel with a nineteen-year-old from Hervey Bay on a hen's night.

I even had rendezvous with a model from Melbourne whose hotel bed I left the morning I got word that my ex-girlfriend was going into labour. It was a busy summer around the pool bar that year in more ways than one.

The reason I am sharing these promiscuous stories is not to brag, but rather to illustrate how looking for love in someone else is a fruitless exercise if you can't find it within yourself.

We all want to be loved, but most of us are searching for it in someone else, instead of inside ourselves. At that point in my life, I was acting from a place of ego and being driven by those insecurities I mentioned earlier.

The fact that I had managed to seduce and sleep with all of these women did very little to quell my insecurities. The instant gratification of the moment felt great, but the second it was over, the vulnerability and insecurities returned.

Dr. Wayne Dyer summed it up perfectly when he related it to fruit. Stick with me. If you squeeze an orange, grapefruit juice doesn't come out. When you squeeze a lemon, apple juice doesn't escape. Whatever is on the inside of the fruit is what comes out. Squeezing an orange gives you orange juice. We are the same.

If we have anger inside us, squeezing us is going to release anger. Likewise, if we are looking for love unless we have love inside for ourselves, it won't come out and can't be shared or enjoyed by anyone else.

We can all show a particular side to our personality, or as entertainers say, "fake it 'till you make it," but when we're put under pressure, like when an orange is squeezed, it is only what is really inside that can come out.

Back when I was jumping the bones of the first girl who paid me attention, I had no love inside for myself. Still to this day, I have no idea why, but regardless, I was insecure and was looking for someone else to fulfill me, instead of being able to do it myself.

So what happened when I was squeezed back then? Insecurities came out and that is what dictated my relationships. Some might say that if you squeezed me, shit comes out coz I'm full of shit, but I'd like to think that these days, love, tolerance, and forgiveness are what would come out. Until we change what is inside, what comes out will never be good.

When I headed off to cruise ships, my insecurities didn't disappear; they were merely hidden more easily. I was adored by passengers and revered as royalty onboard and while this felt amazing, it was masking the real issue.

I thought I was loved and felt like things were perfect. Yes, I was very happy, and I was doing what I loved and travelling the world, but it wasn't until all of that was gone that I realised where the real hole in my life was and that no woman would be able to fill it.

SO THIS IS WHAT FAILURE FEELS LIKE?

In 2008 when I decided that I was going to finish up on cruise ships, I had no idea what I was going to do. I had made the conscious choice to leave ships because I didn't want to be like a few friends who were in their forties, single, with no kids, and had no prospects of either.

CHAPTER 1

I wanted to get out at the top of my game while I was at the peak of my craft. Given that I was used to getting paid ridiculous amounts of money to work one hour per day, I was hardly going to do a three or four-hour gig in a pub or restaurant for $200 - $300 per night while listening to drunks trying to sing along. Once again, I figured that it was time to look for a "real job".

With my extensive travelling to over four-hundred destinations, I managed to land a job with Australia's leading travel agent brand. At first, this was great and while I did enjoy it, something was missing. I had thought that the real job would be just a filler until I discovered what I really wanted to do, post-cruise ships.

I had met with a few entertainment agents in the hope of getting musical theatre work on land, but at the time, there were very few of these types of agents and the ones that did exist were in Sydney or Melbourne. I met with one agent who loved my showreel but was focussed on movies, not theatre.

Even though I have done some acting, I am a singer and dancer who can act, not the other way around. The only acting work I got was as a cop in two different productions. I must have had that useless, arsehole kind of look that most of them have; look who is typecast (and cue the hate mail and harassment from the police force).

The agent recommended that I contact a lady who was in charge of the Australian casting of a hit Broadway musical "Jersey Boys" that was due to open in Australia later in 2009. At the time I had not heard of the show but after a quick Google search, I was hooked.

As we now know, Jersey Boys is the story of Frankie Valli and the Four Seasons. I was due to head to London to stay with my friend Anita for a month while looking for agents there.

Anita is the Aussie who had been a star of London's West End for many years as I mentioned earlier. She was going to introduce me to some of the biggest agents in the industry. I had met one agent while dating another West End star, Sarah the previous year, but I wasn't impressed with what they could offer, so I was looking forward to meeting Anita's contacts.

I'd be more open in dropping names of my female lovers (As above – The West End stars), but that will lead to the police harassing them like they did the others I mentioned in my books "The Blame Game" and "C.R.U.I.S.E". Besides, I'd spend too much time picking up the names I dropped throughout the book if that was the case.

This book is not about conquests. You can read about them and learn their names in my book 'C.R.U.I.S.E'. PMSL. I will say though that both ladies were exceptional talents and two of the biggest names in London's Westend in the preceding decade. (Do your research and you never know what you will find).

I had started rehearsing for the audition in Jersey Boys for a few months and when I landed in London, I noticed that the show was due to open there before setting up in Australia. Anita had a few friends in the lead roles in London, so I bought us tickets to check out the final preview before the official opening night.

As we took our seats in the fourth row, I noticed that directly behind us were Frankie Valli, Bob Gaudio (Two of the Original Four Seasons), and the director Des McAnuff. I recognised Des as I had done extensive research on all aspects of the production in preparing for my audition for the lead role of Frankie Valli.

During the interval, I was leaving a V.I.P. room where Anita had taken me to meet someone when Des walked past me. I introduced myself and told him that I was going to be seeing him in a few weeks in Australia when I was auditioning for the lead role.

He smiled and looked me up and down in a casting director's type of way and said, "Dan. I very much look forward to seeing you then." To me, this chance encounter and the way all of these events had fallen into place was a sign that this role was my destiny.

After the show, Anita took me backstage to meet some of the cast. To say I was a little star-struck was an understatement. I managed to draw on my limited acting ability so that I came off as cool and not too overawed. We hung out in the dressing room of Glenn Carter (Tommy Devito) and had drinks with Glenn, Ryan Malloy (Frankie Valli), and a few other cast members. Shit! Now I have to pick up those names (that I dropped) as well.

I rocked up to the audition a few weeks later in Australia with every ounce of my being believing that this role was what I was destined to do. I had rehearsed harder than ever before and I knew that I had Frankie's distinctly unique and incredibly tough vocal sound down pat.

In my opinion, only two things were standing in my way. The fact that I was supposed to be between 5'6 and 5'9 for the role and that I didn't look Italian at all. I've never been too tall for an audition in my life. In fact, my being 5'10 had made me too short on occasions.

I went into the audition and I smiled when they said that one of the pieces that I had to perform was the falsetto introduction of "Walk like a man" from the show. I had specifically practised that bit in the hope

CHAPTER 1

that it would be used. I nailed both that and my own prepared number and I left the audition certain that I would get the part. After several weeks and months, I learnt that in fact the part had been awarded to Bobby Fox.

I was absolutely devastated. I was certain that the role was what I had dreamed of and it was something I had worked tirelessly for over nine months for. Not getting a role is part and parcel of the entertainment industry.

You can't get every role, no matter how good you are. It's not always your talent that is the determining factor in being cast or not cast. You may not have the right look, or your look or height in relation to the other cast members might not fit.

I have seen Ryan Malloy play the role in London, the original Frankie, John Lloyd Young (Who also played the role in the movie), and Bobby Fox in the role, and while Bobby was great, I did think I had something to offer the role too. Bobby looks more Italian than me and is actually shorter than me so who knows if these were factors or if I simply wasn't the right sound.

Either way, as I said, I was devastated. Besides the fact I truly believed that I was meant to play this role, but didn't get it, this was my very first "failed" audition. Throughout my professional life, I had always landed the roles that I had auditioned for.

I had been offered jobs on the spot at auditions (which rarely happens) and I had gone into auditions pissing around and still got the parts, so this was a massive kick to the ego. I had managed to impress the best directors and choreographers in Australia, the UK, and the USA so this outcome wasn't even on my radar.

I remember one audition while in London where I had prepared to sing "This is the Moment" from Jekyll and Hyde, but when I heard the guy before me sing that song, I decided to change tack. I walked in less prepared than I wanted to be and the lead casting director asked what song I was going to sing. I told them that I wanted to sing This Is the Moment but decided to make a last-minute change. The three casting directors collectively sighed as this song is the most used male audition song everywhere.

I decided to pull out a souped-up version of "Little Deuce Coupe" instead and at the end of the song, the three of them applauded, took a few seconds to confer, and then offered me the role on the spot. Whether I have been lucky, or brilliant at my auditions, failure did not find me until Jersey Boys.

The only other audition that I took on that didn't lead to a role was in one of the stage productions at Jupiter's Casino on the Gold Coast in the early 2000s. The show was a "Latino" show and the part was between myself and Tony Lee Scott who was also from the Gold Coast.

Unfortunately for me, Tony was taller, even more of a lady's man, and was part Maori so he looked more Latino than I did. I saw the show with the directors once it launched and I did enjoy Tony's performance. I wasn't too worried by this lost role because I had been offered a lead role with Princess Cruises, so life moved on quickly.

I've never been one to talk my talent up or have a big head, but I was always quietly confident of my ability. When you know what you are good at and work hard to hone that skill, you will usually have much success.

You always see those people at auditions who prance around and tell everyone how good they are. They are usually the first ones who are shown the door. On countless occasions, when people asked if I was a good singer, I would simply say, "Well that's not for me to say. I'd rather let my singing illustrate whether or not I am good."

I knew I wasn't a great bartender or cabinet maker, but I also knew that I had been given this talent to use. When you have a certain talent, it is a shame to not develop it and share it with the world. For that reason, I now look back and feel that I retired from professional singing and cruise ships far too early.

It is said that it is best for people to ask "Why" did you retire, rather than "Why didn't you," but still, I feel like I let my career die while the music was still in me. That said, my creative ability is now channelled into bringing music to life through feature-length scripts, so while I no longer sing, the music may still be alive.

The setback with Jersey Boys hit hard. I didn't sing a single note for months and apart from one occasion when I was flown to Sydney to perform in Cate Blanchett's theatre in 2010, I have not sung in public since.

Hang on a second while I pick up that name that I just dropped as well. While I am dropping names again, that evening I met one of my musical idols, Glenn A. Baker. For years I had idolised his musical knowledge, so to meet the man that many believe possesses the greatest musical mind in the world was an honour.

It wasn't a conscious choice to stop singing, I think I just related too much pain on a subconscious level with singing after Jersey Boys, so I simply avoided it. Giving up what you love can leave a huge hole in who you are, and I know in my case, I struggled with this loss of identity.

Even though I had a good job and was building a life after having been away for almost ten years, emotionally I wasn't happy. This led to me once again chasing the wrong types of girls and thus a string of failed relationships.

What I now know is that for most of us, we don't have just one calling in life, but rather a few. Most successful people have more than one successful career. We have God-given talents in a particular area for a particular stage in our lives. More often than not this is then replaced with our next 'gift' which takes us into the next season of our lives and so on. While I do regret leaving ships too soon, I can now see the new path that I would not have taken if I was still at sea.

CHAPTER TWO

THE ELEPHANT IN EVERY ROOM

"Being perfect at the <u>science of achievement</u> without being successful at the <u>art of fulfillment</u> is like launching a beautiful boat and forgetting to put the bungs in." - J.D Mo'orea

The underlined words above go hand in hand for some people, but the reality for most of us is that they are polar opposites and precisely why so many of us seemingly have everything but are so miserable. I first heard of these two concepts when attending Tony Robbins' Date with Destiny seminar in 2016. Tony talked about them on day six when we were beginning to tie everything together that we had learnt thus far.

Tony has built an empire on teaching others to achieve success, but what many people don't know is that he also teaches people how to be fulfilled. To achieve success in your business or achieve financial freedom is wonderful, but unless you master the "Art of fulfillment" you will never be truly happy. The distinct difference between the two concepts is simple. There is a science to achievement and an art to fulfillment.

Any successful businessman, C.E.O or entrepreneur will be able to show how there is a scientific formula to success, but when it comes to being fulfilled, it is an art; not a science.

On several occasions, both live and on recordings, I have heard Tony tell a wonderful, yet heartbreaking story of one of the world's most loved comedians who conquered the science of achievement, yet somehow failed at the art of fulfillment.

I am of course talking about the late great Robin Williams. To paraphrase (more importantly to shorten) Tony's story, Tony talks about how Robin Williams set many goals and achieved them in what seemed to be an effortless way. He had goals such as having his own TV show and winning an Academy Award for comedy and then he even wanted to win an Academy Award for the opposite of what he was most famous for by winning the award for a serious role. Williams achieved all of these and so much more, yet as we all know, his life ended in such a tragic way.

Not only was Robin Williams successful and famous, but he was one of the most loved people on the planet. He was adored by millions of people all over the world, yet somehow, he wasn't fulfilled. How can this be the case?

I know that Robin's Lewy Body Dementia that he was suffering with was more than likely a contributing factor in the decision to end his life. Nevertheless, I can't help but feel that perhaps while he nailed the "science" of achievement far beyond anyone in the last half-century, he struggled with the "art" of fulfillment portion of his life.

As Tony teaches, we can have all the money, fame, or success in the world, but if we don't master the art of fulfillment; we have nothing. It is wonderful to be successful and to have money, but all of that means nothing if you can't find real joy in life. In my opinion, true happiness comes from having a purpose that is far beyond yourself.

Something that is for the greater good and that will create such juice in your life, that no challenge is too great to hold you back from jumping out of bed each day. Not being fulfilled is what leads to depression or mental illness. Some of the world's most successful people suffer from mental illness as a result of their not mastering the art of fulfillment.

On that note; Let's talk about the elephant in the room. Not just this room; but every room.

When Breeana first committed suicide in 2013, I made a comment on Facebook about mental illness and how Breeana had managed to cover her battles up from her loved ones and friends. This comment was swiftly met by a nasty response from Breeana's aunty.

I have since come to realise that Breeana's aunty is not only a nasty, spiteful person who attacks anyone who doesn't agree with her, but more to the point she is uninformed in both mental illnesses, but more importantly in her own niece's state of mind before her death.

Even though I am being blunt in my assessment of her actions, when it comes to mental illness, she is not the only person who has it all wrong. As a society, we have a stigma surrounding mental illness. When someone is said to have a mental illness, we tend to think of only the higher end of the scale.

For example, if we hear that someone has a mental illness, we instantly think that they are psychotic or need to be admitted to a mental institution and placed in a straight-jacket or padded cell.

This is not the case at all. Think about the term mental illness for a moment. If we had a physical illness, we would see a doctor, chiropractor, or Osteopath. A physical illness can range from a minor cut finger or migraine, all the way up to broken bones, heart attack, or cancer. Unlike physical illness, we clump mental illness altogether instead of realising that there is a broad range of mental illnesses that range from minor to major, just like physical illnesses.

If we say someone has a mental rather than physical illness, we think something very serious is wrong with the person. Just like physical illness, mental illness has varying degrees. Some are serious and others not so much. Mental illness could be as minor as having infrequent bouts of anxiety or feelings of being overwhelmed.

On the other end of the spectrum yes, mental illness can be very serious and requires professional monitoring around the clock, but for most of us, mental illness is minor and very manageable or curable. It is also something that should not be ridiculed, denied, or suppressed.

I myself have had times of depression or feelings of being overwhelmed. That doesn't mean I am a psychopath. Nor does it mean that you or anyone else is a psychopath for suffering in the same way. We need to remove the stigma surrounding mental illness and treat it like we do with physical illness. Until we do, the rate of suicide will continue to increase at the alarming rate it has over the last ten years.

In Breeana's case, it wasn't necessarily major, however, the fact that it wasn't dealt with correctly by her family or even me, didn't help. In "The Blame Game" I again mentioned Breeana's battle with depression and mental illness. This was met with strenuous denial and condemnation by her family.

I have no idea whether her family feels this way about her situation because they are in complete denial, if they feel guilty about not doing more for her, or if in fact, they had no idea that she was suffering in this way.

CHAPTER 2

As I stated in the book and during my two-hour interview with Channel Seven for the Sunday Night program, Breeana told me on many occasions that she was depressed. It was stated by the family that this was rubbish and it was also brought up by detectives when I was charged with her murder that at no time was Breeana diagnosed with depression.

At no point did I say that Breeana was diagnosed with depression, nor did I claim that I was an expert or authority on mental illness or depression. I simply stated that on several occasions Breeana said to me that she was depressed.

The fact that she may not have said it to her family does not mean what I said in my book or the interview was incorrect. If I had audio recordings of all of my conversations with Breeana then I would have proof of her saying it but for obvious reasons, I don't record things like that.

The reason I remember these words from her was because, to me, Breeana was far from depressed. She was such a happy-go-lucky young woman and on the surface, seemed far from depressed. However, just like Robin Williams, Breeana kept that side of her feelings well hidden from most people.

This is the case with many people who are depressed or suicidal. They are embarrassed to admit that they are struggling or have a problem. Paul Hester; the drummer from the band Crowded House is another classic example. To me, Paul was the happiest member of the band and the least likely to harm himself, yet we all know his story.

Most people who die from suicide have not been diagnosed with depression or mental illness. That is partly due to incorrect diagnosis, but mostly because of a reluctance to seek help. While the incorrect diagnosis is a worry, this can be rectified through a better understanding of the issues involved by health professionals. The main concern is the reluctance of people to seek that help, or diagnosis in the first place.

We need to encourage people to seek help and reassure them that they will not be discriminated against, or ridiculed if they do seek help, or admit that they are not okay.

From my experience, the reason why families are always shocked when a loved one commits suicide is because they simply don't see it coming. The apparent shame of admitting to loved ones that we are suffering in this way is what holds most people back from talking to the people who could possibly help the most.

I know firsthand how as a society we ridicule people with mental illness. In 2010 I was battling with the Child Support Agency over the way they were harassing me over the extreme amount of child support I had to pay in relation to my actual wage.

I absolutely believe that a man should pay a 'fair' amount of child support. Many men don't and I understand that this is a delicate topic for both sexes, but at the time I felt hard done by in this regard.

During a conversation with the C.S.A., I flippantly said "Well the agency clearly doesn't care if I live or die, so why should I." In hindsight, that was a stupid thing to say, even as a joke or flippant remark, but my point was that the people in the agency had no regard whatsoever for the human element of this situation. I know many people who have dealt with the C.S.A. who would have felt the same way and perhaps even taken it to a level beyond my throw-away comment.

After giving up on getting anywhere with this department, I hung up the phone and went about my day around the house. Within half an hour there were three Police officers kicking in my front door and escorting me to the hospital for a mental assessment.

I was stunned at how over the top their actions were, but at the same time, I found it quite funny. I wasn't too pleased with having to replace the entire front door, but I did laugh inwardly (To not have anyone think I was loopy) throughout the next hour or so while I was being assessed.

As is the case in every situation, there was a silver lining and that was that I scored a date with the very cute female doctor from Scotland who was assessing me. Hey! She was very clear that I was of no danger to myself or anyone so perhaps I should have kept the paperwork from her for future reference. I don't mean to make light of mental illness, but let's be honest, if we all laughed more, there would be less mental illness.

FIVE-HUNDRED, TWENTY-FIVE-THOUSAND, SIX-HUNDRED MINUTES

Far too often we think about the way someone died. I personally think it is more important to think about the way they lived. How they died is only but a moment in the grand scheme of things. How they lived, on the other hand, encompasses millions of moments.

In 2003, my contract took me to Tahiti for six months onboard the Tahitian Princess. During rehearsals for the five shows, one set of song lyrics stood out. That song was "Seasons of Love" from the musical Rent.

The opening line of the song goes, "Five-hundred, twenty-five-thousand, six-hundred minutes". At the time, the significance of those lyrics didn't sink in as I had not seen the musical, nor did I know what they represented. Many years later it clicked for me though. Five-hundred, twenty-five-thousand, six-hundred minutes is the number of minutes each of us has in a non-leap year.

You often hear people say that the years went by so fast. That is usually the case because we are either hurrying to get somewhere in our lives, or we're consumed by guilt or regret from things in the past.

It's been said many times in recent years that we must live in the moment and Eckhart Tolle even aimed his best-selling book "The Power of Now" at this precise topic. In a far less serious way, Ferris Bueller captured a similar sentiment in the movie's opening monologue when he said, "Life moves pretty fast. If you don't stop and look around once in a while; you might miss it."

We are given a relatively small amount of time on earth, yet we spend a large portion of it living in the past or dreaming of the future. I love reminiscing about the past, and like many, I have audacious dreams of my future, but I now stop and centre myself throughout the day so that I can be present and in the moment. That is often where life's greatest joys are. We don't know how long we have on this earth, so why waste a moment of it?

Take a moment to study the figures below

11,122,560 mins = 185,376 hours = 7,724 days = 1,103 weeks = 253 months = ?? years

Do you know what the answer is, or the significance of these numbers? Before I tell you, let me ask you this. How often have you wasted several minutes procrastinating, an hour fighting with someone, a day hungover where you couldn't function, or a week worrying about something? How many months have you lost in a bad relationship, or years in a dead-end job?

I don't want you to beat yourself up over your answer. That defeats the purpose of this exercise. I simply want you to realise that life is precious and that we should never waste a single moment on things that are not worth it. Perhaps if I show you another set of numbers you might get where this is headed. I am certain Breeana's family will.

06/12/91 – 29/01/13

For those who don't know, this is Breeana's date of birth and date of death. It doesn't mean much when written that way, but look back at the original set of numbers and you get a far more significant look at how valuable life is.

Breeana lived for twenty-one years and just over one month in total. Seems like a fairly short amount of time, right? Now look back at how few days, hours, and minutes she spent on earth.

Given that I am not certain of Breeana's exact time of birth, I have rounded the minutes and hours to a whole day. I've also taken into account the leap years over that period. Either way, looking at the hours, days, or weeks she spent here on earth is frightening, when we look at how we spend our time.

Even though Breeana crammed quite a bit into her short life, it's still horrific to think that life can disappear so quickly. This, along with Breeana's ever-bubbly personality, it's no wonder her family, friends, and I struggled to come to terms with the fact that she ended her life so prematurely.

If there is a lesson to be taken from this, it is that we really must cherish every moment in life. The "dash" between her dates of birth and death looks so small, but somehow her entire life is right there in that dash. Think about life in that context and make sure that your "dash" is filled with many incredible moments.

YOU'RE NOT THE FIRST AND YOU WON'T BE THE LAST

Have you ever felt like you're the only person in the world with your particular problem? Allow me to shed some light on your problem in a not-so-new way. Songwriters sit down and pour their hearts out in a musical arrangement that they think is one of a kind, only to realise that the chord progression they used has been in dozens of hits over the past five decades. If you don't believe me, search "Axis of Awesome 4 chords" on YouTube. The video will blow your mind.

A screenwriter comes up with a supposedly new story for a movie, only to discover that there have been hundreds of movies with the same basic storyline; told in a slightly different way.

To show you how this is the case when writing a "logline" (a one-sentence summary of what a movie is about) the formula is as such: A story about a [fill in the blank] who must [fill in the blank] in order to [fill in the blank]. That's every single movie you've ever seen.

In the first decade of the twenty-first century musical artists as well as movies and TV shows such as Pitch Perfect and Glee popularised "mash ups" possibly not realising that once again, it's not an original concept.

CHAPTER 2

Two decades before mash-ups were done by everyone, Gene Kelly and his young co-star in the movie Xanadu melded two completely different song genres into the showstopper "Dancin".

Despite what most think, there are only a certain number of combinations of notes that can make a pop song. Similarly, there are only three true genres of movies (Comedy, Drama, and Romance). Like mashups, most good ideas are spawned from old ones and despite what you may think, your problems are not exclusive to you.

The worst thing we can do is to think that our problems, insecurities, and challenges are unique to us. That type of thinking is not only destructive, but it is downright soul-sucking too.

To think we are all alone in going through what we are facing can be worse than the problem itself. The best thing we can do is to realise that almost everyone has the same problems, challenges, and insecurities as we do and to stop feeling like we are being punished.

As Tony Robbins said on the first day of his Date with Destiny seminar that I attended in 2016, "We are all fucked up. It's just the level of fucked-upness that varies."

When you realise that the problems you are facing have been faced by millions of people over previous decades, you discover that there must have been a solution and all you need to do is find it. Work out who has had the same or similar challenges in the past and use their blueprint to overcome it yourself.

I learnt how to rap as a teenager by modelling myself on Run DMC, NWA, and Ice-T. I taught myself how to sing by mimicking John Farnham and other great singers. I learnt how to write screenplays by reading great screenplays and watching the corresponding movies to see how what was on the page translated to the screen. And when it came to problems in life, I either looked for how other people overcame them, or I looked at how I had overcome them myself in the past.

Your problems and insecurities are not unique to only you and neither are the solutions to those problems and insecurities, so stop beating yourself up for having them and start looking for the simple, tried, and true solutions that have helped many others

WHY THE FUCK WOULD YOU DESTROY A PERFECTLY GOOD BIKE?

I have a dear friend Wilfred who I met while working on cruise ships in 2007. Wil is a talented, great-looking, charismatic guy with such a zest for life. He has a gorgeous wife and a beautiful young child, yet despite all this, a few years ago I received a message from Wil on Facebook messenger saying that he had "Had enough and was going to end it." Wil then went on to say that he was going to ride his high-powered and very expensive motorbike into a brick wall.

Let me make this clear. Wil and I had only met a few times on ships when I was a guest entertainer who flew in and out and only ever stayed on board for a week at a time. Wil lived in Sydney and I lived on the Gold Coast, so we hadn't spent much time together but had a bond, despite the distance. We share the same birthday so our personalities are very similar. Our contact was mostly on Facebook and at the time, I hadn't spoken to Wil in several months.

Why Wil contacted me instead of his closest friends or family was baffling at the time but having been through Breeana's suicide I didn't hesitate to act. I asked Wil for his phone number and upon receiving it a moment later, quickly called him.

When Wil answered the phone I asked him what was wrong. He said once again, "I'm driving around Sydney looking for a brick wall to ride into." Without a second thought, I quickly fired back, "Why the fuck would you destroy a perfectly good bike?"

This question was met with total silence down the phone line. After the extended pause, Wil said "What?" at which point I repeated the question.

This time Wil shot back with confusion and anger in his voice, "I'm about to kill myself and all you can think about is my bike." "Yepp," I said. "You're clearly not thinking straight," I said. After a brief pause, I heard him snicker down the phone and say, "You're a mad cunt," to which I replied, "Absolutely. Now. What's the real issue here?"

Unbeknownst to me at the time, what I did in that moment was to break Wil's pattern. This is the first step in changing a person's old patterns and creating a new one. I had learnt this from Tony Robbins and even though I didn't do it consciously, I recalled it on a subconscious level and thankfully it worked.

By breaking Wil's pattern, it allowed me the time to bring Wil back to a more coherent place where he was able to use his cognitive skills more easily while being less reactive to his emotions.

As it turned out Wil had a minor dilemma he was facing, but which had consumed him to the point where he couldn't see clearly. This is what people refer to as 'Fog' or in some cases, the 'Black Dog'. You know, that feeling where something is all-consuming where you can't think clearly or rationally.

We've all been there at some point in our lives; myself included. The way I get myself out of it is simple. Just like Tony teaches, and as I did with Wil, I break my own pattern, so I can create a new one.

The way I break my own pattern is by jolting myself out of the old one. I do this by doing something completely radical like pulling a face, slapping myself in the face, or anything that shakes the shit out of myself and therefore breaks the pattern.

It's like I mentioned the grooves in the record in the previous chapter. Unless we slap the needle across the record, it will follow the pattern until the end of the record.

Step two of this process is to destroy the groove completely so that the needle cannot return to it and follow the old pattern. Once we have done that then you create a brand-new pattern. Step two is very important, because if you don't destroy the old pattern, then you will easily fall back into that pattern EG: The contort zone we previously talked about.

In Wil's case, creating the new pattern was relatively easy. I simply had him focus on what was really important to him. Wil adored his wife and child. Those two gave him joy and a greater purpose to thrive in life. If I seem to be a little vague on the details of Wil's situation, this is because I want to respect his trust in me. His situation was private, and it is up to him to share the details if he chooses to.

The main reason why I share Wil's story is that it dawned on me several weeks later that the reason Wil contacted me and not his wife, family, or close friends was because he felt ashamed to admit his situation to those closest to him. This is a common trait among those suffering in this way.

It's the ones we love and respect the most who we fear the reactions of the most. Our loved ones are more likely to judge us and this is why many people suffering from depression or any form of mental illness keep it bottled up.

I believe that Breeana felt this way too. For some reason, she was able to share her feelings with me when we first met, but not her mother. Without speaking badly of her mother, Breeana did mention that her mother had been overpowering on many occasions and therefore Breeana felt that she couldn't always open up to her.

I am certain that Breeana's mother did the best she knew how and acted accordingly, but this is possibly why Breeana's family is so steadfast in their denial of Breeana's condition. I had to mention this because I want other families to be aware of these types of things so that their loved ones don't feel the way Breeana did when it comes to sharing their battles.

In Wil's case, he also felt that he couldn't share his challenges with a professional. This brings me to another issue that we face in combating suicide. How do we correctly allow those suffering from a mental illness to feel like they can open up, whether it be to a professional or a loved one?

I honestly don't have the answer to this question. It is awesome that organisations like "RUOK" are encouraging people to ask "are you ok" but I think the problem is more complex than that. This concept is a really good start, but I would like some of the country's greatest minds to sit down and find a way where people can open up without fear of ridicule or embarrassment.

I truly believe that the answer lies somewhere in society as a whole letting go of the stigma that surrounds mental illness. Let's start the conversation. Let's bring the topic to the forefront and hopefully, a solution will become more obvious.

When Breeana committed suicide there was not a single newspaper article, or mention of it because back then suicide was even more of a taboo topic. The media and police did not want suicide to be common knowledge for fear of copycat incidents.

While I understand the reasoning behind this, I am glad that there is a little more reporting of suicide as it brings the topic to our attention, which enables us to have that conversation and hopefully find a solution so fewer people feel that they have no other option.

There are several reasons why a person might feel that suicide is the only option. While bullying, harassment, and shaming are common reasons for people committing suicide, I want to focus firstly on the most common reason; a lack of self-worth.

The reason that I feel that this is the most common is that the other reasons would rarely be influencing factors in suicide if those suffering had higher self-esteem or self-worth. I am going to start this topic by making what may seem like an outlandish statement; given the commonality of this topic.

I AM NOT A FAN OF FAKE BREASTS!

Ladies. Before you throw the book against the wall or into a fireplace, let me explain. I don't hate all fake breasts or all women who have fake breasts. There are two simple reasons that I have an issue

CHAPTER 2

with them. They are quite simple and come from a sincere place and a place of love; not hate, or judgement.

I accept that in some cases having breast enhancements or reductions is necessary and in fact lifesaving. For example. If a woman has had cancer or perhaps after breastfeeding the appearance of the breasts might be less than desirable.

I also concede that it is not my right to have an opinion on what another person should do with their body, but please understand that these opinions come from a place of love; not judgement.

Like many young women, Breeana had huge insecurities about her body image and in particular her breasts. Let me say that in my opinion, Breeana's breasts were perfect. All of her was perfect, but unfortunately, like many young men and women, she didn't think so.

The reason I discouraged Breeana from getting breast implants and the reason I disagree with many women getting them comes in two parts. Firstly, in Breeana's case and in many cases, the reason for getting fake breasts is simply to mask an insecurity.

Let's be honest, men would do the same if we could get a penis enlargement as easily as women can get new breasts wouldn't we? But in most cases, this would only be masking a feeling of insecurity. Sure, we'd have a bigger penis, but that would not change the underlying insecurities that led to the person wanting the work done in the first place. (FYI: I am totally cool with what I have. Only the 'caveman' ego inside me would want more down there).

I said to Breeana when the topic came up, that I supported her in having this done, but only if she worked on the underlying issues that made her feel less than perfect. It's like buying a new car. It feels great at first, but it doesn't help in the long term and after a while, you feel the same as you did before (except with bigger breasts or a nice car) The big difference is that you can always sell the car without too much discomfort.

My other reason for not always agreeing with breast enhancements is that in my opinion, every female is perfect just the way they are. I have yet to date a woman who I've thought was not physically perfect in her most natural state.

Women are naturally beautiful creatures and are absolutely perfect as they are. Clothes, makeup, hairstyles, etc can all be nice, but for me and in fact many men, a woman is at her most beautiful when she is just the way God intended her.

Now I have to be a little hypocritical here and state that I'm not wanting my partner to have legs as hairy as mine or armpits as bushy as mine, but like I said; I'm not perfect.

Whether their bum is a little bigger, their breasts are small or not perfectly shaped, their nose is slightly crooked, or there is something else that they might not see as perfect, they are beautiful just the way they are. I sincerely wish that every woman in the world could see that she is perfect precisely how God made her.

Apart from the above-mentioned (hairy legs etc.), every girl and woman is gorgeous as she is. We put such emphasis on looks and while physical attraction is somewhat important, beauty as they say is in the eye of the beholder. We spend so much time worrying about covering up our imperfections instead of embracing all of our unique qualities.

I too have fallen into this trap of worrying about my appearance. When I was on stage, I started dying my hair. Not because it was grey, but because at the time, I wanted to be trendy. One day I watched a video of me on stage and noticed that I looked bald because of the lightness of my hair under the stage lights so I dyed it back to a little darker than my natural colour.

I did this for a year or so and one day when I got it cut in the salon on board, I noticed that I was in fact going grey. As I was only in my mid-thirties, I decided to dye it a little to maintain the current look.

I continued this for several years until one day I got my hair cut and almost fell out of the chair when I saw just how much grey hair I had. I literally went from dark brown all over to completely grey all over in one haircut.

Now that I knew how grey I was, I didn't want to look old, so I kept dying it. My point in mentioning this is simple. My own insecurities and unwillingness to accept my appearance kept me from truly being happy. I was denying who I really was and this itself was causing me more pain than anyone saying "Oh wow. You're very grey".

Just like a woman changing her appearance to mask an insecurity, I was doing the same. Now there is nothing wrong with doing things to make yourself feel better or take care of your appearance. Just remember that we are all perfectly imperfect and this should be embraced.

Love yourself and embrace how you look, and I promise that you will feel much better than any set of breasts, hair dye or new car will make you feel.

Your flaws are, as 'One Direction' sang "What makes you beautiful." Incidentally, Breeana hated that song along with Bruno Mars' "Just the way you are." Read into that what you may, but in my opinion and with the benefit of hindsight is a clear sign of her lack of self-worth.

CHAPTER 2

If I was on social media, I'd spend my day posting about how my shit does stink, how I am sometimes not perfect, and how I am occasionally a complete fucking arsehole for no reason. I am also a hopeless romantic who believes in the fairy-tale love story like in "The Notebook." My point is, whatever quirks or flaws you have, embrace them and realise that they are what attracts people to you; not repels them, so stop being ashamed of them.

We spend our entire lives putting people on a pedestal and worshipping their wonderful qualities, when in fact it is their flaws that make them special. We spend so much effort on promoting our good traits and just as much time covering up our flaws when it should be the other way around. If you want to know what true love is, show someone the absolute worst of you, and if they still love you; that is the safest place you can rest your heart.

MY FIRST BRUSH WITH SUICIDE.

A few years after finishing school I lost one of my good mates to suicide. I finished school over thirty years ago and sadly I had forgotten about this tragic story until I was writing this book. I got home from being released on bail for murder and I was greeted by a disgusting mess at home.

Anyone who knows me knows that I am exceptionally tidy, and my place is never a mess. Ten days earlier the police had disrespected my place and trashed it in a desperate search for something that could make their pathetically weak case against me stronger.

During their search warrant, they had completely trashed my place so upon arriving home, I decided to occupy myself by cleaning up. It was a great way to keep my mind busy so that I didn't break down over the magnitude of the charges I was facing.

It was also the first night in five years that I had been at home without my dogs. Sue had put them in a kennel while I was locked up and I wasn't able to collect them until the following day, so I needed something to distract me so that I didn't freak out without their love and protection.

I was tidying up my office and packing away a large storage container filled with all my paper clippings, show photos, and memorabilia that Mum had collected over the years. As I packed it all away from being thrown all over the floor, I stumbled across a photo from my graduation.

The photo was of me with my four 'T-Birds' from our high school production of Grease. We were all in our tuxedos, standing in the famous Grease-Lightning pose. As I scanned the photo, I remembered that "Doody" (Mark Swinburne) was no longer with us.

Nathan (Sonny), Greg (Putzy), and Jason (Kenickie) were all at our reunion several years earlier, but sadly Mark had committed suicide a few years before our fifteen-year reunion.

Of the four other guys in the photo, Mark was the least likely to take his own life; or so I thought. Nathan was a high-level executive with a stressful job, Jason was kind of normal, but reserved and while Greg was the crazy/funny one, he was slightly unhinged, but somehow that kept him sane.

As is often the case, Mark was the one who seemed happiest, but sadly underneath he was battling demons. Greg was a bigger clown than Mark and me, but Mark was the kid who always had a smile on his face.

Mark came from a very normal and loving family. His parents were lovely people and his younger brother was a nice kid; just like Mark. This made his motivation for committing suicide even more baffling.

Apart from his girlfriend breaking up with him after high school, there weren't any clues at all. He had a gorgeous new girlfriend, so all was well; we thought.

At school, Mark and I didn't become close until the last few years of school, but throughout grade twelve we were close mates. We were in Grease together and our interest in music had us spending much time together at lunch.

At the time, Miami High was a very forward-thinking school. It was the first school in Australia to teach Film and Television and the first to teach dance and even surfing as subjects. The school was often referred to as the "closest thing to an American high school."

Just like American schools, Miami High had a 'Miss Miami High' pageant. It wasn't so much a beauty pageant, but more of a personality pageant. Previous winners dating back to the 1980s were Tiffany Lamb (Co-host of Perfect Match) and Kim Watkins (Channel 7 newsreader). In 1988, well before gender equality was a hot topic, Miami High changed the format of the pageant to include both males and females.

The entire thing was light-hearted but the main idea of it was to raise money for the school and to boost the confidence of students entering. Each contestant had to give a speech and raise a minimum of one hundred dollars to enter the contest. Each contestant chose their

CHAPTER 2

own way to raise money and the one who raised the most also gained the title of 'top fund raiser'.

On a side note, just like in most public speaking circles, I engaged a speechwriter for my speech in the contest. I was very fortunate to have one-half of the funniest duo at school, Richard Wells, write my speech for the night. Richard's speech was brilliant, so all I had to do was deliver it as written. This led to thunderous laughter and wild accolation both on the night and afterward for Richard and myself

In our final year, Mark and I both entered the contest for a laugh and decided to band together for our fundraising. We decided that we would hold a lip-sync competition in the great hall at school and have a $2 admission fee. The hall held around 800 people so we knew if we could fill it, we'd be sweet.

The night was a huge success and upon counting the door's take, we had roughly $800. We looked at each other and without a word said, we smiled, pocketed $100 each for the fundraising, then rallied a heap of friends and headed across the road to the KFC.

Mark and I strolled into KFC like shepherds with our flock behind us. Our flock was hungry, so we ordered every last piece of chicken, copious amounts of chips, plus every side and drink the store had. The management was baffled where two sixteen-year-olds got so much cash, but I'm sure they didn't care as their daily take went through the roof.

How on earth do you spend $600 on KFC? Teenagers are hungry creatures and even though a piece of chicken back then was only $1.50 each, we had very little change by the end of the night.

This was a classic example of what Mark was like as a person. He was an incredibly generous guy and his short life was all about serving others and making other people happy. Mark was a caring, giving guy, and right up until his final days, he was at his happiest doing things for other people.

Mark left school and went straight into a traineeship at a 5-star hotel, before going on to work in and eventually managing high-end restaurants in the exclusive Main Beach dining precinct.

I guess if anything can be learnt from Mark's example and that of Robbin Williams, is that while it is admirable to serve others and put others first, it is also important to take care of yourself. A friend of mine who is a single mother runs herself into the ground taking care of her teenage boys. She is often sick and very frequently stressed.

I completely understand that her kids need her, and she has to do what she has to do, but I often say to her, "You need to take care of yourself, or you won't be around to take care of them."

It is like in the case of an emergency on a plane where the crew tells you that you must fit your own oxygen mask, before helping others. We must strike a balance between taking care of others' needs and making sure that our own welfare is looked after. This is the only conclusion I can draw from the tragic suicides of my friend Mark, Robbin Williams, and many other people who have taken this action.

Suicide is not new, yet we still haven't worked out how to slow it down or stop it. Suicide goes as far back as ancient times. Cleopatra committed suicide, as did her husband Mark Antony in 30 BC, yet it is still happening over two thousand years later. I don't have the answer to stop it, but I believe that it lies in the level of self-love we have for ourselves.

INSECURITIES; IF YOU DISOWN THEM - THEY WILL OWN YOU

"Your worst enemy cannot harm you half as much as your mind left unguarded" – Buddha

Deny it if you wish, but you're only lying to yourself by doing so. Insecurities get the better of all of us at some stage. Heck, my first book "All at Sea – Confessions of a neurotic cruise ship singer" exposed many of mine. While I openly admit to most of my insecurities, most people deny them or project them onto others to avoid confronting them.

From a young age, I have always been an honest person. I say what I think, regardless of whether it is good or bad. When it comes to the opposite sex and dating, I have no problem telling a girl if she is beautiful. I am openly unashamed to say to a stranger or a girlfriend that they are beautiful, their hair looks nice, or if I like their outfit.

I guess where I got in trouble was because these traits are traditionally reserved for gay guys and not straight ones like myself. I heard it a lot from girlfriends that guys never say nice things, never compliment them and never notice their hair or clothes. Perhaps those guys are ignorant and self-centred, or perhaps they are frightened to say so; for good reason.

Guys, have you ever said something nice to a girl, only to have her tell you that you're a sleaze or a liar? I bet you thought twice the next time you went to say anything nice; if you ever did it again at all. On countless occasions, I have complimented a girl only to have her throw it back in my face, or to say, "No I am not beautiful."

For the most part, they think that my nice compliments are a sleazy attempt to get in their pants, but this could not be further from

CHAPTER 2

the truth. Sure, on many occasions, this has led to me getting a little action, but this is more a byproduct, rather than an intention.

I've often asked girlfriends why they don't like compliments and the same responses keep coming up. They are either not used to hearing them, their ex-partners never said nice things (or only said bad things), or If you read between the lines, the girl didn't believe what was being said to them. When I say that they didn't believe it, I don't mean that they didn't believe that the guy or myself didn't mean it. I mean that they didn't believe that what was being said about them was true about them.

I experienced a disturbing case of this when I worked for the country's largest timeshare company in their travel club. I hopped in the elevator of the company building after lunch one day and was joined by a girl from the accounts department. This girl was reasonably attractive and if I am completely honest, she had the most incredible breasts I had seen.

Despite the previous comment, at no point had I ever made it obvious that I thought that, and I hadn't even said a word to her on any previous passings in the hallways of the building. The fact that her breasts were well out of proportion for her slim body is no doubt a bone of contention for her as I am sure that most men would spend more time focusing on her breasts than her face or personality.

The girl was subsequently a little shy but nonetheless appeared to be a nice girl. This particular day, I joined her in the lift and noticed that she had a new hairstyle. She looked very attractive and as I often do, I said "You look very nice today. I love your hair."

As the elevator doors opened, she gave a nervous kind of smile as she looked towards the ground while exiting the lift. I went back to work feeling good about myself, thinking that I had genuinely given a compliment that had hopefully made her day.

Not twenty minutes after returning to my desk, my supervisor Anne called me into a meeting room. To my shock, Anne explained that the girl had made a complaint to her supervisor about my comment and he had contacted Anne requesting that I be reprimanded over what he called sexual harassment. "What the fuck," I said to Anne. "Since when is giving someone a genuine compliment, harassment?"

There was no major issue after that discussion and I agreed that I would not engage in any discussions with the girl so as to protect myself from further issues, but it was terribly disturbing that we lived in a world where people would be scolded for saying nice things.

WHAT OTHER PEOPLE THINK OF YOU IS NONE OF YOUR BUSINESS

I completely understand that some guys overstep the mark and say things that could be seen as sleazy, but what I said was completely innocent. If I had said, "Nice tits" then throw me to the lions, sack me, and mark my papers as "never to be hired" but I said her hair looked nice.

This is a classic example of someone's insecurities getting in the way of them having healthy functioning interactions with people. We can all be cynical from time to time, but to project our own insecurities on other people in this way only hurts us.

I wasn't expecting anything from the girl; not even a thank you. I didn't compliment her to get something in return and I certainly wasn't saying it to get into her pants. It was just a genuine compliment because I felt it.

This type of thing is more common than most people realise and there is a very good reason for it being the case. You see, while I am very complimentary and say lots of nice things, I have on occasions, said things that are not so nice.

The funny thing is that while the girl I say the nice things to may not believe them, on any occasion I have said something that was not so nice; they absolutely took these words as gospel. Why is that?

I can tell you why. It is because we don't compliment ourselves or have positive self-talk or a positive self-image of ourselves. We subconsciously put ourselves down and refuse to embrace our flaws while minimising our amazing attributes. Something I discovered many years ago was that whenever I got pissed off with something someone said about me, it was because that thing was a trait that I had not yet owned.

For example, if someone said to me that I was a shit singer, there is no way I would get upset because I knew on a deeper level that this is not true. If someone said something like that to me, I knew that it had everything to do with them and nothing to do with me.

On the other hand, if someone said to me that I am short and ugly, I might get pissed off. I'm five foot ten and certainly not a yeti, so neither of these things are true, but these things are subjective, and over the years I have questioned them too, so yes, they may cut a little.

There are many reasons why we have insecurities, but when we don't own all of our traits, that is when other people have the power to cut us down. In most cases, women have insecurities surrounding the size of their bum, so if a man said she had a fat ass, you would be sure that this would cut deep. In contrast, if you said to Nigella Lawson that she was a shit cook, I doubt she would do anything but laugh.

CHAPTER 2

It is only when the traits that we have disowned are criticized, that we feel hurt over them. For example, my ex-girlfriend Klara was the sweetest blonde Swedish girl who stood only five feet tall. She had been with very few men so if I tried to call her a slut, it would not upset her at all because she knew that it was not true. If I said she was short, this may upset her.

On the other hand, another ex-girlfriend Casey who had slept with a lot of partners would have stabbed me if I suggested that she was a slut. Now, there is nothing wrong with how many partners she had been with. The difference is that in her mind, she had not owned that trait and therefore anyone suggesting it was a bad thing would cut her deeply.

I've known women who have slept with dozens of guys, but if you called them a slut, it wouldn't bother them at all. The reason for this is that these girls have owned that trait and accepted it, instead of questioning their actions or having insecurities over it.

If you have a fat ass, a small dick, a big nose, or tiny tits; embrace them and accept them. If you're a slut, a player, or a neurotic cruise ship singer; own it. As soon as you own those traits, no one will have the power to "own" you.

When we own all of our traits, no one has the power to bring us down. Not even ourselves. This is why bullies are so successful. They see a flaw in a person and know that this person has not yet owned it. Words can't hurt you; unless you believe them.

That is why certain words hurt so much. It's only the things we believe subconsciously that can infiltrate our feelings. Next time someone says something to you that really hurts, instead of hating them and contemplating suicide, take a moment to look at the trait in question and see how you can own it and accept it.

In my book "C.R.U.I.S.E" I tell a story of when my Cruise Director Chris Nichol said that my voice wasn't up to Princes Cruises standards. At the time I was devastated, but instead of saying "Fuck you" to Chris, I took a different approach. I first called my director William Forsyth back in Sydney, who reminded me of why he cast me in the lead role, then I worked so hard that three years later when I crossed paths with Chris again, he said that my voice was one of the best he had heard at sea.

If you don't like one of your traits, change it, or own it. Then no one can ever push your buttons. We are all perfect, but we need to see that and stop giving other people access to hurt us.

WHAT OTHER PEOPLE THINK OF YOU IS NONE OF YOUR BUSINESS

F.A.A.F.I.A.S.S (FUNNY AS A FART IN A SPACE SUIT)

"Nothing binds you except your thoughts. Nothing limits you except your fears and nothing controls you except your beliefs"
– Marianne Williamson

Carrying on from the last topic, nothing is true other than what you believe to be true. Someone calling you a murderer makes it no more a fact or the truth than wearing an astronaut costume to a fancy-dress party and believing you are an astronaut. Okay. So you're probably wondering what this paragraph title is about and how it pertains to the overall story. Just roll with it and hopefully, it will make sense in a minute.

I had to 'crowbar' this story in because it makes me laugh as do most of my antics over forty years of friendship with my former best mate. We were attending a fancy-dress party for his sister-in-law's twenty-first birthday which was an "A-party." You had to dress up as something or someone beginning with the letter "A".

Even though we could both have attended as "assholes," we decided to go as astronauts. We decorated our spacesuits with similar logos to that of N.A.S.A, except our logo was "F.A.A.F.I.A.S.S" (Funny As A Fart In A Space Suit) instead of N.A.S.A, and instead of N.A.S.A's unofficial motto which was "Failure is not an option" we had "Farting is not an option."

John and I had a history of this kind of antics at parties. In fact, we even attended a 'Hollywood' party (where he was invited but I wasn't) where he turned up as 'Shrek' and I came as a donkey (Shrek's annoying best friend).

Throughout our friendship, we portrayed ourselves as Gynecologists when checking into hotels, and even setting up radio station disc jockeys in order to win free lunches and dinners.

Ask Gold Coast radio announcer Paul Gayle about his number three all-time best 'crazy call' and he will say it was 'The jealous ex-boyfriend' that he did on-air in 1995. These calls were typically where friends secretly set their mates up for Paul to call and prank them, but in our case, I knew the call was coming as John and I set it up to win a free meal. Subsequently, it has been played many times over the years.

Getting back on topic. People may think we were scammers or clowns for what we did on these occasions, but just like wearing a

CHAPTER 2

spacesuit doesn't make us astronauts, what other people thought of us, or what other people think of you, does not make it so.

I don't need to get into a debate over my innocence or guilt over Breeana's death. Even though I am innocent and have been proven to be, it is of no concern to me if someone disagrees with that.

Someone thinking I am a murderer based on their own justification is no different from me thinking that they are uneducated for thinking or saying so. Their opinion, whether expressed or not, does not make me a murderer so why would I pay it any mind?

The same can be said for what other people think of you. Someone calling you fat or ugly, stupid, or an arsehole doesn't make you fat, ugly, stupid, or an arsehole.

Only your acceptance of those thoughts and statements by them can make it so. People will always have opinions on things. Some of those opinions may be based on fact and some purely on their perception, or what they are projecting onto you.

The only way their comments or thoughts of you can be true is if you let them infiltrate your mind. At the end of the day, the only thing that is true is the way we perceive it to be. There ain't no black or white.

There ain't no "this is fact." There is only perception. You, me, and everyone on this earth all see things through our own flavour of perception. That's why two people can experience the same set of circumstances, yet have vastly different views on it.

It's been said before that perception equals reality, and in my opinion, this is the only truth there is. If your reality sux, then this is because you perceive it to be that way. If you want to change your reality, then all you have to do is change the way you perceive things to be. There is no good or bad; only how you perceive it.

As the late, great master of all things spiritual - Dr. Wayne Dyer said, "When you change the way you look at things; the things you look at change." Or as Henry Ford was once quoted as saying, "Whether you think you can or you can't; either way you are right."

If you believe you are good, you will act in a good way. If you believe you are a failure, you're destined to fail. If you see the world as either good or bad, that's the way it will seem to you. And if you believe life sux then that's precisely what you will attract to confirm your perception.

Start right now by flipping your perception of events on their head and watch how those things suddenly change. As I wrote in my book

WHAT OTHER PEOPLE THINK OF YOU IS NONE OF YOUR BUSINESS

"The No B.S Approach to Create the Life You Want," Tony Robbins framed the simplest, but most profound paragraph in his 2016 Date with Destiny promo video that I had ever read.

Tony asks: "What if? What if problems were all gifts? What if every problem you ever had was life happening for you, not to you? What if everything in our lives was guided? What if everything in our lives was divine timing? Everything; even the pain!"

I'm sure you've been through as much shit as I have and I'm sure you thought most of it was a burden and not a blessing. Reality is (if you perceive it to be that way) that every last piece of shit you've had to go through and deal with has been a blessing and a gift. The secret is to see it that way. Once you can do that; Game over! Life becomes the joy that most people strive for, but never achieve.

"THE MILE-HIGH CLUB"

As I wrote this section's title, I wasn't sure how this story would fit, or where in the book it might go, but let's run with the train of thought for a moment and see where it leads. Everyone knows what the mile-high club is and some even profess to be a member of it. What most don't realise is that even though some think they have joined it at some point, hardly anyone has.

You see, becoming a member of the elusive mile-high club is not as easy as most people think. Most people believe that all you have to do to join the club is to have sex on a plane. While that is one of the main criteria, it is only a quarter of the equation to qualify for the official mile-high club.

Here's the deal. Back when I worked as a concierge at a couple of five-star hotels, one of my hotels had a contract with Qantas and the other with Virgin Australia. This meant that each night we had between ten and twenty airline staff staying with us. During that time the concierge team became good mates with Ryan who was cabin crew with one of those airlines. I've purposely not mentioned which one so he doesn't get in trouble. Ryan, like most airline crew, had different "girlfriends" in each city he stayed in and was very much a playboy. Ryan used to have a laugh with us either when checking in, or when waiting to be collected to go to the airport for his flight.

During one of our chats, the topic of the mile-high club came up, and here's what I learnt. According to Ryan (which was confirmed by

Dan; another cabin crew mate with the other airline) in order to be an official member of the mile-high club, you must satisfy the following three criteria.

1. Not in the loo.
2. Not with the crew.
3. With someone new.

In other words, you can't have sex in the toilet. This is a favourite place for most people trying to achieve this goal. You can't shag the crew. This would be too easy because the crew has secret spots you could have sex in. And lastly, it has to be someone with whom you have not yet had sex.

Basically, if you want to join the official mile-high club you have to meet someone on board or have a partner with whom you have not yet had sex, and either have sex in your seat or wait until the curtains to the galley close after meal service and the rest of the passengers have fallen asleep, then hope that no one comes looking for a cookie or a beer while you're in the middle of it.

I've had sex in a plane toilet with my ex (who played Scary Spice in the Australian "Spiced Girls" show) while I was touring as the Australian Backstreet Boys (I might unpack that bit later). I also got a blowjob from a different ex en route (I said route, not root) from London to Brisbane. Despite these, sadly I am not an official member of the club either.

I have however been fortunate enough to have flown almost half a million miles, including flying over one hundred thousand miles in one calendar year (2007). Sad that I know these figures, but when you spend a combined total of 168 hours (one full week) with your ass in a plane seat in a year, you need to kill the time somehow; if you're not joining the mile-high club. Thank god I keep lists of figures like this.

Flying has always fascinated me, as has travel, and having seen over 400 destinations around the world, you can't help but look at things differently. Travel is the only thing you can buy that enriches your life, so therefore I would have to be the most ungrateful person alive if I didn't feel that my life is extremely blessed.

For all but two flights, (the two I mentioned where I got naughty with girlfriends) I've always travelled alone. When being flown to cruise ship contracts, I've mostly been alone on the flight. When travelling to travel agent trips for free I usually don't know who the other agents are until we land; even if they are in the row behind me.

WHAT OTHER PEOPLE THINK OF YOU IS NONE OF YOUR BUSINESS

And these days when I travel, I have no problem travelling alone too. This forces me to talk to strangers and meet people along the way. This can be confronting but is the part of travel that really enriches your life.

Often, we live in our own bubble with our group of friends, and our favourite places to eat or visit, and rarely do we actually learn or grow. By travelling alone, I am instantly outside of my comfort zone and each situation is challenging and exciting. Meeting new people and learning how they live, experiencing new cultures, and seeing how the rest of the world lives, gives life meaning.

Whether you join the official or unofficial mile-high club or not, the greatest piece of advice I could give any young person, or not-so-young person, is to travel as much as possible.

Whenever I meet people in their late teens and early twenties, I almost beg them to go and travel. I know so many people in their forties who have travelled so little and they regret it so much. Kids, families, mortgages, and possessions get in the way and before they know it, they've missed that chance.

While possessions may seem to make you happy, that happiness will fade as do the possessions, but when you travel, the experiences you gain will bring such joy to your life and teach you so much about life and yourself. These lessons and memories will stay with you until the day you die.

I once dated a girl from a little country town called Lismore. She was in her mid-thirties and had never travelled outside of Australia. I asked her where her ultimate holiday would be to which she replied "New Zealand." Now there is nothing wrong with New Zealand and we are blessed in Australia to have such an incredible geographical neighbour, but it blew my mind that she had no idea what was out there. I don't mean that as an insult to her; she just didn't know any better.

While our relationship turned to crap, I did manage to get her to travel to Hawaii with me for a week. I must say that even though we had broken up by the time we travelled, it was a huge joy for me to take her there and see her experience a different culture for the very first time. That's the one thing I do look back fondly on from our time together. Her mind opened so much during that trip, as did mine over the course of seeing so many places around the world.

Whether it be swimming with stingrays in Tahiti, playing with monkeys on the rock of Gibraltar, watching the Bolshoi Ballet in

Russia, or partying in 'Temple Bar' in Dublin, my life is so much richer for having had these experiences in my life and yours will be also when you do the same.

So, while this section may have started off being about sex on a plane, despite the old saying to the contrary, sometimes the destination does become the journey.

UNCOMPLICATE' SHIT

Speaking of journeys, one of the reasons people struggle to embrace the big picture and enjoy the journey is because they get so caught up in the day-to-day crap. A tear in a stocking, a stubbed toe, or spilt coffee, begins a spiral that would make a "John McLean from Diehard day" look trivial, but this needn't be the case.

While scrolling through thousands of audiobooks on the free library app looking for my seven-hundredth book to read, I saw a book titled "How to have a good day." Out of curiosity, I clicked on the book to get some more details. Given the topic and what I had learnt in relation to that topic, I was shocked to see that the audiobook was more than thirteen hours long.

Now I am not saying that the author is overly crapping on to fill out the pages, but from my experience, I know that I could wrap that entire topic up in less than two hours. In fact, I don't think it would even take half an hour or even more than a paragraph. Actually, even though I've not read the book I can condense it and provide you with everything you need to know to gain the same results in just one word. That word is "choose."

Take the first word of the book title (how) and replace it with "choose" and you have the answer to "how to have a good day." Choose to have a good day. Choose to be happy and not let things turn your day into a bad day.

Yes. People will do things to piss you off and situations will unfold that will more than likely test your faith, but at the end of the day whether you have a good day or a bad day comes down to whether or not you "choose" to have a good day.

This may sound too simple to be correct, but if you talk to any of the greatest mentors and life coaches in the world, they will all tell you that it doesn't matter what happens to you. It only matters how to choose to see those events or how you choose to react to them. If you choose to have a good day no matter what, then that is precisely what you will have.

WHAT OTHER PEOPLE THINK OF YOU IS NONE OF YOUR BUSINESS

I must apologise to Caroline Webb, the author of the before-mentioned book as I may have put a dent in her sales by way of the previous paragraphs. I'm sure it's a very informative book and most likely goes into great detail for those who need a little extra help in achieving what I said should be simple.

For those who are extraordinary and can take a simple concept and run with it, all you have to do is decide to "Choose to have a good day." If someone pushes your buttons at work or screws something up that costs you time and or money, you can choose to let it upset you and frustrate you (which will lead to you having a bad day) or you can use it to grow and develop your personal and professional skills.

I had a female singer on Saga Cruises in 2007 who I knew from when her brother employed me as the live-in manager of his famous motel (The one Farlie Arrow faked her abduction in on the Gold Coast).

This singer (not Farlie Arrow) was probably the biggest bitch I had ever met. She was very insecure and overly loud and obnoxious. Most of the time these traits go hand in hand as a way of compensating for an insecurity. She was a cow to most of the crew on board but she was particularly nasty towards me. According to other cast members, this woman was constantly saying horrible things about me and constantly taunting me to get a reaction or piss me off.

The funny thing was that after I heard her say one less-than-nice thing on day one of a six-month contract, I tuned her out so regardless of what she said from that point on, it simply washed over without having any effect on me. It was like she didn't even exist.

Other cast members would come up to me and say "How have you not punched that bitch out" to which I'd reply, "I actually didn't really hear what she said and even if I did, I wouldn't let her know I did."

One thing I learnt after dealing with my daughter's mother for several years is that you should never let your opponent know when they have upset you or injured you. In boxing or martial arts, if an opponent sees your injury, they will target it. In life, your opponent can do the same, so it is best to never let them see that you are injured. With my female singer in 2007, even though her actions had very little effect on me, even if they did, I would have never let her see that.

This was how I chose to have a good day. I could have bitch-slapped the mole or made her life hell, but that would be lowering myself to her standards while ensuring that my days weren't that good as a result of my focusing on her behaviour.

The funny thing is, that even though it's been more than fifteen years, she still yells abuse across crowded shopping centres these days when she sees me. Well, at least I think that's what she is yelling because I tune her out when I see her downturned mouth and crumpled facial expressions.

Back on ships, I was too busy enjoying the life I was living and experiencing the ship and crew, while she was locked in her cabin all day, except to rehearse, eat, or perform. I chose to ignore her and tune her out and that pissed her off even more which led to me having a good day and her still holding so much anger inside of her, more than a decade later. Now tell me. Of the two of us, who do you think will develop cancer through harbouring that type of acidic environment in our bodies for so long?

No matter what happens, choose to have a good day and choose to act in a way that no matter what happens you will have a good day and that is exactly what you will have.

K.I.S.S (KEEP IT SIMPLE STUPID)

There is a story going around about John Lennon as a child in school that is not one hundred percent confirmed as being true but regardless is one we should learn from. Apparently one of John's teachers asked the class to write down what they wanted to be when they grew up.

As the teacher checked John's response, she saw a problem. The teacher said, "What do you want to be when you grow up John?" John simply said, "Happy." With a slightly puzzled look, the teacher said, "I don't think you understand the question." After a short pause, John looked up at his teacher and said, "No. You're the one who doesn't understand the question."

As both an amateur and professional singer I was blessed to be able to sing some of the most incredible songs. I got to perform songs by men who have changed people's emotions and inspired millions with their lyrics and melody. Not just good singers and songwriters; but great ones. Men like Billy Joel, Frank Sinatra, Dean Martin, Elton John, George Gershwin, Paul McCartney, Nat King Cole, and John Lennon.

Each of their songs was a timeless hit that became that way because of their ability to share a unique message that people related to. None more so than in a song that even though it has been over fifty years since its release, is just as relevant today as it was in 1971. In many great songs the message is deeper than we may think but the profound message of John Lennon's song "Imagine", could not be simpler.

When Yoko Ono penned the words that John later turned into the song, Yoko asked a simple question. Imagine all the things in the world that divide us, no longer existing. It's that simple.

Even though the song is considered by many to be the greatest song ever written, both the chords and the lyrics are so simple; yet so powerful. Likewise, in life itself, far too often we overcomplicate things, but if we strip things back to their bare essentials, that is where we find all of the answers to all of our problems.

I AM PERFECT. WE ARE ALL PERFECT; JUST THE WAY WE ARE

"I am beautiful, no matter what they say. Words can't bring me down"
Linda Perry via Christina Aguilera's song "Beautiful"

The song "Beautiful", written by Linda Perry of "4-non-blondes" fame is in my opinion the poster child of how we need to talk to ourselves daily. Fuck the world and fuck what anyone else thinks. If you believe in yourself and proactively provide positive self-talk to yourself, then no amount of hate, abuse, or spiteful words can ever have an impact on your state of mind.

While the song itself is about physical abuse at the hands of a family member, it could just as easily be interpreted as a battle between the words of others and our own self-talk. We carry the shame of either physical or emotional abuse and somehow it consumes us to the point where everything that we hear is building on that negative self-assessment.

The way to overcome this is to ensure that the voices within are greater than the outside voices trying to bring us down. In order to create this, you don't need to publicly or outwardly say anything to anyone or object to everything. You simply need to make sure that your inner knowing and self-talk are steadfast and more prominent in your world than all of the contradicting voices.

I am under no illusion that this state of mind does not come easily. Like anything in life, it takes mastering. We all have self-doubt and no matter how much we tell ourselves that we are worthy, our subconscious will always try to tell us otherwise.

As Tony Robbins says, "Either you master your mind, or your mind will master you." You need to be the gatekeeper to your mind and

CHAPTER 2

only allow useful and positive thoughts in. Anytime you find yourself talking negatively, stop yourself and say "Hey! Fuck you mind. I am in charge; not you."

Growing up when I got in trouble for doing something stupid, I would say to Mum, "But so and so told me to do it," to which I always got the reply, "So if he told you to jump off a cliff, would you do that too?"

We all know the story, so why do we go through our adult life letting the opinions and ideas of others guide us? You and your words are in charge so if you've let other people's words or thoughts control your life up until now, it's time to take the reins back.

This leads me right to the title of the main chapter of this book.

CHAPTER THREE

WHAT OTHER PEOPLE THINK OF YOU; IS NONE OF YOUR BUSINESS.

"If you can't eat it or fuck it; piss on it and walk away."
Bailey & Bella's "dog-osophy" to life

I know that the above quote is crude and tasteless, but so is the way we let life get the better of us. Simple situations turn into life-changing catastrophes purely because we overcomplicate them. I used the above quote and told a more in-depth story in "The No B.S Approach to Create the Life You Want," but here is a summary. My two awesome kelpies, Bailey and Bella have a simple "dog-osophy" to life and one that I live by and recommend to you.

When Bailey and Bella see something new, something intriguing, or a problem, they do exactly what the above quote says. They size it up and if they can't eat it or fuck it, they piss on it and walk away.

I love this approach to life that I wrote and directed a short "Dogumentary" about it as part of my diploma in directing. Life is that simple. Anytime you encounter a problem, look at it, and if you can't eat it or shag it, figuratively lift your leg on it and don't pay it another thought.

I have lost count of how many times I have used this approach in recent years and I am much happier that this simplistic way of dealing with problems not only makes my life better, but it makes me smile when I think about Bailey and Bella's theory for everything.

One of the biggest challenges we face these days, and one we should "piss on" more often is how we worry about what other people think of us. Why do we put such emphasis on someone else's opinion of us and not our own opinion of ourselves? It's one thing to say that we should believe in ourselves and have positive self-worth, but what about when others think or say less than positive things about us?

In recent years, with the advent of social media, it is no coincidence that suicide rates have shot up with the success of these mostly destructive platforms. I am certain that when Mark Zuckerberg created Facebook, his intention was for it to be a "social network", not the "Anti-Social Network" that it has morphed into.

We live in a world where people think that it is their right to voice their opinion on any platform they wish to, regardless of their expertise (or lack thereof) on the subject. Yes, we should embrace freedom of speech and everyone has the right to an opinion, but that doesn't mean you should always use it.

There is a quote by Lao Tzu that I read in his book "Tao Te Ching" that says "He who knows, does not speak. He who speaks does not know." To put my twist on a modern (crude) version, "Opinions are like arseholes. Everyone has one, but some are better off blocked".

The more I learn and the more I read, the less I feel the need to share my opinion; especially on social media. Even though I know much more now than I did a few years ago, I honestly don't feel the need to show off or share my thoughts on every topic.

I am sharing my learnings in this book in case they may benefit someone who is searching for similar answers to what I was. Most of the time people sharing their opinions so freely are searching for some sort of significance, or validation, as a result of a lack of self-worth.

On any given day if you look at any media outlet's pages, or visit Twitter or Facebook posts, you will see hundreds of comments and opinions on various topics. In most cases, the comments are not only irrelevant, but they are incorrect and make the person contributing the comments look less than intelligent.

Another fabulous quote on this is, "It is better to remain silent and be thought a fool than to speak and remove all doubt."

When it was first incorrectly reported in late 2014, about my situation with Breeana, the number of nasty comments that people posted on social media was concerning. While at first, it was alarming to read what other people thought, what was most disturbing was that these people actually thought they were correct, or more disturbingly; they thought they were intelligent for thinking and writing it.

Not only were their comments wrong, but they were based on their perceptions of my situation and not the facts. It didn't help that the Gold Coast Bullshitten deliberately misled the public when a rookie reporter named Megan Wheymes embellished the facts that were provided in court, to make the story appear saucier so she could make a name for herself. FYI: She apologised for her behaviour the next time I saw her.

At first, I was quite upset, to say the least, that complete strangers were saying completely incorrect things. As time went on and the same people kept saying the same things, I worried less and less about their comments.

The funny thing was that if you went on social media regularly and trolled the media outlets' pages or feeds, you would have seen the same trolls commenting over and over on a variety of different topics.

More often than not they said the same things and displayed the same amount of anger and hatred towards different people. I make this point because this is the most obvious example of how people deal with their own issues.

There is an old saying that goes, there are two ways to have the tallest building in town. 1. Build the tallest building or 2. Tear down everyone else's building so yours is the tallest. What took me a while to realise was that those people who were attacking me and others were doing so because of their own insecurities.

They weren't attacking me. They were projecting their insecurities onto me and lashing out because they didn't know how to deal with their own issues or triggers concerning similar traits in their own lives.

I know this is the case because I too had done this in the past. Thankfully I saw how I was projecting my insecurities outwardly by attacking others, instead of dealing with my issues internally.

When we lost Charlotte Dawson to suicide in 2014, my heart broke because she wasn't able to see that the trolls who were attacking her were doing so because of their own shit and not anything she did or stood for.

The trolls' comments had very little to do with Charlotte and everything to do with the trolls' own insecurities and their own battle with mental illness. With all due respect to Charlotte for taking the trolls on, I think that this was a foolish move. It was admirable for her to stand up to them and she was extremely brave for doing so, but it was a battle that she was never going to win on her own.

Continuing on from the previous chapter where I talked about self-image and trying to impress others, we need to stop giving a shit about what other people think or say about us and worry more about what we think and say about ourselves.

CHAPTER 3

It doesn't matter what other people think of you. What matters is what you think of yourself. The title of the chapter and book came from my brother when he flew down from Mackay to visit me immediately after Breeana's death.

The topic about what Breeana's family thought of me came up when my brother blurted out the words "What other people think of you, is none of your business." My brother is no Oxford scholar and God knows we've had our issues, but for all his faults, that one line has been more valuable to me than he will ever know.

Truth be known, that line, along with a comment by a friend who was a police officer the night after Breeana committed suicide are the reason that I am alive today to tell this story. My female police friend told me that I was not responsible for someone else's actions and as sad as the situation was, both hers and my brother's comments were spot on.

We worry so much about what other people think. This is why we go to great lengths in an attempt to make others happy, make them love us, and have them think nice things about us. The problem with that is that we end up spending our entire lives trying to please other people, instead of pleasing ourselves.

No one wants to be hated; me included, but as I have always said, "I would rather be hated for my honesty than loved for my lies." Gary Vaynerchuck once said that he holds the opinion he has of himself higher than the opinions of other people. This is exactly what this book is all about. When you stop giving a fuck about what others think of you, your life will become so much better.

I would have called this book "The (not-so) subtle art of not giving a fuck" but Mark Manson beat me to it. Incidentally, I read Mark's book before it became a best-seller and I was surprised that while the book started off the way you would imagine it would (based on the title), it nicely morphs into quite a spiritual book by the end. I highly recommend it, if you've not already read it.

I remember on my fortieth birthday when I was sitting on my balcony with friends, and I discovered what people mean when they say, "Life begins at forty." My understanding of that statement is simply that at age forty, you stop giving a fuck about what other people think and you start worrying only about what you think of yourself.

This is not to say that you live your life being completely self-centred and act in a way that is disrespectful to others. It simply means that other people's opinions have very little bearing on your happiness, how you live your life, or your state of mind.

Since being released from prison on bail for the murder charge, I have stopped dying my hair and I occasionally grow the beard that I had while I had no access to a razor in the watch house. This is my way of letting go of the last bit of resistance to not worrying about what other people think of me. It is also me accepting myself as I am as a perfectly imperfect human being.

One of my favourite movies recently was "The Greatest Showman". For those living under a rock, the story is about how P.T Barnum discovered what we now know as the circus. To some, he was a scam, but to many, Phineas T. Barnum became a hero. We'll talk about becoming a hero later, but in the movie, he unearthed what many believed to be "freaks" but whom we now embrace as equals in our society.

Embrace who you are and love all that you have; both good and bad. We'll get into this later in the book, but for now, I want to share one of the movie's songs that typifies what I believe is the key to happiness.

The song is called "This is Me" and is performed by the bearded lady and her fellow 'freaks' as they step out of the shadows and refuse to hide their flaws. They are ready to accept themselves as they are and don't care what anyone else thinks of them.

I urge you to do the same. Stop looking at what you think is wrong with you physically and learn to love all of you. Just like I did by colouring my hair and as Breeana did by wearing cosmetic contact lenses to cover what she thought were defective eyes, we all try to cover our flaws, but the way to true happiness is to embrace all of ourselves; not just the bits we like.

I wish that Breeana was around to see this movie and hear this song. She was a huge fan of 'Highschool Musical', all of the 'Step-up' films, and any film with singing and dancing in it. I also know she had a crush on Zac Efron (what young woman didn't) so I'm sure this movie would have been worn out in no time. She would have loved this movie and I know that the lyrics would have deeply touched her to the point where she may have been able to embrace what she saw as flaws in herself.

"THIS IS ME"
by Keala Settle & the ensemble of The Greatest Showman

I am not a stranger to the dark
Hide away, they say
'Cause we don't want your broken parts
I've learned to be ashamed of all my scars
Run away, they say
No one'll love you as you are
But, I won't let them break me down to dust
I know that there's a place for us
For we are glorious

Chorus:
When the sharpest words wanna cut me down
I'm gonna send a flood, gonna drown them out
I am brave, I am bruised
I am who I'm meant to be, this is me
Look out 'cause here I come
And I'm marching on to the beat I drum
I'm not scared to be seen
I make no apologies, this is me

Another round of bullets hits my skin
Well, fire away 'cause today, I won't let the shame sink in
We are bursting through the barricades and
Reaching for the sun (we are warriors)
Yeah, that's what we've become (yeah, that's what we've become)
I won't let them break me down to dust
I know that there's a place for us
For we are glorious

WHAT OTHER PEOPLE THINK OF YOU IS NONE OF YOUR BUSINESS

Chorus x 1
This is me
And I know that I deserve your love
There's nothing I'm not worthy of

Chorus x 1
(When the sharpest words wanna cut me down)
(I'm gonna send a flood, gonna drown them out)
I'm gonna send a flood
Gonna drown them out

This is me

I don't think much can be added to those lyrics as they are so incredible when it comes to how we should be with our own opinion of ourselves. One line I want to highlight though is in the chorus "When the sharpest words wanna cut me down. Gonna send a flood, gonna drown them out." For me, this sums up exactly how I have lived my life since being thrust into the public spotlight. This is precisely how I deal with defamatory or negative comments if I see them.

When people say things about me or to me to try to hurt me or get a reaction, I handle it in a simple, yet effective way. As Keala sings "When the sharpest words wanna cut me down" I flood their negativity out with my own self-talk. I am self-assured about who I am, and I send a flood of my own thoughts to drown out any negative words that others say.

As I stated earlier, we put far too much emphasis on what others think of us and not enough on what we think of ourselves. I discussed this topic in "The Blame Game" as well as in "The No B.S Approach to Create the Life You Want" when referring to our self-esteem as a bank account.

When other people make deposits into our self-esteem bank account, each comment is equivalent to one dollar, but when we deposit into our bank account by way of positive self-talk, each such deposit is worth twice as much.

Unfortunately, most people, see it as the other way around. They see others' comments as more valuable than their own. They therefore

CHAPTER 3

give power to other people and are dictated by how other people treat them as to how they feel about themselves. Make sure you always stand guard at the doorway of your mind.

Do not allow the media, your enemies, or even your friends to infiltrate your mind or poison your thoughts. Even friends with the best of intentions can poison our minds. Control what you are subjected to.

Instead of social media or the news, read books or listen to podcasts that nourish your mind; not poison it. If you feed the plants in your garden poison, they will die but if you feed them fertiliser, they will flourish. We are the same as plants. You can't allow your mind to be fed negative or destructive thoughts (poison), otherwise, it may literally kill you.

Besides the media and other people, we can be the most poisonous to our own well-being. Train yourself to use supportive words, not negative words about yourself. Watch what you say to yourself daily.

The word "disease" when broken down is literally a dis-ease of the mind. Almost all illnesses and diseases originally stem from a 'dis-ease' of the mind, so be careful what type of thoughts you allow your mind to take in on a regular basis.

A great way to ensure negative thoughts don't easily infiltrate your mind is to surround yourself with people who support you and who will hold you to account if they see you talking badly about yourself. They will always lift you up, but at the same time ensure that you are doing most of the 'heavy lifting' when it comes to your own self-image.

One of the hidden blessings of the horrific way the media distorted the facts surrounding Breeana's suicide is that I no longer have fake friends around me. I lost many friends when things were incorrectly reported and most of them disappeared without even a word or explanation. At the time this was disturbing, but in hindsight, it has been a huge blessing.

The friends that I had back then had a lower standard for themselves than I had for myself. For me to keep them as my peer group, either I had to lower my standards, or they had to raise theirs.

With my experience in personal development, I tried to help many of them raise their standards, but they weren't on the same level or didn't want to make small sacrifices to improve their lives. That led to resentment and when push came to shove, we parted ways.

Even a friendship that had spanned almost forty years disappeared and while that was truly devastating at the time, in hindsight, that was a blessing too. It took me more than a year to see how I had been dragged down for many years by the relentless negative thoughts that seemed to engulf their life.

I wanted so much happiness for this person and did everything I could to lift them up and give them a better way to look at life, but it was like they were resigned to "Life is just that way," or "Life is not meant to be good," or their favourite saying "That's just Murphy's Law" (Except they would insert their own surname, instead of Murphy).

Don't misunderstand what I am saying here. This person was and is a great person who does a lot for other people, but as I look back over forty years, on almost every occasion that I looked at whatever life was presenting us with a positive attitude, it was swiftly met with a negative response.

I have always been a very positive person. Some people call me a dreamer, but I'd rather be a dreamer than be constantly thinking "Woe is me." At that time, I used to think that perhaps this friend's negative attitude was a good balance for my 'King of wishful thinking' attitude to everything in life and therefore keeping my feet planted firmly on the ground. In hindsight though, it just deflated me.

This not only made me question my own thoughts, but it was an emotional drain constantly trying to negate their "glass half empty" outlook. It is no coincidence that things never seemed to work out for them when that was their state of mind. If you look at life as being hard and bad, that is exactly what you will get. You will always get what you focus on, so why focus on the negative?

Like I said a moment ago, I sincerely hope that they will one day see that life really isn't all bad. What is wrong is always available, but so is what is right if you look at it from a different perspective.

I am by no means suggesting that this person or any of my former friends were holding me back. I chose the friends I had, and I am responsible for what that brought with it. I am thankful though that I was dealt that hand and that the decision to lose those friends was beyond my control because, like most people, I probably would have stayed loyal to them, despite the harm it was doing to my life.

As a result of losing those friends, I have established new friendships that are far more mutually beneficial than the previous ones. While I often wonder how those old friends are doing, I know that the people who I surround myself with these days know everything there is to know about me and they support me and love me for exactly who I am.

CHAPTER 3

I've often said that this is the meaning of true love. Someone who knows everything about you and who loves you because of that and not despite it. There are no people in my life these days who could poison my mind like before and not one of my current friends is too gutless to confront me if they want to know something about me, us, or my situation.

I guess that is what was most disappointing about losing the old friends. I have always been the most honest person. I don't sugar-coat shit and I speak my mind. This has gotten me in trouble, but as I keep saying, I'd rather be hated for my honesty; than loved for my lies.

I would have hoped that if a 'friend' had any issues with me or my situation that they would say something. Instead, they just disappeared. Every single one of them. Not one even said, "Hey is any of this true?"

Not one of them had the balls to question me about anything or give me the opportunity to show them that things weren't how it was portrayed in the media. They just disappeared. That in itself showed how gutless they were and that they weren't real friends in the first place.

If you want to improve your life, you must surround yourself with people who stretch you emotionally. If you hang with people who settle for less than they deserve, then you too will create that in your life. If you hang with people who have a higher standard than you, then you will lift your game.

They say that you always want to be the dumbest person in a room. Why? Well, if you're the dumbest then you're the one who will benefit the most from those brilliant minds around you. They will ensure that you must lift your game to a higher level to associate with them.

If you want to be the world's best tennis player, you don't practice against lower-ranked players. You practice against the best. Stretching ourselves and growing is an essential part of the "art of fulfillment" that I discussed earlier.

I first heard Tony Robbins say something along these lines, but I've recently interpreted a particular verse of the Bible as saying something similar. "Everything in the universe must grow. If it doesn't grow; it dies. Once it dies, it then becomes fertiliser so that other things can grow." If you're not growing, you're dying, so find friends who make you stretch and grow and ditch the ones who are holding you back.

NEGATIVE VERSUS POSITIVE

One of the more difficult things that I've had to deal with throughout this process is what is at the core of mental illness; negative thoughts. Like most people, I've had negative thoughts and even though I have always professed to be one of the most optimistic people around, at times I have struggled with this too.

As Tony Robbins says, our ten-thousand-year-old brain is designed to save us; not make us happy. Our default thought is negative, which is a protection mechanism. We were designed to look for danger by way of dinosaurs all those years ago and even today, that is still how we are hard-wired; minus the dinosaurs.

Many gurus like to preach that you should eliminate negative thoughts, but as I've learnt, these thoughts can be useful. Tony bangs into us that there is no point in saying "there are no weeds" in the garden, all the while weeds are growing.

Tony teaches us how to identify the weeds and then rip the fuckers out. The same goes for our thoughts. Don't ignore them. Hear the negative thoughts, assess if they are helpful, or truly warning us of danger and if so, act upon them. If they're not useful, then get rid of them.

Even though I have known of my innocence in relation to Breeana's death from the beginning of this whole saga, the natural negative thoughts have tried to infiltrate my daily existence for several years; especially since being charged with murder.

It has taken lots of practise for me to be able to hear the thoughts and in most cases, remove them before they start to fuck with my mental health. This is not easy to do, and it has taken me some time to get good enough at it that I can dismiss the thoughts, or deal with them before they have any effect on me.

The first step is to identify the negative thought and establish if there is something you need to act on, or if it is simply the case that your mind is trying to screw with you. If there is real danger or something you need to act on, then see it as a blessing and act on it.

In many cases, the thought enables us to protect ourselves from a situation or safeguard us before disasters hit. If it is the latter and is just a useless thought, then it's just a case of saying "piss off. I won't let you stay here in my mind."

The only issue with this is that if this is all you do, then you will have another negative thought take its place soon after. The key is to replace that useless negative thought with a more positive one, or one that will serve you better.

Let me be very clear. This is not about being positive and pretending that everything is rosy. If you do this then seemingly out of nowhere, shit is going to go down. Negative thoughts have their place and trying to be only positive all the time is worse than being negative because you also become delusional.

Negative thoughts can be productive and helpful, but don't let them take over. Some examples of better thoughts might be as follows. If your initial negative thought is "I am fat," you might replace it with "I am working towards my ultimate body." Notice I didn't say replace it with "I am fit and fabulous with an awesome body."

Our mind knows a lie and will call 'bullshit' on you unless it is the case that you have an awesome body. If you are overweight and you say "I'm fit" as the replacement thought, your mind will fire back with, "No, you're a fat fuck" at which time you will more than likely agree and feel even more depressed.

You don't want to falsely puff yourself up because that will bring more counter-negative thoughts. Being realistic (with a slight tilt towards the positive) is the key. You want to replace the negative thought with a slightly positive one, but not a lie. It's kind of like a compromise. You're not all the way to where you want to be, but you and your mind will more than likely accept a compromise over a blatant lie.

If your initial negative thought is "I am always broke" don't say "I have lots of money" but instead try something like "I will find a way to earn more money." In both these cases, the better thought will also activate the reticular activating system in your mind which will begin looking for ways to make these things happen.

For example, in the case of money, once you say "I will find a way to earn more money" your mind will automatically take that as a challenge to go looking for opportunities for you to earn more money. Don't believe me? Try it.

Once your mind is given a directive, the reticular activating system finds examples and opportunities everywhere. It is like the old story where you buy a red VW and as soon as you drive it out of the car yard, you start seeing the same car everywhere.

At first, this process will be hard, but like any muscle, the more you practise, the easier it gets and the stronger you become. As I said, there is nothing wrong with negative thoughts. Don't just dismiss them all and pretend that everything is rainbows and unicorns because they will come back and bite you in the arse eventually. Hear the thought.

Identify its validity or usefulness, then deal with it or squash it and replace it with a more useful one.

Rather than calling them 'negative' or 'positive' thoughts, I like to refer to them as 'empowering' or 'disempowering'. If you can catch yourself when you think disempowering thoughts, quickly replace them with empowering ones. It becomes a little game and before you know it, the mind starts to do it automatically. The same goes for questions. If you find yourself asking a dumb question, replace it with a better question.

Here are some examples:

DISEMPOWERING	EMPOWERING
I am ugly.	I am perfect the way I am.
I can't do that.	I will find a way to achieve that.
I am always broke.	I will attract abundance.
Why is this happening to me?	How can this benefit me?
Nobody loves me.	There is love around me, even if I don't realise it.
Why did they do this to me?	What can I learn from this?

IS THERE A "P.R ANONYMOUS"?

"Hi. My name is Dan and I'm a pathological rescuer." It sounds like an opening confession or something like alcoholics anonymous for rescuers. Unfortunately, this has been the case in almost all my relationships. It is said that "with great knowledge, comes great responsibility" but that doesn't mean it is my responsibility to save every sick animal I run into. Oh dear! I can hear the feminists screaming now, "He refers to women as animals." For those too angry or precious to see my sense of humour; IT WAS A JOKE! Not a joke about women being animals, but about how we all want to rescue all the sick puppies in the world, but if we did, we'd end up having a house full of dog hair, crap, and fleas.

Now let's see if I can segue from sick puppies to ex-girlfriends as seamlessly as I did between songs on stage.

CHAPTER 3

As an entertainer, I often had to tap into my feminine energy to convey a character. Therefore, unlike many men, I developed a more sensitive side to my personality. This meant that (like most women) I tended to see a partner for her potential; not who she currently was.

It's a great quality to see the best in people, but when all you see is who you think you can help them to be, it's a recipe for disaster. There's an old joke that a man marries a woman, hoping she will never change, but a woman marries a man, hoping she can change him. I never wanted to change anyone. I only wanted to 'save' them from what they may have been currently going through when I met them.

Subconsciously I believed that if I saved the women I met, then they would love me and not abandon me. My friend Meagan, not Megan who promised to pay for my USA trip but Meagan, who I broke the balcony chair with having sex, claims that I saved her from a violent relationship.

Meagan used to always say that she was the girl who attracted the arseholes and I was the guy who attracted the girls who had previously attracted the arseholes. I'm not saying that every single woman I've dated needed rescuing, but in most instances, it was a case of them seeing in me the ability to provide them with tools to overcome their previous relationship hurt.

It's not my place to help or fix anyone but my nature is a caring one and I hate seeing people hurting or not able to move beyond their limiting beliefs. My natural instinct is to help people who seem stuck in an area of their life.

I know that it is a common mistake that men make and it wasn't until I read "Men Are from Mars and Women Are from Venus" by John Grey that I discovered that women don't want a man to fix their issues; they just want you to listen. Read that line again fellas.

I first learnt this fact during Tony Robbins' seminar, on relationship day. Just like John Grey's book suggests, Tony discussed how women will talk about their problems, and men see that as a green light to get to work to fix it. It's not bad that a man wants to fix things for his partner, but.... Yeah, it's a bad thing.

"Shut up and just listen" is what I learnt from Tony. Be totally present with her and make sure that she does not feel the '3-U's'. Unseen, (Not) Understood, and Unsafe.

While I always ensured that my partners were never 'unseen' in our relationship, I concede that my wanting to help them and save them meant that they may not have felt understood.

As for "unsafe", well we could debate the various meanings of that and whether or not this occurred in our relationships, but at the end of the day, I could certainly have done better in this area too and most certainly will in the future, now that I have an understanding of this important concept.

For those curious ones, Tony also provides the women in the seminar with the '3-C's' that a woman must never make a man feel, for the relationship to thrive. They are:

Criticized: Solution - Admire him and appreciate him; don't criticize him.

Closed: Solution - Be open and playful with him,

Controlled: Solution - Give him freedom and love.

On the final one; Controlled. This was the most powerful part of the entire six-day seminar. No amount of describing it in a book can do the final hour of this day justice, but in short, Tony explained that if a woman gives her man freedom, he will always honour her because that is how we men are wired.

A man's ultimate desire is to honour and protect his partner, but this can only happen when he is given freedom. It sounds contradictory, but a man's natural instinct when given freedom is to honour that, and never betray it. That's not to say every man in the world will do it, but most will.

Two other points that I will never forget about that evening were how Tony explained that inside every woman, is a scared little girl who desires to be loved and to feel safe. He also illustrated that in every man, is a little boy.

To the women in the room, Tony then said, "Nurture the boy, and the man will appear." We often forget that the most confident women or the strongest of men still have insecurities that need to be dealt with in a caring way.

When it came to my friends, I would help any of them with tools to turn any part of their life around if they wanted. It's not my place, but you can't help but want the best for them.

My wanting to help my former partners was the same. Unfortunately, when a partner in an intimate relationship wants to help, it can be interpreted as controlling or that you're trying to change the person.

CHAPTER 5

This was never my intention, but I can see that someone who may have insecurities might see my wanting to help, as me wanting to change or control them.

This can then lead to the person thinking that you believe that they are not good enough. They believe that this is why you want to help/fix them, and they then push back and that's not a good place for a relationship to be.

Instead of thinking I was Tony Robbins and wanting to help all of them, I should have listened and walked away when I realised that they weren't right for me, instead of staying and trying to help because, at the end of the day, you can lead a horse to water, but .... (you know the rest).

WHEN YOU CHANGE HOW YOU LOOK AT THINGS; THE THINGS THAT YOU LOOK AT CHANGE

Possibly the coolest thing I've learnt from travelling the world and capturing images as a photographer is to find the beauty in everything and every situation. Most people only take photos when the sun is shining or the scenery is perfect, but sometimes it is when things aren't so perfect that they are at their most beautiful. Try shooting long-exposure photography on a bright sunny day and you will know what I mean.

For example; I've sailed through Milford Sound in New Zealand on two occasions and each time offered something different. The first time we entered the fjord, the weather was perfect with not a cloud in the sky.

The fjord was stunning and offered many opportunities to capture its beauty. The blue sky contrasted with the lush green mountains and the white cascading waterfalls that spilled from the top of the cliffs into the ocean below.

On the second occasion we sailed up the fjord it was dark, cloudy, rainy, and in complete contrast to the first occasion. Despite this, I must say that I found this visit to be more spectacular.

The low clouds and mist meant that there were not the contrasting colours from the previous visit, but this gave the fjord a Lord of the Rings kind of feel to it. It was mystical, eerie, and incredibly peaceful.

When I talked with people about my visits there it was always the second visit that I thought of. From a photographer's point of view, it was stunning, but from a philosophical angle, it's enlightening.

WHAT OTHER PEOPLE THINK OF YOU IS NONE OF YOUR BUSINESS

It's easy to find the beauty in life when everything is perfect and things are going well, but if you can find the beauty in anything, regardless of the circumstances, that is when life becomes exciting. As Tony says, "Life is always happening for you; not to you."

As they say, "When life gives you lemons, make lemonade" or as I prefer; "make yourself a margarita." I guess that is why I love photography so much because no matter what the situation, I can always experience the beauty, and each time I do, I am reminded that life can be the same if you allow it to be.

In one of my screenplays, a real turning point for the protagonist's journey was when they were getting something framed in a framing shop. The scene started off looking like an unimportant one, but it became a pivotal part of the story when the staff member doing the framing asked, "How would you like it framed?" to which the protagonist replied, "It doesn't really matter."

At this point, the staff member says, "Are you sure? The way you frame something can make a huge difference to how it looks." This seemingly off-the-cuff comment had a much deeper meaning to the protagonist and became the cornerstone of their "hero's journey" which we will look further into later in this book.

We all have the choice to choose how we want to frame everything that happens in our lives and how we frame an event can make a huge difference to how it looks to us

BEING RIGHT VERSUS BEING HAPPY

> Dorothy: "How can you talk without a brain?"
> Scarecrow: "I don't know, but a lot of people without a brain do a lot of talking." – The Wizard of Oz

God gave us two eyes, two ears, and two nostrils; but only one mouth. I believe that this means that he intended for us to look, listen, and breathe twice as much as we should speak. For most people these days it is the exact opposite. They think that if they're not speaking their mind, voicing their opinion, or explaining their point of view, this makes them less of a person than everyone else.

The fact of the matter is that no one ever got in trouble by listening, looking, or breathing, but everyone has landed themselves in some bad situation by speaking; me included.

In my opinion, you don't learn anything by speaking, but you learn a lot by listening. There is a consensus that everyone has a right to speak their mind and while this may be true, it doesn't mean we have to activate this right to be happy.

Most people would rather be right than be happy. A classic example of this is the ongoing battle between drivers and bicycle riders across Australia. Bicycle riders have suddenly felt the need to ride on the road instead of in designated bike lanes (where available).

While I drive a car and don't ride a bike, my thoughts here are purely from a logical perspective. The bicycle riders claim that it is their right to use the car lanes as they pay registration and insurance for their cars.

Unfortunately, their argument in this case, is extremely flawed because they pay rego, etc. for their cars, but not their bicycles. Regardless, the laws actually allow them to ride on the road. The problem is that there is growing frustration and anger between drivers and bike riders over some riders pushing this loophole too far.

While bicycle riders may be allowed to ride in the middle of most roads, I personally couldn't think of anything more stupid. Yes, if I was riding on the road and was hit by a car, it would more than likely be the car driver's fault. The issue I face is that if I am dead, then I'm hardly going to get to be "right" am I?

Sadly, as I write this, I just read twenty minutes ago that a cyclist was hit and killed by a car on a road. The driver was charged and it is yet to be determined if they were guilty or not, but either way, the cyclist is dead. As sad as this story is, once again I ask the question; Is it more important to be right, or happy?

Another classic example of this type of thinking is when a woman says it is her right to wear provocative clothing in public, almost to the point of tempting fate and risking her safety for the sake of making a point.

I completely agree that a man or woman is entitled to wear anything they wish within the law and should be able to do so without fear of rape, sexual assault, harassment, or cat-calling.

However, this does not mean that she will be safe in doing so. We live in an age where men and women are equal and men's million-year-old primitive brains are now ruled by respect and ethics, rather than his right to take a woman any way he pleases. This does not mean that every single man can cognitively process a woman respectfully wearing such attire and not act in a less-than-respectful way.

Of course, any such man who harms a woman should be reprimanded, locked up, or institutionalised if he does act in a derogatory way, but while this should be the case, I don't believe any woman should put herself in any potentially harmful situation, just because it's her 'right'.

As previously stated, yes, it is a woman's right to dress how she pleases without fear or reprise by men, but it is still smarter to do so cautiously, because at the end of the day, if something terrible happens to you, then it is you who suffers the most.

We all know sharks kill, but sharks don't swim on land. If you want to swim in the water, you do run a slight risk of being attacked. While I urge women to exercise their rights, once again it comes down to whether or not you wish to be right or be happy.

When the black woman Rosa Parks famously refused to give up her seat to a white man on a bus in Alabama in 1955, she was not intending to change the civil rights movement. She was simply tired. Yes, her actions changed the course of the world, but at the time, she put herself at great risk. Thankfully we now live in a world where she and any other black man or woman can, for the most part, live as equals.

If you want to be a Rosa Parks, a cyclist, or anyone else enforcing your rights, then I applaud you. All I am saying is to think about what is most important; to be happy, or to be right. When you give up having to be right, you will be much happier. I certainly have.

I could pursue the media, Breeana's family, or Queensland politician Ros Bates for blatant defamation, abuse, and harassment, or the police for wrongful imprisonment, but do I really want to put myself through that, just because I want to be right? I am not saying any of these things won't happen, but I would much rather be happy than be right.

In many cases throughout life, we feel the need to be right, rather than to be happy. This causes conflict and anguish in our lives and leads to anger, frustrations, and in turn, illness and disease. I personally would rather be happy than feel the need to be right. It doesn't mean that I concede or give in to everyone. It simply means that I don't feel the need to push my point or my opinion and be right to feel better about myself.

This is where most couples fail and relationships break down; my previous relationships included. We would rather get our point across and be right during an argument than be happy.

It really doesn't matter who is right or wrong, in fact, both people could be right (or wrong) and neither one would concede or be happy. There is nothing wrong with saying sorry regardless of who is right.

I know I used to be the worst at this, so I can hardly claim to be a role model for this argument, but I can promise you that the sooner a couple says sorry and puts being happy before being right, the sooner the relationship will be a good one.

Sorry doesn't mean you are conceding or are wrong. It simply means that your partner's happiness is more important to you than whatever it is you're arguing about; which in most cases is not important.

Now let's use this in relation to one of the world's biggest social issues at the moment; online bullying. With the advent of social media, there is a new set of challenges that both the users and the law enforcement agencies have to adjust to.

Never before have we given complete strangers such intimate access to our personal lives. Not long after Facebook exploded with users, a friend gave what I believe to be excellent advice when it comes to who you let in on that platform. He said, "You should never be friends on Facebook with anyone who you would not invite into your home."

You would never let someone into your home if all they were going to do was abuse you or harm you emotionally or physically. So why would you give them the same opportunities online?

If someone was rude to you, you would throw them out of your house. The same should be done online. The best advice I can give anyone pertaining to online is to surround yourself only with those who are good for your mental health.

One good thing about social media is that you can easily remove people from your sphere which disables their ability to abuse or threaten you. Even better, you can remove yourself from the platform altogether.

Everyone has the right to express their opinion, but more importantly, you have the right to feel safe and not be attacked; or defamed. Many people seem to think that if they get off social media their life will be less enjoyable or less meaningful. I can tell you from personal experience that the complete opposite is true.

My life became much better and my happiness and mental state dramatically improved after going off all forms of social media. People are leaving social media as fast as they are leaving private health cover. While it can be argued that some good things do come from social media, the bad easily outweighs the good that stems from being on these platforms.

WHAT OTHER PEOPLE THINK OF YOU IS NONE OF YOUR BUSINESS

If you do stay on social media, you need to be smart about how and who you interact with on your profile and in public forums. You have the right to defend yourself against bullying etc., but do you need to engage them for the sake of being right? By ignoring, not responding, or blocking them it may appear that you are giving in to them. But, by not feeling the need to defend yourself or your rights, you can disempower them.

Most people who say horrible things online would never have the guts to say the same things to your face. I know this for a fact. For all the thousands of hateful comments and threats levelled at me online, not one person has said a single thing to me face to face. Once you realise that the people who attack you are nothing more than gutless insecure people, you realise that they are of no real harm to you.

They are simply struggling to come to terms with their own lives in comparison to what they see on social media and are simply lashing out at you as a result of their own insecurities. What they say should have no bearing on you and in almost every case, they are too gutless to continue their abuse in person. How do I know this?

There once was a time when I was coming to terms with my life transitioning from being a highly paid singer to establishing myself in the travel and cruise industry on land. It was during this time that I too was part of the idiots arguing about so many things that had no bearing on my own life. I felt that by stating my point, I was giving my life one of the basic human needs that we all require; significance.

Significance is why many people spend their life trying to convince others on social media that their life is so great. Don't fall into that trap and don't compare yourself to anyone else.

As Ralph Waldo Emerson said, "Envy is ignorance and imitation is suicide." Live your life according to your rules, your timeline, and your values, not someone else's. There is a divine plan for you that is different from anyone else. Your timeline may differ from someone else so stop giving a shit about what they have.

While listening to an episode of Dr. John Demartini's podcast recently, John asked the question, "Would you rather be the second Elvis; or the first you?" There is no one else like you in the world, so find those unique skills that make you who you are and become the best 'first you'.

CHAPTER FOUR

FROM THE PENTHOUSE TO THE JAILHOUSE

"Everybody has a plan; until they get punched in the mouth"
- Mike Tyson

In the past, it has been suggested that cruise ship singers are not of the same calibre as Broadway singers or West End performers, but I can tell you that this is simply not the case. I'm not particularly talking about myself, although I'm hardly going to say that myself or any of my fellow cruise ship performers were crap.

Perhaps in the 1990s singers that couldn't get a gig on Broadway would run off to sea, and if you watched The Love Boat you would swear all cruise ship entertainers were crap. These days though, the competition for roles and the quality of shows onboard cruise ships rival any Broadway or West End production. There is also a significant crossover with many Broadway stars performing on ships as well as on Broadway.

Before I delve deeper into this story, I should clarify something. For the most part, the media has portrayed me as a "Cruise Ship Crooner". This title implies that I may have been some sort of lounge singer, sitting on a stool wooing the ladies with tunes by Frank Sinatra and from an era where only men voted and women stayed in the kitchen, etc.

The title they gave me paints a picture of a smoky room, filled with the stench of stale alcohol, a few drunks at the bar, and some crew who have knocked off for the evening, sitting in booths, drowning their sorrows as a reluctant pianist accompanies me as I sing.

Towards the end of my career at sea, I did develop my own one-man show, singing all the biggest big-band hits of the golden era of swing, with my big-band, but this was as a headline act in the main theatre on board.

When doing this, I was paid incredible amounts of money for one hour's work per week. That's right. A one-hour show, star billing, and a paid holiday after. On the night of my show, I was the show. The headline act for that night and the one by who the entire ship came to be entertained.

That said, that portion of my career was a minuscule part of my time at sea. For the majority of my time on cruise ships, I was the leading male in over thirty Broadway-style shows. These shows were the pinnacle of entertainment onboard and were produced, directed, and choreographed by some of the greatest names in the world.

The funny thing about the comments about the quality of cruise ship performers is that you never hear it from entertainers. Professional entertainers know that having a gig is a wonderful thing. The nature of the industry is that even if you star in a hit Broadway show, or have a residency in Vegas, you still have to tread the boards and audition for each gig. Having a well-paid long-term gig of any kind is what we dream of.

My ex-partner Sarah, who has starred as the lead in Les Miserable and Phantom of the Opera in London, did several gigs on cruise ships. My friend Anita who has toured with Take That and starred in Chicago and Saturday Night Fever in the West End also enjoyed several contracts on cruise ships. Shit! Some ships even have full Broadway versions of Grease, Jersey Boys, Cats, Hairspray, and Chicago on board. Not to mention acts like Blue Man Group.

Having recently watched all five seasons of The Love Boat on DVD, I can see why people may think cruise ship entertainment is rubbish, but that was over forty years ago. FYI: Those in Australia shouldn't judge cruise ships by the standard of entertainment that Aussie ships have, because they really do lag behind the overseas ships these days.

That is partly because of the standard of shows and entertainers in Australia, but sadly it is also because we are not as "theatrically sophisticated" as the Americans and British.

To backtrack for a moment. When I worked on Australian ships, Australian entertainers were allowed to work onboard. This changed in roughly 2008 when the Australian government tried to close a loophole in the industry, whereby crew on board did not legally have to pay tax. Rather than pander to the Australian government, the cruise lines told them to shove it up their arse and decided that unless a crew member held a dual passport, then only international crew could work in Australian waters.

With this being the case, the best of the Aussies went overseas to the international ships and international waters, while the Australian ships were sent substandard entertainers; mostly from Britain.

Now that I've offended many Brits. Let me make it clear. British entertainers are good, however, in comparison to Australian and American singers and dancers, they are a step-down, as such. That said, many of them are still of a good enough standard to not warrant people thinking that their working on ships is due to a lack of ability, or inability to gain high-quality gigs on land.

In comparison to cruise ship work, the girl who was my "Sandy" in my high school production of Grease was well entrenched in the recording industry by the time she left school. Her former boyfriend was a member of a well-known Brisbane-based pop band "Indecent Obsession" in the late '80s and she toured with them along with Kylie Minogue. Several years later she signed a record deal with Sony Music and had a couple of top 20 hits, yet despite this success, she told me that she and her bandmates only made $500 each.

Now I'm not knocking her at all for this. She was an incredible singer and a dear friend at the time. She got further than I did in that particular part of the industry, but in hindsight, I am glad that this path didn't work out for me because my professional singing career stretched for two decades, while hers was fleeting at best. Plus, while she made $500 over many years, I was making double that; per hour!

Either way, both my friend and myself were always so grateful for the success we had, doing what we loved so as you can probably surmise, we would both rather have been on the journey we embarked on than that of those who make such comments. Both of us attended our fifteen-year high school reunion and were met with several comments about how we actually went out and did what we said we were going to do with our lives.

I am by no means saying that someone who doesn't follow their dreams is less of a person. My point is that those who do should be applauded; not discouraged for not hitting the highest peak of their industry. As I like to say, "Reach for the stars, and even if you don't get all the way there, at least you won't just have a handful of dirt."

The only people I have ever heard say that a job as an entertainer on a cruise ship is second-rate are those who gave up on their dreams.

The type of people who weren't as brave as the entertainers who never let negativity or occasional failure stop them.

The people I have seen or heard make comments about cruise ships have always been those who are unhappy with the choices they made in their own lives and feel the need to try to bring other people down to lift themselves up.

Not everyone is destined to be a mega-hit recording artist, a Broadway star, or a cruise ship performer. That doesn't make you less of a person. It means you have different talents, passions, and purposes. I constantly meet people who say how exciting and awesome my life is and how they wish they had such a life.

While I am always humbled to hear this, I often rebut with how I often feel the same about how people can do certain jobs that I would suck at, or not have the patience for.

I am always in awe of nurses, artists, architects, mechanics, and any profession where the person is in love with what they do. That to me is the secret to a happy life. Not how famous you are, or if your career is glamorous. It's whether or not you love what you do.

"Either do what you love to do, or find a way to love what you do"

Seriously, anyone who still believes that cruise ship performers aren't of the same quality has more than likely not seen both a Broadway show and a cruise ship show in recent years. Some of the best singers and dancers in the business have worked on ships.

I myself have worked with the likes of Jackie Love, Lucky Grills, Aled Jones, Anita Louise Combes, and even Neil Sedaka as well as some of the best musicians, who in turn have worked with Liza Minelli, Frank Sinatra, and Dean Martin, to name a few.

Even Lee Mead, who won Andrew Lloyd Webber's 'Any Dream Will Do' show and went on to star in London's West End as Joseph, was one of my cast members in 2002 when I was Cruise Director.

When I worked at sea, I wore costumes designed by world-famous designers Bob Mackie and Nolan Miller. I worked with world-renowned choreographers both here and in the USA and U.K. Stilletto Entertainment that produces shows for Holland America Line manages artists like Barry Manilow, and has even won Tony awards.

The bonus of being a cruise ship performer is that you get all your meals paid for, you get to see the world, in most cases, the pay is tax-

CHAPTER 4

free and you don't have the monotony of performing the same show eight times a week. Not to mention that in many cases, the pay is better than on Broadway, hence why the best of the best goes to sea at least once.

As I mentioned in my last book "C.R.U.I.S.E", a singer onboard a cruise ship is treated like royalty. You get your own large passenger cabin. You can eat and drink anywhere on the ship; just like the passengers. You have no duties to do other than the shows and you arrive and depart the ship in a limousine. Besides all of that you are adored by passengers who (unlike with Broadway stars) get to meet and mingle with you if you're willing to make yourself available.

Almost all of my female singers would hide after a show and throughout the cruise, whereas I would make a habit of always de-greeting the show and hearing what the passengers had to say. Who wouldn't want to hear how awesome you were right lol?

On the flip side, even if I had an average show I would still race out to the front of the theatre and cop any average comments on the chin (Trust me the passengers weren't shy to share their opinion either way).

The passengers were quite happy to chat and buy you a drink and they showed a real interest in the behind-the-scenes secrets that made the shows so spectacular. Throughout my time working as a professional singer, people often asked me how I managed to retain so many lyrics and dance steps. I guess as they say, "repetition is the mother of all skills.

During rehearsals of any show, each step and every note is broken down and practised until it is as second nature as breathing. While I could remember all lyrics and dances for five shows at a time and have performed in over thirty shows at sea, these days there are very few lyrics and next to no dance routines that I could bust into if needed.

One that I do still remember, is the patter that I used to say before I performed 'Mr. Bojangles' in my own show. Full disclosure, I completely plagiarised the entire verse straight from Robbie Williams' live concert at the Albert Hall in 2001 because the way he did it was sheer perfection.

The fact that he had done it word for word mattered little to my audience as they felt that it was just like an artist singing another artist's song. Even more than ten years after the last time I performed the song, these words still roll effortlessly off my tongue anytime I think of the song.

WHAT OTHER PEOPLE THINK OF YOU IS NONE OF YOUR BUSINESS

The introduction went as follows.

The next song I'd like to sing was written about the greatest tap dancer that ever lived. His name was Bill Robinson and he was born in Harlem. He tapped his way from the Whitehouse to the Jailhouse. He was a drinker a brawler and a womaniser [chuckle] – so we're in good company. When he died, his coffin was carried by Duke Ellington, Cole Porter, and Irving Berlin. [Sigh] Ladies and Gentlemen, it gives me great pleasure to sing this song. [Smile] This is Mister Bojangles.

These days the above lines make me giggle because even though I haven't performed in the Whitehouse as Bill Robinson did, I have experienced firsthand the highs and lows of life; going from the Penthouse (being royalty on ships) to the Jailhouse. From all accounts and through my interpretation of the song, neither of those events defined Bill Robinson, and likewise, neither of mine defined me.

I don't define my life by having experienced such highs doing what I loved and living the dreams that many people are too afraid to go after. Nor do I define myself by the two unfortunate short stints in prison that I have experienced. Both of these examples just are. I have learnt a lot from both, and that is what is most important.

Life is how we perceive it. Nothing in life is either good or bad; it just is. You can have two people who have the same experience and have completely different perceived outcomes. I have made it my mission since Breeana's death to find the good in the situation and to promote love and forgiveness.

I refuse to harbour anger towards Breeana, or her family these days. On the other side of the coin, you have some of Breeana's family who have so much anger, hatred, and venom in their hearts. It is a tragic situation for all concerned, but my point is simple; The only meaning anything has in life; is the meaning we give it.

Even just one of the things that have happened to me in the past eight years would send most people over the edge; let alone having to deal with all of them. Despite this, I have managed to overcome them, find a way to move forward, and somehow stay calm and at peace throughout the process. How I have been able to be this way has surprised both my family and even me.

If anyone said to me a decade ago that I would witness my girlfriend commit suicide, be wrongly jailed for 10 days, be targeted by police for six years, have my entire personal life scrutinized beyond excess, be harassed by media from all over the world, then be charged with murder, I would have probably done myself in right then and there. I certainly wouldn't have thought I would be able to remain calm throughout all of it.

Knowing that I was innocent and have been harshly done by, has been the main motivating factor, but my desire to be some sort of inspiration for anyone else facing drastic challenges is also a big factor in my wanting to overcome these challenges.

I'm also a very stubborn person and the fact that Breeana's aunt and her band of angry people have been so misguided in their attacks is more fuel than I could ever need to conquer these challenges.

I often wonder if Breeana's aunt's behaviour is driven by what she claims it to be, or if her eldest daughter's fame is more her motivation. If you dig below the surface she appears to be more interested in fueling her daughter's aspiring influencer/porn career on as many occasions as she is trying to convince herself and others that I am responsible for her niece's death.

Either way, I would never give them the satisfaction of giving in, as many victims of bullies do. And let's be honest. Breeana's aunt is nothing more than a bully and a coward, and I have no problem calling her or anyone else on it because the world has too many cowardly bullies like her in it.

Steve Harvey, who famously and monumentally fucked up the crowning of Miss Universe in front of a worldwide audience in 2015 said, "A moment of crisis showed me exactly who I was (and it will do the same for you)."

Speaking of beauty pageants and things being a matter of perception. (Oh this is going to be my worst segue in the book yet). During the early 2000's I was called upon to be a celebrity judge for the national finals of Miss Hawaiian Tropics, Queen of Clubs, Miss Indy, and Miss Nude.

I was also asked to compère the national final of 'Miss Exotic Angel' in 2004 & 2006. For those unsure of what this is, it is the culmination of a national search for the country's best female exotic dancer. Laugh as you may, to these women, it was quite prestigious.

To most men, this would be a dream come true, but for me....Oh, who the fuck am I trying to fool. It was a dream gig for me too. It was nearly as cool as managing Hooters when it opened on the Gold Coast.

As the compère, I was given tickets to give to friends so my brother and best mate came along to watch me perform. Yeah right. They didn't even notice me doing my job. All they noticed was each naked woman on stage.

Speaking of this, halfway through the evening, a woman was performing on stage when I received a text from my mate saying I needed to get out there and see this girl. At the time I was backstage reviewing my notes for the next performer.

There were twenty girls in the competition and only one on stage, so I sent my mate the following reply. "One naked woman on stage. Where do you think the other nineteen naked women are?" Of course, the answer was that the other nineteen were naked backstage; with me.

Here's where my segue makes sense. To him, he was focused on one naked woman, but me, I could see nineteen of them. Life is all about perception. You can change your perception and therefore change your entire life.

While most people see stripping as degrading and sleazy, I can also see the talent that these women have. Sure, they have to undress to show off their talent, but this doesn't make them less talented than a woman who is clothed.

When I managed Hooters, most of the young ladies working there were also pin-up models, nude models, or strippers. Without fail, each one of them was the sweetest, most respectful girl you could meet. Even the Playboy Bunnies who I arranged to fly in from the U.S.A for the grand opening were regular, nice women. They just chose to remove their clothes for their profession.

To further reiterate my point, when in Thailand on a cruise ship, I visited a 'Ping-pong' show with Sue (my biological mother), and on a separate occasion, I also took my Swedish girlfriend Klara to the same show. Let me clarify. I did not want to take them to this type of show, but the gay dancers on board said that if I didn't; then they would. So, I thought it best for me to supervise them lol.

To most, these shows are the lowest form of degradation to women in the world. While I did agree with this sentiment, I altered my perception and looked beyond that. To us in the Western world, these women are seen as sex objects and pieces of meat, but perhaps in their country, they are revered in a higher manner.

I would dare say that these girls also get paid a lot more than many women in Thailand thus providing their families with a better quality of life than otherwise possible, so who are we to judge?

CHAPTER 4

At the end of the day, everything in life is how we perceive it. Whether you're a stripper, a Thai hooker, a ladyboy, or someone who has been thrown in jail. It matters not what happens to you, or what you see, but rather how you perceive it that will ultimately decide whether you will be happy or not. In my opinion, the way to change your perception of almost anything in life is summed up in the next sub-chapter.

THE DEEPER YOU GO; THE MORE JUICE YOU FIND IN THE FRUIT

An interesting thing that I learnt while ploughing through every single episode of both 'Two and a Half Men' and 'Glee' recently, is that things aren't always as they appear on the surface. When both shows were on TV, I often watched Two and a Half Men but rarely saw five minutes of Glee.

Half a decade after both shows ended, I turned to the DVD box sets and was surprised by what I learnt. On the surface, Glee appeared to be a wholesome singing show and Two and a Half Men seemed like a raunchy bachelor-targeted show.

When both shows were on the air, my best friend at the time had two daughters who were aged between nine and fifteen during the shows' lifetimes. At the time he would let his daughters watch Two and a Half Men, but forbid them from watching Glee. Given that the girls were precisely the target demographic for Glee, I was baffled at his reasoning for this. In his words "Glee is full of smutty innuendo and graphic content".

Somehow though, he thought that Two and a Half Men was more sanitised. I thought at the time that his assumption and rule were purely based on the fact that he loved Two and a Half Men and didn't want to sit through the singing on Glee. I thought he disguised this with the previously stated thoughts on why the girls should only watch one.

Having sat through hundreds of episodes of both shows, it appears that he was closer to the mark than I gave him credit for. As it turned out, Glee was full of sexual innuendo and graphic themes, but to most children and adults who watch shows on a superficial level, such content is easily missed.

Two and a Half Men on the other hand, while appearing to be all smut and little substance, actually tackled some rarely addressed men's issues and issues that men, boys, and even women and girls face on a daily basis, but rarely broach with friends or colleagues.

WHAT OTHER PEOPLE THINK OF YOU IS NONE OF YOUR BUSINESS

Both Glee and Two and a Half Men ran on one premise, while bravely tackling societal issues rarely seen on TV. I didn't realise how many issues Glee in particular faced head-on.

These range from the obvious same-sex relationships and homosexuality, right through to gender identification, bullying, religious beliefs, and domestic violence. Two and a Half Men tackled its issues in a way that men can watch and relate to without feeling completely uncomfortable because the messages are hidden behind brilliantly witty humour.

The two shows were polar opposites so far as their demographics, yet beneath their surface differences, they were one and the same. Both shows also lost their leading men at the height of their popularity, and while the circumstances were different, the way both shows tackled the subject and refused to shy away from what happened was a lesson to all of us.

Trying to hide the truth, shying away from what is real, or suppressing the real issue is a surefire way to prolong the pain. This is why I refused to dwell on what happened to Breeana. We all grieve differently and while her family dealt with her death in their way, I did it my way and neither of us is wrong for that.

Besides the above lesson from two seemingly flippant shows, there is another valuable thing that can be learnt from these prime-time hits. If you look at something or someone only on the surface, you will be quick to judge and perhaps form a positive or negative opinion of them.

But if you take the time to look deeper and notice all the hidden secrets and traits, you will learn a lot more about them and yourself. We are so quick to judge without knowing anything more than the 'surface fluff' of a person. Look for the subtleties in people and life takes on a new meaning.

I've been blessed as a singer, songwriter, scriptwriter and now director to have learnt these intricate crafts. As a result of this, when I hear a song or watch a movie, I see and hear so much more than many people do.

I notice the subtle random funny prop or facial expression from an extra on a movie or show that most people either miss or think it's a mistake. I see it and know it's an inside joke by the writer or director.

The vanity cards that Chuck Lorre puts at the end of each episode of 'Two and a Half Men', 'Big Bang Theory' & 'Mom', or the inter-scene beach shot on Two and a Half Men where the poor guy in a white shirt with a dog who never gets real far along the beach are two examples.

I notice the light and shade in a singer's voice and their storytelling ability. Instead of hearing a song as a whole, I also switch to a listening mode where I can hear every single instrument push through individually to the front of my conscious hearing as if that instrument is playing solo and not part of an arrangement. This is where life gets its juice.

Take the time to notice the small things in every situation and life turns into one big awesome celebration. Don't just notice the beautiful flower. Take the time to notice the stems and the plant holding them up.

Don't just eat or drink your food. Notice the texture of it and how good it feels as you devour it. When getting to know someone, don't just hear what they say, but notice all the tiny idiosyncrasies that make them who they really are. Look beyond the facade that you see in the mirror and see how amazing you are and all the unique and incredible traits that make you special.

For me personally, the deeper I look at something or a situation, the more exciting it gets, which in turn makes life juicier. I know I tend to look at things in an abstract way compared to most people, but that is often where I learn the most and subsequently grow the most.

I was listening to the classic 80's song 'Kyrie' by Mister Mister one day when it dawned on me that I had no frickin' clue what Richard Page was singing in the chorus. "Kyrie Eleison", which is at the start of each line in the chorus is Greek for "Lord, have mercy." When I translated it and read it with each line of the chorus, the song took on a much deeper and spiritual meaning. Substitute the Greek translation in each line and the song makes perfect sense.

Translation:

[Kyrie Eleison]
[Lord have mercy] down the road that I must travel
[Lord have mercy] through the darkness of the night
[Lord have mercy] where I'm going will you follow
[Lord have mercy] on the highway in the night

WHAT OTHER PEOPLE THINK OF YOU IS NONE OF YOUR BUSINESS

I guess it was no coincidence that this curiosity about the song's origins was around the same time that I read both the new and old testaments of the Bible along with over three hundred spiritual and religious books. Now when I listen to the song, I feel completely different than before this realisation.

What I am trying to get across in this short story is that we often go through life barely scratching the surface and therefore are easily swept up in superficial things that leave us susceptible. Take the time to look a little deeper and this will become your foundation of stability and joy in life so that when tough times show up, you will be able to find peace of mind to get you through it.

FRANK'S WAY, MICHAEL'S WAY, AND MY WAY.

Along with being the leading male in over thirty different production shows on cruise ships, I was allowed the opportunity to develop my own show while on board. This began in 2005 while onboard the ill-fated Pacific Sky in which we were the last cast ever to sail on that old girl. I had just discovered the wonderful genre of big band and swing in one of our shows and I wanted to develop a show around that genre.

Incidentally, it was on my previous contract in Tahiti that I became engaged to a Canadian girl whose brother-in-law was friends with a local singer who was about to release his first major album through a record label. Myself and my fiancée were having dinner with her sister and brother-in-law in Vancouver in early 2004 when they told me of this friend of theirs and his upcoming project.

Their friend had already released an independent CD, but they believed that this, his first album through a major label was going to launch their friend into the music stratosphere. They told me that this album was going to be all remakes of classic swing songs made famous many decades earlier.

My first reaction was that I thought Robbie Williams had beaten him to the punch with his "Swing When You're Winning" album in 2001. Having said that, it was Canada, and not many British artists crack the big time with album sales across the pond, so Robbie wasn't that well known there at that stage. That said, I still didn't see the validity of the idea.

He said that his mate Michael had a real gift for the genre and that I should keep my eye out for him. I thought nothing of it and got on

CHAPTER 4

with life. I moved my fiancée over to Australia and six months later I discovered that not only was my fiancé's brother-in-law right but that the world had unearthed the most brilliant swing voice since Francis Albert Sinatra himself. That friend they were talking about was none other than Michael Bublé.

In almost two decades, Michael has covered most of Frank's repertoire in his albums, but one song he has only done as a tribute occasionally live is "My Way". Written by Paul Anka, "My Way" along with the classic "One for My Baby" was Frank's greatest song. Well, okay. Add "New York New York" to that list, but let's not open that can of worms.

Incidentally, in 2007 when I was invited to perform my own show with some of the greatest UK jazz musicians of the past fifty years, I was fortunate enough to have Duncan Lamont play saxophone when I sang "One for my Baby". Duncan played saxophone on the original recording of the song and toured with Frank Sinatra for more than a decade, so it was a huge honour to share a stage and such an intimate song with him.

By the time Duncan performed with me, he was seventy-six years old, but even still, he had the musical chops to rival any much younger musician. Sadly, Duncan passed away twelve years later, but true to his passion, he was still playing gigs only hours before he died. That in itself shows that when you're doing what you love, you will never really work a day in your life.

When my show "A Little Bit of Swing" developed at sea I quickly discovered that if I was to do a show based around swing and big band music then I should omit My Way from the playlist at my own peril.

The audience loved the song and expected it somewhere in the show. To me, there was only one place to put the song, and that was to be as an encore; leaving the audience on a high. As it turned out, I too was left on a high by finishing with that song.

The lyrics in My Way are humbling and reflective and I personally couldn't help but relate to them as I delivered them to my audiences. Frank Sinatra was said to have never felt comfortable with the lyrics because he felt that they were self-righteous, but I see them as inspiring. To live a life that is full and on your terms is an inspirational life and one to be proud of.

He sings "I've loved, I've laughed I've cried. I've had my fill, my share of losing." We've all had those moments and I myself have had many losses. As the lyric suggests, I don't shy away from them because they have made me who I am.

In the second verse, Frank sings, "Regrets, I've had a few, but then again, too few to mention". I too have had very few regrets in life. Sure, there are things that I might not do again, but I don't regret them.

At the end of the day, everything that I have been through has been a part of making me who I am; and for that, I am grateful.

By far, my favourite verse in the song is the last one. "For what is a man, what has he got. If not himself, then he has not, to say the things, he truly feels, and not the words, of one who kneels". If you can't be yourself, then what is the point of living? As they say, "It's better to die on your feet than live on your knees".

You will only be truly happy when you are being truly authentic to yourself. Live the life you always dreamed of living and the world will feel like a much better place to you than if you're living someone else's dreams.

THE "M-WORD"

"The only constant in life is change" – Heraclitus

Isn't it amazing how quickly things can change in life? No one knows this better than I do. Thankfully, two things early in my life had prepared me for dealing with this fact of life; working at sea and the changing of a hotel brand.

Any sailor will tell you that the sea deserves the utmost respect. You can be sailing along in the most pristine conditions, then suddenly all hell breaks loose and you wonder if you will make it back to shore alive. I learnt this on many occasions, both growing up on boats as well as throughout the one million miles that I sailed while working on cruise ships.

At a moment's notice, you had to be ready for things to change.

Even before I went to sea, I was fortunate to have been taught the importance of embracing change. It was in my early twenties when I was working at a five-star hotel when the hotel was rebranded as part of the world's largest hotel chain taking it over. On the day that the hotel changed names, our new executive team addressed the nervous staff in the grand ballroom. None of us knew if our jobs were safe, or what the future held for us and the hotel.

When the new General Manager stood on stage, his first sentence not only equipped me for a successful transition into the new culture that was expected of me, but it has sat prominently in my mind for more than three decades since and allowed me to navigate many changes in my life. These changes might have destroyed some people; but not me. Thanks to him, I look forward to change and in fact, thrive when it arrives.

Our GM's message was simple. He said "I need each and every one of you to get used to change. Nothing is going to remain the same, but everything is going to work out."

Over the next six months, he was dead right. Everything we did at the hotel changed, but it taught me that change is more often than not a good thing that leads to great opportunities.

When I first sat down and started mapping out the contents of this book, I wrote down the chapter ideas. All of the chapters in the book as of now were the ones I had on day one of this project. As I wrote the book though, all of the chapters came together with relative ease; except this one.

Just to clarify, chapter 5 of the book was supposed to be "The M-Word". I had planned to devote an entire chapter to how I was charged with murder, held in custody for ten days, and then subjected to extreme bail conditions.

As the book took shape, it changed direction, and by the time I had finished all but this chapter, the original title of this chapter didn't seem relevant. You see, in the beginning, I had the idea that I wanted to talk about how badly I was treated by the detective who thought it was a smart idea to charge me with murder. I wanted to correct some things and put some truth into what was reported in the media.

Things changed when I read Schapelle Corby's book. I thoroughly enjoyed her book, however, I felt that a large portion of it was spent defending herself and correcting media reports. I totally get it and I too did that in "The Blame Game" so I am hardly going to judge her for it.

I will say though that in my opinion, Schapelle didn't need to do this. In her eyes, she was innocent. Therefore, the only person she needed to justify herself to, is Schapelle Corby. My point here is simple. If you believe in yourself, then you don't need to justify your stance to anyone.

Schapelle's book was a very interesting read and I am thankful for having taken the time to read it. The book made me realise how I too had spent much of my previous book on this topic defending myself and trying to correct wrong information.

I am now very comfortable with myself and no longer feel the need to explain myself, or my actions, defend myself, or spend time correcting facts or people. When it came time to go back and write this last chapter (chronologically) I decided to keep the original chapter title but use it as a sub-title, rather than an entire chapter while using it to illustrate the importance of embracing change.

We get set in our ways and for the most part, hate to change, but from my experience, this is where some of my greatest moments have occurred. My mindset has changed since the original concept of this book and subsequently, I have pivoted and adjusted course accordingly.

Good leaders make decisions and remain rock-solid in their pursuit of them, but great leaders and visionaries are those who can identify when a change is required. They can see that the original course may need a change of tact and they act accordingly. To stay steadfast to a cause when you know there is a better alternative is crazy.

This book is about helping other people; not clearing my name. My name is already clear in my mind so why would I waste any more time trying to change anyone else's mind? Before getting back to the real purpose of this book, I will make a few obvious points because they need to be said.

WE ARE ALL HUMAN AND WE ALL MAKE MISTAKES

Charging me with murder based on the mindset that the ignorant detectives used is akin to launching a cruise ship with no rudder, no propeller, and half a hull. At best you might go around in circles or aimlessly drift along. At worst, it will become a disaster of Titanic proportions.

This was a classic example of how even people that we believe are trained to think logically and rationally can let their ego and emotions get in the way in order to further their career; with no regard to how it affects other lives.

It was not just me, my life, my livelihood, and financial loss that was at stake. Imagine Breeana's family. They've lost a loved one. They had no answers and only a lot of speculation for eight years. Then they got their hopes up when I was charged with murder, only to find out that the police had no evidence.

CHAPTER 4

They only had a bunch of other people's opinions about me as a person and what they thought may have happened, but very little actual evidence to base the entire case on. Like I've said before. I may be many things and people are entitled to their opinion of me, but none of that makes me or anyone else a murderer.

That to me is incredibly irresponsible behaviour by the lead detective and he should be dealt with by the full force of the law for his inadequacies. You may notice that I did not name and shame him. I originally had his name in this chapter, but no matter how badly he screwed up, I decided not to let my emotions dictate my rash behaviour, as he did.

He screwed up, but we need to stop this culture of naming and shaming people for their mistakes. With the lead of the media, we have become obsessed with defaming and ridiculing people and it's just fucking wrong.

I don't hate the guy or his team. Even though he was highly irresponsible and even cocky and egotistical during and leading up to my arrest, he's only human. We've all let our ego take over and want to fast-track our career, fame, or fortunes at some point in our lives and he was no different.

We buy lotto tickets to get rich quickly, step on a co-worker to get promoted, or in this case, fabricate facts to justify a very foolish decision in order to make himself look more capable than perhaps he was.

I'm not the first person to have faced a corrupt police force. Both Lindy and Schapelle were up against police and prosecutors who manipulated evidence while ignoring crucial evidence that would have easily acquitted them. This is not the case with all Police Officers.

I had four cousins who were Police Officers and two of them worked in forensics at one time, so I know that there are many amazing Police Officers who are doing a fantastic job. My daughter's aunt is also a police officer and I even dated a police officer many years ago so I know that the "bad eggs" mentioned a moment ago are the exception to the rule.

Unfortunately, in this case, the lead detective was too cocky for his own good. The same emotions that clouded his judgement, also made his flimsy case unwinnable for the Police. This poor judgement cost taxpayers close to millions of dollars by the time the whole saga was over.

These are not my legal fees I am talking about. Tax-payers did not have to pay a cent for my legal defence. I am talking about the money that detectives and prosecution wasted on an unwinnable case. That money could have been spent on suicide prevention.

As I mentioned in the previous story, it is foolish to pursue a losing position. You must realise that you made the wrong choice originally, and then pivot. You might be able to bluff your way out of a really bad hand in poker, but you can't bluff your way out of prosecuting someone with no relevant evidence.

I've made mistakes at work and in life so I'd hate to see the detective punished too badly, however, I do hope that he learns from this gross error of judgement so that he doesn't put other people through what I and Breeana's family have been through.

Justice should always be served, but people with the power to incarcerate and charge people, which in turn affects lives, should be held to account. I am innocent and this has been proven, but the toll on myself, my family, and other families is of no concern to this detective.

He goes home at night with no concern at all for the bad decisions that he made. He still has a job, perhaps a promotion for somehow wrongly charging someone with murder and he has hardly any recourse over the grossly wrong judgements that he made.

If a famous sportsperson did something even slightly distasteful, the media and public are up in arms, calling for their sacking. When I worked in the travel industry, if I fucked up and sent a client to the wrong airport or booked the wrong date; I had to pay for it. If the rest of the world is supposed to be held accountable, then why aren't the police, who have the greatest power?

I know it is a bugbear of many in the legal fraternity that their clients get charged and acquitted, yet their clients have no means of reimbursement or compensation. Perhaps if the police were held to account financially more often, then the courts wouldn't be so clogged with bullshit charges that never should have been brought before the court in the first place.

For those of you not lucky enough to have experienced a night in the watchhouse or a stint in jail, men and women are segregated in the watchhouse and housed in completely separate jails once sent to prison. This is where the old "Soap on a rope" or "Bubba" jokes come from because I'd guess that spending an extended period of time in prison would make anyone look worthy of doing lol.

Thankfully I have not been that desperate by having spent ten days in the watch house on two occasions, I can tell you that even the ugliest or oldest of female guards starts looking pretty hot. Peter, (Not Peter

Foster) with whom I was in the cell with for ten days had his girlfriend in a nearby cell as she was also being held on the same charges as him.

On a few occasions, we would see a guard walking his girlfriend down the corridor. This would be a welcome change of sight from burly-looking blokes covered in tattoos.

Any sight of a female was welcomed by day five of my stint, so when the cell door opened and my name was called to see my lawyer, I instinctively paused to take a second look at the female guard.

As much as the guard was female and therefore attractive, my reason for pausing was because her face was worryingly familiar. Her uniform which comprised of a police-issue polo top and pants were practical and therefore quite masculine and she was a little more solid/muscular than I remembered the body attached to the face to be, but the smile was unforgettable.

After a moment it hit me. It was my very first kiss; Angela Graham. (I told you to remember that name). She too was processing who I was as my surname had changed from what she knew from school, so while she knew my face, the name didn't match. "Hey Ange", I said, as the realisation of who I was dawned on her. With a wry smile, Angela ushered me out of the cell and around to the visiting room nearby.

"Funny who you run into in strange places hey?" I said as we made our way along the hallway. "You'd be surprised in this job," she replied. I wasn't sure if I should use my usually cheeky personality to crack a joke, but either way, I doubted that I would be getting another kiss like the one more than thirty years earlier.

I am neither proud nor ashamed of having spent time in prison. The circumstances of me spending time there have nothing to do with my actions. They were beyond my control, so to attach any type of feelings towards that time spent in prison is inconsequential.

I am however extremely proud that having spent time in prison has not defined me, nor has it ruined me, as is the case with many people who have been thrust into that situation.

As Joseph said to his brothers in The Bible in Genesis, Chapter 50, Verse 20, "You meant evil against me, but God meant it for good." I knew that when this downright evil situation was thrust upon me on the day that I was charged over Breeana's death, it was somehow meant for good.

The media, Breeana's hate-filled family, and the ego-driven police officers responsible all wished evil upon me. What they didn't know was that God had a plan all along to turn this terrible situation for both Breeana and myself into something good.

This book is testament to that

Not only was the charge of murder wrong but knowing that they had no case, the police desperately threw in nine stalking charges dating back two decades to try to strengthen their case. These additional charges only came about when they realised that I had a good chance of getting bail after my arrest.

After slapping me with the additional charges, the lead detective took me back to my cell and said (with a cocky smile on his face) "How do you think your bail application will go now?" I simply looked at him with a deadpan expression and said, "Why don't you ask the judge tomorrow?"

Sadly, I didn't get the chance to properly answer his question because I was released on bail and I have not spoken to him since. Given that it is now five years later, I thought I had better do the right thing and give him my response. So here it is; "Pretty good don't you think?"

> "Money can't buy freedom, but it does cost money if you want it"
> - JD Moorea

One of the conditions of me being released on bail was that I was fitted with a GPS tracking device. While these devices are uncomfortable and at times, downright annoying, they certainly beat the other option; being locked up. After wearing the device for fifteen months, my case was still more than three years away from being put to bed, so I decided to bite the bullet and apply to have that part of my bail condition removed.

This would allow me to wear shorts without people looking at me like I was some kind of paedophile and it would mean I didn't have to charge the fucking thing every single night so that the monitoring company didn't call to say it wasn't responding. If this happened, then more often than not the police would also come over to check to see if I was home after dark.

From my point of view, the bail variation wasn't too difficult, other than me having to pony up a considerable amount of money for my barrister to appear on my behalf. Me trying to do this in front of a judge on my own would have inevitably ended up with an unsuccessful result.

CHAPTER 4

My barrister was one of the best around, so while it was an expensive process, in the end, the application breezed through with the prosecution and judge not objecting to it at all.

Even though I still had other restrictions on me until the case was over, in essence, I was free to live a more normal life. As I said, money can't buy you freedom, but it sure does cost you money to be free.

The day we successfully had my conditions altered; my lawyer arranged for me to attend the watchhouse to have the GPS device removed. Knowing that the media would be waiting, we arranged for it to be after dark.

Unfortunately, one of the watchhouse guards leaked the time and information to the local crappy newspaper so they could have a photographer waiting to get a photo for the following morning's front cover.

As I got ready, I decided to wear one of my own "C.R.U.I.S.E" branded hoodies, a "C.R.U.I.S.E" cap, and sunnies so if the photographer got a photo, at least I would get some free publicity. I really didn't want them taking photos of me, but at least this way, I benefited from it.

I parked around the back of the watchhouse and walked to the security gate to get buzzed in. I had my head down and sunnies on with the hoodie pulled over my head, fully expecting the photographer that I had seen waiting up the street to come running down with his camera shoved in my face.

As the gate automatically opened, I walked up the long pathway to the entrance of the watchhouse and as I turned around for a quick glimpse, I noticed that there was no photographer at the gate. Somehow, he must not have seen me walk in from the other side. I went in and had the device removed and left half an hour later.

Once again, I prepared myself to be ambushed by the photographer, either as I walked down the fenced pathway, or while I waited for the officer to remotely open the security gate at the bottom of the pathway. Somehow, I managed to get all the way down the pathway, ring the buzzer, wait, and then walk out and down the street without the dopey photographer even seeing me.

It's not like I tried to hide. He was only twenty metres up the street and the gate was in full view from where he was. I walked to my car and thought I'd have a bit of fun. I drove around the block, and past the spot where the photographer was waiting. As I drove past, he was talking on his phone; probably to his boss saying that I was nowhere to be seen. As I drove past, I wound down the passenger side window, tooted my horn, and yelled out, "Hey buddy. You looking for me?"

WHAT OTHER PEOPLE THINK OF YOU IS NONE OF YOUR BUSINESS

The photographer turned his head, lowered his phone from his ear, and watched dumbfounded as I drove off in the distance. While it was nowhere as epic as Schapelle Corby's deception of the media, to me it was still a hilarious win. Once again, this illustrates that we are humans. The media would love for us to believe that they are somehow above the rest of us, but as my next story shows; they aren't.

THE "RISE AND FALL" OF ME?

If you haven't worked out by now, I don't take myself too seriously and I certainly don't take the media seriously; and neither should you. I've always been highly entertained by some of the crap the GC Bullshittin writes, but what Lea Emery published the day after my committal hearing finished was particularly humorous.

The funny thing about what Lea, the man-hating feminist (her own description on her LinkedIn page) wrote in the piece, was that not only did it expose her jealousy and insecurities, but it showcased her ignorance and pinpointed why many people don't achieve financial freedom in their lives. Okay so I added the "Man-hating" bit, but she does call herself a feminist, and aren't they one and the same?

In her story, Lea attempted to paint a picture that I had somehow gone from living the high life to apparently living a lesser life now. If she did more than just troll my street pestering my neighbours for some comments, she may have worked out that my life now is far better (superficially) than it was back in 2013. My life is far better in every area now, but for the purposes of this story, to stay on par with what she wrote, I'm only talking about financially.

My life's focus is not on possessions and the measure of someone's success is not their possessions or level of wealth. That said, my possessions and level of wealth are far superior now than they were in 2013.

Back then, I lived in a small two-bedroom apartment with pretty average furniture and no savings or investments. Now, I am in a much larger house, furnished with beautiful new furniture and all the toys I could ever want.

A huge TV/home theatre, piano, beautiful artwork and photography on the walls, massage chair, leather lounge, home gym, jetski, and other toys are nice, and I love having them, but they are not how I measure my success.

Of more importance to me is that I have now built an investment portfolio and am securing my financial future at the same time as the before-mentioned possessions. The fact the journalist wanted to suggest that I was somehow worse off these days was laughable though.

What was even more worrying was that her opinion that I once worked four jobs (it was only ever two jobs) was a bad thing. That is disturbing because it is a sentiment that is shared by most people. Unfortunately, it is the same people who are struggling financially.

The only reason I make this point is to change people's mindsets concerning money. If you work more than one job, have a side hustle, or do whatever it takes to build a secure future for yourself and your family; I applaud you.

To me, it's not important if you have one high-paying job or three that pay an equal amount. What matters is that you're not a lazy fuck who complains about having no money, yet sits on their ass doing nothing about it; like the entire family of dole-bludgers who I used to live next to for a decade.

If, like this particular journalist, you think that a person who does whatever it takes to be financially independent is a bad thing; then I feel sorry for you. I have no clue what this woman's financial situation is, but based on her attitude towards money and other people's financial outlook, I'd guess that she does not travel much (for lack of money), and when she does, it definitely isn't business class.

I'd guess that she most likely doesn't have at least six months' worth of cash savings. She doesn't contribute at least 20% each week to either her superannuation or savings, and she doesn't have a solid investment portfolio to take care of her in retirement.

I no longer have to work two jobs to be able to do all those things listed above. When I did work two jobs, it was mostly because I was spending over ten thousand dollars each year on trips to the Maldives, the Caribbean, or various cruises, plus an additional 10k-20k on investments.

I'll also bet that I was, and still am earning three times what she does, so maybe she should grab an extra job, or based on her research skills; a new career.

Lea. If you would like some free advice on how to improve your financial situation, I'll gladly send you a free copy of my book "The No B.S Approach to Create the Life You Want" which has an entire chapter dedicated to finances and how to build wealth. Oh. And it also has a chapter on happiness.

The fact that the media have become so obsessed with me, is adorable, if not sad. Since coming to terms with the media attention,

WHAT OTHER PEOPLE THINK OF YOU IS NONE OF YOUR BUSINESS

I have found many ways to have fun with them; even if they are not aware of it.

For example, when Lea started doorknocking my street and asking my neighbours for comments about me, my neighbours asked me what I wanted them to say. I said that I didn't really care, what they said, but I'd love it if they had fun with the media who came around.

On one occasion, when a neighbour was asked about me, they said that I kept to myself, apart from each night, just before eight o'clock, when my curfew began. They said that each night, I did a nudie run around the street to celebrate my curfew starting, then right at 8 pm, I climbed the tree in my front yard and started "yanking it like a monkey in a mango tree".

I'm sure you can work out what they were referring to when they said "Yanking it". Of course, this wasn't the case, but it was nice to see my neighbours joining in the fun with the media. I am surprised that those things weren't printed somewhere, because God knows the media have printed far worse.

In January 2021 during my committal hearing, I decided to stay focused and tune out the outside noise. This included stupid questions by the media on my way in and out of court each day, as well as any misdirected anger by Bree's Aunt, or her misinformed followers.

I knew that my every reaction was being watched and that the media would do their best to elicit some sort of reaction. I was determined to stay focused on the job at hand. This meant that emotions of any kind were off the table.

If I smiled, I would have been reported as showing little respect for Breeana. If I acted angrily, it would have been reported that I was showing signs of cracking under pressure.

Each day, as I entered and exited the court, I listened to music to help me focus. This quickly caught the attention of the journalists, who pestered my Lawyer Chris as to what I was listening to.

Like my neighbours, Chris likes to play with the media, so he told them that I was listening to one of my audiobooks and a podcast about my next cruise. The truth of the matter was that I was listening to inspiring and uplifting songs to make sure I was primed for whatever the day held for me.

This plan of action worked, but it also had an unexpected benefit. After the first day of me wearing EarPods, the media realised that it was futile for them to ask me questions because I simply couldn't hear a word they were saying.

CHAPTER 4

For the entire two weeks, not one of the reporters outside court approached me. I did laugh when my lawyer Chris told me on the first morning that my favourite parasite from ACA (Chris Allen) asked me "Are you worried about what might happen today?" To which my lawyer instantly shot back, "No. We're more worried about the shit you will publish tonight."

For those wondering, over the ten days, I listened to the following songs: Eye of the Tiger (Survivor). Gonna fly now (Theme from Rocky). Hold on (Wilson Phillips). Kyrie (Mister Mister). Drive (Incubus). Don't stop believing (Glee). I'm still standing (Elton John), and This is the moment (Anthony Warlow).

A REAL SIGN FROM ABOVE

"Sometimes our cup of life needs to be completely emptied so that it can be filled with something better. It's when the ego says that life is over that God can say okay, let's begin" – Marianne Williamson

About four days into my stint in the watchhouse while awaiting my Supreme Court bail hearing for the murder charge, I was sat on my three large cushions early in the evening and wondering how this situation had happened. I would have to say that this was the lowest point of this entire experience and also my life.

The three of us in the bulk holding cell had finished our dinner and were pretty much waiting for the lights to go out for the evening. I sat cross-legged against the steel wall and closed my eyes. I was thinking about the situation, my dogs, how I was going to get out of this mess, and if I was strong enough to deal with everything that was coming in the future.

As was the case during my stint at a Christian school many years earlier, I had always been reluctant to talk about God and couldn't recall ever praying up to that point. The only time I had held a Bible was when a fellow prisoner four years prior had asked me to carry the Bible into my cell so he could use the pages to make homemade cigarettes the following day.

I had always thought that perhaps there was a God, but I wasn't certain. Despite this, I began asking for guidance. I don't recall my exact thoughts, but I asked for assistance in getting through my current predicament and I prayed for God to help me to overcome the horrible set of circumstances that I had been thrust into.

At the end of my disjointed mumbling of thoughts in the form of a prayer, I said in my mind "I need your help. If you are truly real God, then give me a sign." Unsure if my prayers were good enough, or able to be heard in a dark, dingy cell, I opened my eyes and cast my mind to a different topic.

Time in the watchhouse is difficult to judge, but it was no more than five minutes later when the small flap in the steel cell door opened. This opening was around 50cm wide and no more than 15cm high. It's only big enough to push a small food container through and only ever opens at meal times, so when it opened after dinner, it caught my attention.

As I peered at the opening, I could see an elderly man peering through the gap in the door. He asked how we were doing and if there was anything he could talk to us about. The man was gentle in nature and definitely not a prison guard.

The man introduced himself as Allan and told us that he was from the local church. "What the fucking fuck" was all I thought. I laughed to myself and then thought, "Well played God; you smart ass."

I spent the next hour talking to Allan. He talked to us about his troubled early years and how he turned his life around with the help of God. He also said a very meaningful prayer for me upon learning of my predicament.

The situation reminded me of the poem "Footprints in the Sand". That poem was my Mum's favourite. In particular, I was reminded of the final line of the scripture where the man questioned God's love, before God told the man that it was during his darkest times, that God carried him. That night, I was also reminded of the classic saying "The teacher will appear when the student is ready."

Until that moment, I wasn't ready for the teacher to appear, but as you can imagine, my eyes are now open to a whole different mindset. Upon being released on bail a few days later, I obtained a copy of the Bible. I also borrowed the entire King James Version of the audio Bible from the library and listened to all sixty-three discs of the Old and New Testaments. That seemingly coincidental meeting was no coincidence and neither was the fact that it was me who had been thrust into this situation.

I have been given a certain set of skills, along with a particular message to share; whether it is with one person or one hundred million people. I am still somewhat reluctant to label myself as religious because I feel that we too often rely on labels to identify with to feel significant.

I've always seen myself as a bit of a rebel, or a maverick. I've never been one to conform and my religious beliefs follow suit. I now

CHAPTER 4

have very strong beliefs, but that doesn't mean I will be knocking on everyone's doors and sharing the good news.

Just like any relationship, your relationship with your God, or 'higher source' is between you and him/her/them. Unless you're an attention seeker or sadist, you don't tell the whole world every intimate detail about your marriage or relationship and the same goes for your faith.

If you want to preach it to everyone then so be it, but that doesn't make you a better Christian, Catholic, Muslim, or whatever category you put yourself in.

In my opinion, the biggest problem with religion is that many who follow a religion feel that they must act in a certain way and give themselves whatever title their religion dictates. People feel that to fit in, they have to have a title.

They feel that if they are going to be true to their faith, they must go to church, preach the gospel, and make their faith public for all the world to see. This, in my opinion, is why so many people are reluctant to talk about their religious beliefs.

My Godfather is a very religious man. He and his wife did all the things that typify someone with religious faith. They even took it further by founding an incredible Christian radio station to support like-minded people in the community. Radio 4CRB is still going strong over forty years later.

My mother on the other hand rarely went to church. I can't ever remember her talking about God and other than being told that she was Catholic, I would never have thought that she was one. That said, she was just as religious as my Godparents.

Mum had her faith and she shared it with the world by being a good person, a loyal friend, a loving mother, a devoted wife, and a supportive member of the community. That to me is what is important to God.

I am not saying that people who go to church aren't close to God, or religious, but we have all met those who attend church once a week, yet for the other six days live life more like they are rooting for the opposite team.

In my opinion, your relationship with your creator is personal. You don't need to shout it from the rooftops for it to be special. I also believe that you don't have to call yourself "God-Fearing" as many do, for it to be right.

To me, it doesn't make sense that any father would want their child to be fearful of them. I would rather be "God-Loving", rather than fearing, because a relationship based on fear is not a healthy one. That said, your faith is your faith and it is up to you to develop it the way you want to and not how I or anyone else suggests.

CHAPTER FIVE

THE REAL LAW OF ATTRACTION AND HOW TO USE IT

"Life begins at the end of your comfort zone" – Neale Donald Walsch

Before we delve deeper into this chapter, I want to start by setting it up with two words; What + if. These two words may not seem special, but if you use them in the right way, they can change your life.

I told a story in "The No B.S Approach to Create the Life You Want" where Tony Robbins used these words to flip our thinking around in his "Date with Destiny 2016" promotional video on YouTube. Search "Date with Destiny 2016 promo" on YouTube to see the video I am referring to.

Whenever I watch this video, I get goosebumps and well up with tears of excitement. Please. Do yourself a favour. Watch this video. Not just once. But as many times as it takes until you too find yourself getting goosebumps and tearing up. Once this happens you will know that the truest meaning of Tony's words has sunk in.

STOP READING AND TAKE TWO MINUTES TO CHANGE YOUR LIFE BY ABSORBING THAT SHORT VIDEO

The video is a very powerful two-minute video and recently it got me thinking if I could create something similar to flip the narrative on how people see their lives and their circumstances. The biggest hurdle for people in taking charge of their life, is them thinking that they have little control over what happens, or what they attract.

So here's what I jotted down in the hope that before we dive into some controversial topics, you might be able to see the power of those two words. If you can, then I promise you that your life will never be the same again.

Open your mind and ask yourself:

What if <u>we</u> had the power to create the life we wanted?
What if <u>we</u> were responsible for how others treated us?
What if <u>we</u> were the only reason we succeeded or failed?
What if <u>we</u> somehow attracted everything that has happened in our life?
What if <u>we</u> stopped using excuses and stopped blaming others?
What if <u>nothing was our fault</u>, but <u>everything was our responsibility</u>?

And most importantly….

What if all of this was actually true?

Would you do things differently?
Would you be more careful with what you attract?
Would you choose more wisely when making decisions in all areas of your life?

If we can grasp the concept that in some way <u>we are responsible</u> for everything that happens to us, then <u>we have the power</u> to attract <u>anything we want</u> into our lives.

No matter what happens, no one is to blame for your failures and no one deserves the credit for your successes; Except you.

The most important "What ifs" in life

"Instead of comparing yourself to someone else today, compare yourself today with who you were yesterday" - J.D Moorea

A little while after writing the above paragraphs, I was driving along and the following question came to mind. I touched on this earlier, but I really want to explore this because it may just be the solution to a problem that we've all been searching for as the suicide rate climbs around the world.

Almost every day since Breeana took her life, I have asked myself, "What makes someone want to commit suicide? I know that every person affected by suicide has asked this same question; as have lawmakers, psychologists, and medical professionals around the world. It's something that we can all take a stab at, but really, at best; it's a guess.

I have come to believe that a person decides to take their own life when they feel that there is no other alternative. My great mentor, Dr. John Demartini suggests that this feeling of hopelessness comes when a person's fantasy of what their life should look like, doesn't match the reality of what their life is.

Think about that for a second.

"A feeling of hopelessness comes when a person's fantasy of what their life should look like, doesn't match the reality of what their life is."

Dr. Demartini believes that this is what leads to depression and suicide. If what Dr. Demartini is saying is true, then those two words that Tony Robbins so eloquently used and that I mentioned a moment ago (What if) are applied to this situation, then we may have something very powerful in combatting suicide.

There are so many reasons why someone might feel like they want to commit suicide. Examples are listed below:

- My partner doesn't love me.
- My mother abandoned me. (My favourite 'go to' excuse)
- I can't make enough money to live.
- I am ugly / I am fat / I am stupid.

To most of us, these reasons might seem silly, but to anyone bogged down in depression, these thoughts about their situation seem insurmountable. There are dozens of reasons like these that make people feel like life sux and is not worth living. The key here is for the individual (or the person assisting the individual) to see that no matter what, there is always an alternative.

If you drive your car into a dead-end street, you don't stop and say "Well that's my life over". You turn the car around and backtrack until you see a better option. Life is the same. Sometimes you have to backtrack, but no matter what, you are never stuck with no alternative.

WHAT OTHER PEOPLE THINK OF YOU IS NONE OF YOUR BUSINESS

If you drink too much, you can decide not to do that again, or keep making the same mistake. If you make a bad investment, you can throw good money after bad, or cut your losses. There is almost always an alternative to every situation in life. We just need to find it.

As I have said before, the difference between success or failure, good or bad; is perception. The way we perceive things dictates how we feel, and in many cases how we act in relation to that. The best way to turn things around is to flip things on their head. The way we do this is with those two magic words; what if.

Let's take the above examples and let's say these are issues that we are dealing with ourselves. If we use the "what if" principles and all we do is ask the opposite of what we currently believe, then things look and feel a lot different.

My partner doesn't love me!
- What if my partner does love me, but struggles to communicate their feelings?
- What if my partner has their own insecurities and fears like I do?
- What if this person shows love in a different way from how I do?
- What if the universe has someone better planned for me and they are on their way?
- What if instead of relying on someone else's love, I learn to love myself?

My mother abandoned me!
- What if she was scared of what life might look like if she didn't give me up?
- What if she kept me and our lives were miserable and filled with poverty and pain?
- What if she believed that she was doing the right thing?
- What if she made the most incredible sacrifice so that I could have a better life?

I can't make enough money to live!
- What if I could make enough money?
- What if I could find a way to spend less?
- What if I worked harder and saved more?

CHAPTER 5

- What if I already have all the abundance I need?
- What if all the money I ever wanted could flow to me?

I am ugly / I am fat / I am stupid!
- What if I just can't see how truly beautiful, I really am?
- What if I can lose weight, but I just haven't worked out the best way yet?
- What if I learn differently from most people and I just need to do it my way?

None of these are direct answers to your problems, however, they will open up your mind to new possibilities that will trigger your mind to get to work to find the solutions. The thing about these "what if" questions is that they can provide clarity, but most importantly they can break the pattern we get stuck in. When you change the way you look at a thing, the thing you look at changes.

More importantly, the words what and if are incredibly powerful words. The reason they are so powerful is because they give hope. The hope of something better. The hope of a way out. The hope of our dreams coming true. The hope of a life beyond pain and struggle.

Hope is what people suffering from depression or suicidal thoughts are missing. Give yourself or someone you know who is suffering the gift of hope by sharing those two simple, yet powerful words and see what a difference it makes in their life or yours.

THE REAL SECRET

"You get what you tolerate in life" - Tony Robbins

One of the greatest lessons that I have ever learnt came when I discovered how the law of attraction really worked. Most people have seen "The Secret" and have some idea of it. While Rhonda Byrne did a fantastic job of bringing this information to the attention of the masses, most of what the law of attraction is really about was left out.

The problem Rhonda faced was that if she wanted to accurately share the law of attraction, which is based on the teachings of Abraham/Hicks, the movie would have gone for two days and not two hours.

WHAT OTHER PEOPLE THINK OF YOU IS NONE OF YOUR BUSINESS

When I talk to people about The Secret the most common response I get is that they tried it and think it's a load of crap. If they only did what was suggested in the movie or the book, then of course they would think that, because there was so much crucial information missing.

When I talk about the difference between The Secret and the real law of attraction, I explain that The Secret is like the trailer of a movie. It tells you what the film is about, but it doesn't give the entire story away.

To fully understand how the law of attraction works, you must go a lot deeper than Rhonda Byrnes went. I was fortunate to stumble upon the proper teachings of Abraham/Hicks in 2007 and got a hold of the entire catalogue of audio by probably the world's foremost experts on the topic; Esther and Jerry Hicks.

Apart from learning about how to use the teachings, the most important thing that I learnt was that we are responsible in some way, for everything that is in our lives. At that point in my life, this sounded way too far-fetched, just like I am sure that as you read this, you will think the same thing. Despite my disbelief that this could be true, I decided to have an open mind and suspend my judgement until I knew more.

As I began thinking about this seemingly absurd philosophy, I started thinking about things that had happened in my life and if it could be at all true that I may have been responsible for them in some way.

At the time, my Swedish girlfriend who was living in my apartment in Surfers had just told me she was going home to Sweden and that same day (The day before I had learnt this new information about the law of attraction), I had a major flood in my cruise ship cabin and lost thousands of dollars of sheet music.

As I sat looking out over the Norwegian fjords, I realised that I had in fact been partly responsible for manifesting these things. I had spent so much mental energy agonising over a minor leak in the overhead pipes outside my cabin and had also been getting friendly with a female dancer on board, so yeah, it made sense that I had been in some way responsible for these events. Coincidence? Maybe. But stick with me.

I began looking at other things (both good and bad) that had happened in my life and sure enough, if I was honest enough, I was somehow responsible for those too. The key word in that last sentence is honest.

Unless you're willing to be brutally honest with yourself and confront your darkest thoughts, you will never be able to grasp this concept. You will continue to make excuses and blame people and circumstances.

Let's be clear here. There is a difference between something being your responsibility and it being your fault. I am not suggesting that bad things that happen in your life are your fault. I am however saying that you are responsible in some way for them being in your life.

This is going to take a little time to explain properly so stick with me and please continue to suspend your judgement for the time being.

As discussed earlier, a woman is entitled to wear provocative clothing and walk down a dark alley at night, but that doesn't mean that nothing bad is going to happen to her. It is not her fault if someone attacks her, or rapes her, but that doesn't negate her responsibility in this situation.

She can't control what another person might do, but she can take steps to avoid the situation. That is the difference between something being your fault and it being your responsibility.

In almost anything in life, the same applies. We can't control how people act, how the weather is, or how the stock market performs. What we can do is take responsibility for how we act, what we do, and how we place ourselves in these situations. This will dictate our experience in any given situation.

In the teachings of Abraham/Hicks, Esther and Jerry Hicks talk about 'Co-creating.' This is where we create with other people. For example; if you're driving along and have a car accident, you have co-created this with the other driver. It doesn't matter who is at fault, the accident would not have happened if both parties were not there at that exact moment.

When you bump into someone who becomes your soul mate, this is co-creating. The event that led to your meeting would not have occurred if you were not both present.

You're probably thinking, "Well that's chance, not co-creating." That's fine if you believe that everything in life is by chance. I, along with many people believe that we manifest the circumstances in our lives by the most prominent thoughts that we hold.

Have you ever been so worried about falling over, that it actually happened? Or, have you focused so much on someone leaving you, that they did? These are examples of the law of attraction and co-creating.

If I asked you why you got a promotion at work or have a killer body, you would no doubt say that you are responsible for them. On the other hand, if I asked you why you're in a crappy relationship, I have no doubt that you would say that it's because the other person is a relationship retard. Trust me, that was my excuse once upon a time too.

We love to take credit for the good things in our lives, but quickly blame others or circumstances for the bad. The truth is that we are responsible for all of it. As I said a moment ago, it doesn't mean it is our fault, or that we deserve it.

It simply means that we have somehow manifested it in our lives, either by our most predominant thoughts and actions or by combining them with someone else and therefore co-creating.

I know that this is not the easiest concept to grasp, but I promise that if you can accept it, your life will be completely different. Once you understand that you are responsible for everything in your life, then it is you who has the power to create only the things that you want.

That's not to say that you won't screw up and create some shit, but if you understand that you are responsible for it then you can look at how you created it and not do the same thing in the future.

By blaming someone else for your situation, you are taking away your power. If you blame someone else, you may be able to remove yourself from the situation or behaviour, but you won't be able to remove the situation or behaviour from yourself.

It will keep appearing until you take back the power and accept that you are in some way responsible for this behaviour showing up. You will then be empowered to make it disappear too.

THE REAL ISSUE WITH DOMESTIC VIOLENCE

"When you don't love yourself, that's when people can hurt you."

Now that you hopefully have a grasp on how you may have created things in your life, let's look at how this pertains to domestic violence. Those who don't yet grasp this concept may say, "How is a woman responsible for a man hitting her?" The answer to this and similar situations where there are what people call a "victim" is varied depending on the situation, but let me provide this school of thought.

Once again, we must differentiate between fault and responsibility. Before I make this point, I want to be clear. I am providing this information not to blame anyone, but rather to provide them with the tools to avoid such situations.

In this specific example of domestic violence, (Or violence of any kind, such as rape) there will always be extreme examples where no matter what a woman does, a man is going to be violent towards her. These ideas are not going to eliminate every single case, but they will go a long way to avoiding them in many cases.

In the case of violence in a relationship, at some point both people met, and liked each other and things were probably fine. This first meeting and deciding to form a relationship is co-creating. It didn't happen with just one person.

From the point of view of the "Victim", she (I am generalising that the female is the victim for this example) chose her partner. The woman had the opportunity to not engage in a relationship with him. Perhaps her radar was off so far as spotting the red flags that he had, or maybe he was good at hiding them. Either way, the relationship began.

Over time, the partner may have displayed qualities that the female didn't like, but she chose to ignore them for whatever reason. These qualities may have worsened in nature, or perhaps the female may have acted in ways that were also not good for creating a loving relationship.

Again. I am not suggesting that this is anyone's fault. The point is to illustrate how we could possibly have co-created the final outcome. Perhaps as the relationship grew, so did the jealousy and abuse. The female may have felt that she couldn't leave or maybe thought that her partner might change.

If the female ignored her partner's abuse, there is every chance that he may have continued to use this tactic and more than likely increased the frequency, or level of abuse used to get what he wanted.

Long story short, throughout a violent relationship, there are many choices that both parties have made. This begins at the very first encounter, right up until the relationship becomes what we would refer to as domestic violence.

While the final act of physical or emotional abuse is not excusable in any way, if we look back over the timeline, we see that the end result is a product of many choices and co-created scenarios.

I know that it is often hard to leave a partner; especially one where your life is in danger, or if children are involved. My point is that by understanding how we all create everything in our lives, we then have the power to stop these situations from happening before it gets to that point.

This chapter and in fact this entire book is about empowering people so that we can prevent violence of any kind, but most importantly in intimate relationships. Just like cancer, there is so much focus on treatment, but hardly any on prevention.

We will never stop domestic violence by making punishments harsher. We will only reduce it, or stop it by implementing preventative measures. This means going right back to how we educate children on real subjects like co-creating, self-esteem, and respect.

The so-called "fight" against domestic violence has it all wrong. Instead of talking about the real issue which is how we are all acting, we are simply saying that a man should not hit a woman. Of course, he shouldn't.

The problem is that in intimate relationships, emotions take over and both men and women act in ways that create anger in a relationship, instead of love. There is no excuse for violence of any kind in any relationship and no matter what a woman says or does to a man, he should never be violent, but let's be brutally honest; women are not helping in many cases.

Like I said earlier, there will always be cases where no matter what a woman does, a man will be violent. That stems from his own issues and may never change, no matter how wonderful his partner is.

However, instead of trying to "Band-Aid" the situation by saying don't hit a woman, we need to go much deeper and look at how we treat each other, in an attempt to avoid getting to the point where anyone would be that violent.

Instead of "fighting" domestic violence, let's "create" love. As per the law of attraction, we create what we focus on; whether we want it or not. When we focus on what we don't want, all that does is attract more of what we don't want.

It therefore makes sense that if we want to stop domestic violence then we need to focus on the opposite of what we don't want and that is love and peaceful relationships.

In my opinion, we need to come from a place of love and compassion, not anger and hatred. It's like when I did three days of intensive fire-fighting training in the U.K. before one of my cruise ship contracts. The first thing that we learnt was that a fire needs three elements to survive; heat, fuel, and oxygen. If we take one or more of these elements away, the fire goes out.

You don't see firefighters throwing more fuel, such as timber on a fire that they want to extinguish. You don't see them with big fans blowing oxygen onto the fire either. They remove fuel where possible, try to reduce the heat with water or smother the flames.

CHAPTER 5

Domestic violence is the same. As a society, we're fueling the fire by making men feel like it is all their fault and women play no part whatsoever in the lead-up.

The final act of violence that gets the most attention is the man's fault because we have the choice to react or not react to our partner's actions (If she did or said something), but as previously stated, there is usually a lot before this event that we need to change if we're serious about stamping out domestic violence.

As I said a moment ago, we are failing to stop domestic violence because we are treating it the same way the world treats cancer. Cancer will never be cured when all we do is detect and treat cancer once it is in a person's body.

There is no money in finding out why cancer is caused so therefore this disease will never be stopped until we go back and look at the causes and not just detection and treatment. Detection and treatment are helping, but that's not the problem. Finding out why people get cancer is where the focus should be.

The same thing is happening with domestic violence. We are focusing on detecting it and punishing offenders when we should also be looking further into why this happens and how we can help men and women in preventing relationships from getting to the point where they become violent.

The stigma of blaming men without finding out what causes this has to be putting pressure on men, which would in return surely have them in such a tense state that they may react, instead of having control. We need to take a step back from all the blaming and look at this from a place of love and compassion, rather than hatred and blame.

So far as the oxygen part of this analogy, the media are giving the situation far too much of the wrong type of oxygen. Yes, we need to be having the conversation, but the media want to constantly play the "man-bashing" and negative card in order to boost ratings.

This is just creating more anger among men and women and isn't helping at all. If the media were serious about their claims of being "for the best interests of the public" like many outlets proclaim, then they would change their approach.

Lastly. The best way to reduce violence in any situation is to give it love. Corny sounding, I know, but nonetheless true. Like the fire, remove the heat and it goes out. As Saint Francis of Assisi said, "Lord make me an instrument of your peace. Where there is hatred; let me sow love."

In other words, give love to hatred and hatred disappears. It is only in rare circumstances that you can have a fight with someone who is not fighting back.

The more often we give love in the face of anger, or simply walk away, the faster the violence will be extinguished. The natural instinct of men and women is to stand up for themselves and give as good as they get.

As I said earlier, we seem to think it is better to be right; than to be happy. I'm not suggesting that you should cop abuse or not stand up for your safety, but what is more important; to be right – or to be happy?

In a nutshell, when it comes to domestic violence and bullying, we are coming at it from the wrong angle. When you're in the ring with Mike Tyson, you don't stand toe to toe with him. Trying to fight violence with violence or standing up and fighting bullies will never work.

The best way to approach it is to worry less about the opponent and more about yourself. When you focus on violence, you attract violence. When you focus on love, you attract love. In a relationship, when you spend your time on what the other person is or isn't doing, you're not spending enough time worrying about what you are doing to improve the relationship.

When two people are focusing on the other's faults, or how little the other person is giving or contributing, then the relationship breaks down. When you worry more about how you can give to the relationship, it will thrive.

As Mother Teresa famously said when asked if she would march against war, she said, "If you have a march for peace, then count me in." Instead of being against Domestic Violence, why not be for loving and nurturing relationships?

MY GIFT TO YOU - THE ANSWER TO STOPPING DOMESTIC VIOLENCE

"We don't get rid of darkness by hitting it with a baseball bat. We only get rid of darkness by turning on the light"
– Marianne Williamson

If you've made it this far into the book, then clearly you're either a glutton for punishment or someone who stands out from the crowd and is more interested in the deep truth, as opposed to the surface "fluff" that most people focus on.

CHAPTER 5

Having spent many years wondering what went wrong in relationships and being on the wrong side of a violent relationship in Canada, it finally dawned on me recently where we're going wrong with stemming the incidents of domestic violence.

Many so-called experts, authorities, practitioners, and powers that be, have used all their "wisdom" and power to come up with what I believe is a big steaming pile of crap when it comes to how they think domestic violence can be stopped.

We also have the "Me too" movement that is disempowering women, by making them all out to be victims instead of empowering women to make better choices. We have media campaigns stating that "A man shouldn't hit a woman" and telling men to pull their mates into line if they act violently towards a woman, but all of these things are missing the mark by a long way.

The most astounding thing I have learnt from reading over fifteen hundred books in recent years is that the most complex of problems can always be solved by the simplest of solutions. When discussing how to achieve something complex, my former best mate would often say, "If it was that simple, everyone would be doing it."

Unfortunately, in many cases, that is true. Not because what he is saying is necessarily correct, but more so because the person applying the solution believes it to be too simple to be true and therefore, doesn't pay it a second thought. They move on with their lives and wonder why nothing has changed.

I read a quote in one book that was as follows. "All the water of all the oceans in the world cannot sink a ship; unless the water is let in." My interpretation of this is that the entire world can hate me all they like, but because I choose to not let their hate in, they can never affect me.

This is at the core of how I believe we can reduce domestic violence dramatically. Let me preface what I am about to say by stating that this concept applies to how others treat you, how you treat others, and most importantly, how you treat yourself.

The only reason someone would act violently towards another person is because they are scared, feel threatened, or vulnerable. The main reason why anyone would feel these feelings is from not loving themselves. When we don't love ourselves, we "let the water in" which sinks our ship (Our relation-ship).

My two kelpies will run around and be the friendliest mutts when they know they are safe, but if I have them held tightly on a lead around a bigger dog, my dogs will go ballistic. They are beautifully-natured dogs, but when they feel threatened, they lash out.

Humans are the same. We are all nice people for the most part, but when our ego takes over, we feel anxious or threatened, we will instinctively lash out verbally or physically to protect our ego.

When my dogs are at home, they feel safe, but outside my home, they are naturally anxious, and this can lead to aggression. My job is to make sure they always feel safe. I choose environments that encourage calmness for them.

Humans need to do the same thing. Embarking on relationships that make us feel anxious or unloved may cause us or our partner to lash out. Keep in mind though that this will only occur if we let ourselves feel this way. This often occurs when we have self-doubt. This may sound strange, but selecting the right partner is half the battle. The other half is nothing more than self-love.

Love each other and love yourself. It's that fucking simple. Take full reasonability for your actions and the situation, instead of blaming your partner. I'm not talking about the physical or psychological act of domestic violence. I am talking about what creates a situation where two people treat each other badly.

Society wants us to focus on the act of abuse when we should be focusing on what causes it. When you love yourself and have love in your heart, you will be less likely to attract someone with hatred or anger in their heart. That is the starting point. If you have low self-esteem, you are more likely to accept people into your life who might be more inclined to be violent.

I now know this to be the case when I attracted violence into my life in 2004. At the time of meeting my Canadian ex in Tahiti, I was insecure and not loving myself as I should have. With this being the case, when she showed me the type of love and attention that I was not giving myself, I fell for her, while subconsciously ignoring all of the signs of her aggressiveness and emotionally violent personality.

That said, I am sure she can be a wonderful person and in fact, I saw how awesome she was as well. We all have both sides, however, in hindsight, I could see that she too was insecure and the combination of neither of us providing ourselves with the love we needed, led to us looking for it in each other and eventually lashing out at each other. This is what I was talking about earlier in relation to co-creating and everything being your responsibility.

From my point of view, if I was emotionally stronger as I am these days, there is no way that I would have attracted her into my life. I would not have pursued a relationship and therefore would never have been in a situation where she could have been emotionally and then physically violent toward me in Canada.

Like attracts like. Water seeks its own level. If you are attracting certain things into your life that you don't like, it is because that same trait is lurking disowned somewhere inside of you.

Even if I had started a relationship with my ex while loving myself more, I would not have accepted such behaviour for very long. Notice that I am not blaming her. I am putting the onus on me and that gives me the power to understand my part in attracting the violence so that I can not attract it into my life in the future.

It's not about saying your partner was an arse, but rather that you missed an opportunity to not put yourself into that situation. When you blame others, you take away your power, but when you take responsibility for everything you attract in your life, then you give yourself all the power.

I get that not everyone will embrace this way of living and there will always be some level of violence in some people's lives, but that doesn't mean that it has to be a part of yours.

We often rely on other people to make us feel good, and if they don't, we feel hurt. At the end of the day, it is not our partner's responsibility to make us feel good. It is ours. I know this to be a fact from my own experience.

If you love yourself, and your partner loves themself, then you heighten each other's happiness, rather than rely on it from each other. If you rely on someone else for you to be happy, then inevitably there will come a time when you are let down.

If you love yourself as well as them, and they love themselves as well as you, then I am 100% certain that there won't be any form of domestic violence in your relationship. Yes, I know, it's not necessarily that easy. It is that simple, but not that easy when we're dealing with millions of people.

My point here is that we need to educate the whole of society that these are the changes that we need to make. If we do this and the collective consciousness moves in that direction, domestic violence will decrease. If we love each other in general, then this will breed more love in other areas.

We need to love everyone and most importantly; love ourselves. As I have previously stated, fighting fire with fire only creates more fire.

As the quote at the beginning of this sub-chapter says, we only get rid of darkness by turning on the light.

We will never get rid of domestic violence in our lives by "fighting" it. When we learn to love ourselves and turn on the light, the darkness of domestic violence will disappear.

A DIFFERENT APPROACH TO DOMESTIC VIOLENCE

No, I wasn't born black, a woman, gay, transgender, in a third world country, of ethnic background in a white culture, disabled, mentally impaired, blind, deaf, missing limbs, or suffering from any birth defects. As a white male, I've had it easier than some, but I've also experienced what it's like to be looked down on, laughed at, abused, cast aside, and looked at as some sort of predator. Therefore, I can empathise with those who have faced the beforementioned challenges in their lives.

In recent years we have created a society where men have to take unprecedented steps to protect themselves and their reputation like never before. No longer can a man help a woman in distress, or a child who is lost, without the fear of being accused of a sinister act.

At a time when the world needs men to stand up in these areas to protect women and children, men are too afraid to do so for fear of accusations or untoward behaviour. Many men would also rather avoid dating than risk being accused of rape or sexual harassment at the first sign of a fling or sexual encounter going pear-shaped. It's the saddest statement to make, but nonetheless; it's true.

While I am not playing the blame game or defending any man who is violent towards a partner, for every abusive man, there is a woman somewhere who is treating a man in different but somewhat still horrible ways.

Women can be just as emotionally abusive or use sex or money as a way to manipulate a partner as men can. Unfortunately, this type of behaviour is not made as public or scrutinized by the media as much. This is why we need to change the narrative around domestic violence.

We can argue all day about who treats who worse, but until both sexes accept responsibility for issues and violence in a relationship, then it won't end. With all sincerity, I hope that comment offends people and pisses them off because maybe then both men and women will take a real hard look at themselves and stop blaming each other and start taking positive steps towards treating each other better in relationships.

CHAPTER 5

When I sat through a Men's Domestic Violence program in 2015, almost every single man there came up with excuses for why he was violent towards his partner. Excuses like, "The bitch fucked another guy." Or "The slut spent all my money and smoked all my drugs."

I lost count of how many times I stepped in and said to one of them, "Mate, it doesn't matter what she did. What matters is how you reacted to it." I get what they're saying and I feel for them, but at the end of the day, it doesn't matter what anyone does to you. The only thing that matters is how you act or react to what they do.

We are all human and partners can do things that hurt like fucking hell. But you still have control over your own actions. I have had partners who have done some horrific things in our relationships. That doesn't matter. All that matters is how I react to it.

When men and women start accepting responsibility for how they treat themselves and take charge of their own self-esteem, this will directly reflect how they treat their partners. When we rely on someone else to prop up our self-esteem, we are certain to have it fall sooner or later.

I'm not saying it is a perfect strategy that will always stop violence in every situation, but I am certain that it's a better solution than has been put forward thus far by authorities who are supposed to know better than me.

Every time a woman dies at the hands of a partner, people cry out for harsher penalties for offenders like that would solve everything. That's like saying you should close the stable gate after the horse has already bolted.

For far too long the focus has been on punishment instead of what causes a relationship to get to this level of anger and what (for the purposes of this discussion) leads a man to be violent towards his partner.

If I seem to be repeating myself that is because it needs to be repeated over and over until someone in power or the collective consciousness understands that we will never stop domestic violence until we identify and rectify what causes people to get to a point where they feel they have no other option, but to act with violence.

For too long the only mindset we have had is the mindset that if someone offends, then we lock them up. I agree that in some cases this is the best option, but what if we put more energy into education, support, and help for both men and women?

Plus, having spent time in custody recently I can tell you that 70% of male offenders in Queensland prisons are there for domestic violence relation matters. Now tell me. Have domestic violence numbers ever decreased in the past decade? Any idiot can answer that question and see we are going about it all the wrong way.

We need to create a network where couples can work through issues individually or collectively when the issues are minor. That way things don't escalate to the point where someone dies and someone else ends up in jail.

Authorities and Police will try to argue that there are already support networks for men in this area, but I can tell you that they are a complete pile of steaming shit! The officers who claim to be there for males spend more time harassing the men and trying to compile information to use against them. Yet they wonder why men are not willing to use these services. This whole situation is counter-productive and a waste of taxpayers' money.

I've had the team visit my house a couple of times and each time they try to pretend that they are looking out for my needs. I simply say to them, "Cut the crap. What do you really want?" They don't like that very much, but once they realise that I am onto them, they usually leave with their tails between their legs and leave me alone for another six months.

Instead of the only solution being that we demonise men, what if we went further back and made "communication" a subject at primary school? Most agree that the education system is not as relevant as it was fifty years ago and needs to be overhauled. English and Maths are important but so is teaching kids finance and how to treat each other and themselves.

My girlfriend Nicky who was twenty when I was finishing high school told me that I'd learn more in the first three years after school than I did in twelve years at school. Guess what? She was spot on.

School didn't teach me discipline, self-esteem, how to create real wealth, or how to have supportive relationships free of insecurities and violence. I know we can't teach everything in school but if we get rid of some of the irrelevant subjects and give students real-life skills then I'll bet the rates of suicide, poverty, and domestic violence decrease dramatically by the time their generation is running the world.

Some might say that it is a parent's job to educate their children in these areas. The problem with that theory is that many parents weren't taught these things in the first place.

How can an adult teach a child something that they themselves were never correctly taught?

These problems will take a generation to be fully corrected, but we need to start somewhere and do it the right way, instead of band-aiding the problem with short-term solutions that cure nothing.

NOT ALL GIFTS CAN BE TAKEN BACK

As Buddha once said after receiving criticism and negativity from one of his critics, "If someone offers you a gift and you don't accept it; to whom does the gift belong?" In other words, if someone belittles you, criticises you, or projects anger towards you and you don't accept it; where does it go?

In my opinion, it returns to the person who is trying to give it to you. Or, as Dr. Wayne Dyer adds, "Why would you accept something that belongs to someone else that is not yours?" If someone offers you the gift of criticism or hateful words or actions, simply don't accept it. That way it will not only have little effect on you, but it will remain with them.

For years Breeana's family have tried their best to hurt, bully, defame, harass, and project anger my way, but because I have not ever accepted it; it sits with them. They own it. They are holding onto it. They are carrying all of these feelings around and it is them who are suffering from it; not me.

I'm not affected by their anger. I'm not having gut-wrenching feelings or stress and anxiety from their hatred; they are. It's like Tony Robbins always says, "hating someone is like drinking poison and expecting them to die."

If those people who are living their lives with so much hate knew anything about how cancer is allowed to develop and survive in our bodies, they would not be holding onto such hate and venom. They are creating the perfect environment in their bodies for cancers and diseases to develop. Why would anyone want to do that to themselves?

The same goes for the media or online trolls. For either of them to affect me, three things have to occur:

1: I have to turn on the news, or go on social media; which I refuse to do.
2: I have to read or listen to what they say; which I won't.
3: I have to let what is said affect me; which will never happen.

WHAT OTHER PEOPLE THINK OF YOU IS NONE OF YOUR BUSINESS

If you've noticed, in all three cases, for anything to affect me, it comes down to my actions and not the actions of someone else. That is essentially what this book is about. Whether we're talking about suicide, bullying, or domestic violence, it all comes down to how you react to anything that happens in life.

It doesn't matter what anyone else says or does. It only matters how you react or let yourself feel about what someone says or does that counts. I am going to repeat that last sentence and put it in bold, because if you remember only one line in this book; this is the one.

It only matters how you react or let yourself feel about what someone says or does that counts.

From a man's point of view, it doesn't matter if your wife spends all your money, won't give you sex, nags you constantly, belittles you in front of your children and friends or does anything else to you. It only matters how you react.

Whether it be that someone is harassing you at work, bullying you online or at school, or showing much anger toward you in a relationship. These things can only hurt you if you let them. This is not to say that this process is easy. It will take practise, but I promise you that your life will change when you follow through with this simple yet effective concept.

In the case of domestic violence, if you don't accept these "gifts" from your partner from the beginning, then it won't get to the level of physical or emotional abuse that we see in many cases before the courts and in the media. If you're not accepting their anger and hatred etc., then you will act in a different way than that of someone who is "fighting domestic violence".

Instead of fighting it, you will more than likely walk away, resolve it, or not attract it into your relationship or your life in the first place. It is only when you don't love yourself that someone else can hurt you. If you truly love yourself, then there is no way you would accept or tolerate anything less than complete love in a relationship. No ifs or buts; this is fact.

How do I know? I have done it myself. I have been in relationships where I didn't love myself and I spent the entire time letting them treat me badly. Why would I do that? Because I was so desperate to be loved that I would turn a blind eye to how badly they were treating me.

It's like having a puppy or a small child. The puppy or child will play up because even though they get in trouble, the attention we give them when they play up is better than no attention at all. As humans, we would subconsciously prefer bad love, to the feeling of having no love at all.

If I loved myself during those bad relationships, there is no way known I would have tolerated any of their behaviour. Sure, I thought I was not tolerating it, but really all I was doing was making it worse by fighting with them, instead of walking away out of respect for myself.

THE WORLD AND ALL OF US ARE IN PERFECT BALANCE

"We get what we truly believe we deserve in life, whether we realise it or not."
Dr. John Demartini

Imagine a magnet with only a south pole, life without death, a conversation with only questions and no answers, or a world where the only season was summer. Ok. The last example is a bad one because I think we would all enjoy it, but I think you get my point.

As Newton's third law states: "For every action, there is an equal and opposite reaction." Polar opposites are not only a fact of life; they are law. We can't have one with the other.

The human personality is the same. While we all differ in many ways, we all have both good and bad traits; whether we want to admit it or not. The world and everyone within it is in perfect balance. When it comes to our personality traits, we spend most of our lives embracing the good and denying the bad, or building up the good while trying to suppress the bad.

Yes, it is better to be good, but to deny that we have the opposite trait is a complete lie. I used to be "Mr. Positive" and while I am still a very positive person, I no longer dislike the seemingly bad traits that I possess. Yes, I strive to be good, but I accept that I have the opposite inside me too. We all do. We are in perfect balance at all times.

It is in the opening paragraph of the famous scripture the Tao Te Ching; Lao Tsu says (I paraphrase) that it is only through witnessing evil, that we can see the good. It is only by knowing hate, that we can feel love. It is when we have been in darkness, that we can notice the dawn of a new day.

Society tells us to be good and not bad, but unless we experience one, we can't appreciate the other. For thirty-nine years I thought that I knew what life was about, but it wasn't until I saw death when Breeana took her last breath metres away from me as she jumped from our balcony, that I was truly able to appreciate life.

Let me take a brief detour here to clarify something that I said in the previous sentence that has caused much debate by everyone from the media to the Police. At the time of Breeana's suicide, when I witnessed her "jump" from our eleventh-floor balcony, I stated that Breeana "jumped".

At the time and as things happened so quickly, I believed that she in fact jumped. Given the shock that I was in at that moment, that is what I believed happened.

After a decade of reflection, over that timeframe, I have replayed that moment over and over in order to definitively understand precisely what happened. At some point in a book, interview, or in a statement to the Police, I have been told that I may have used a different word to "jumped".

This has caused much controversy and as I understand this is one of the main reasons why the Police wrongly charged me with murder. They believed that it was my "change of story" that suggested to them that I might be responsible for her death.

When Breeana committed suicide, by the time I saw her, she was already over the balcony rail railing. At the instant I turned to see her, she disappeared from sight. To this day I am not 100% whether Breeana jumped from the chair that she pushed against the railing and that happened to be at the exact moment I saw her, whether she climbed over the railing and stood on the ledge before jumping off, or if she was standing on the other side and stepped off the ledge or slipped.

All I know is that she disappeared from sight in an intentional manner at the exact moment that I turned and saw her.

For the sake of Breeana's family, the media, and the Police I have tried my best to recall the exact details of this event, but even now I find it impossible to do so. I gave my best recollection to the Police on the night of Breeana's death, but in hindsight and due to possibly suffering from PTSD, for which I was not given any treatment, this may have not been exactly correct. My point then and now is that Breeana plunged to her death after intentionally climbing/jumping over the railing eleven floors up.

CHAPTER 5

Back to the current topic:

When it comes to life, we can't have one (good/bad) thing without the other. It's a fact of life and is the case everywhere we look. If someone is in pain, we automatically show kindness. If a friend loses a relationship, we instantly replace that love with our own to fill that void. Even one of the most horrific events in history; 9/11 had both sides of the spectrum.

While the death and pain of that event were unprecedented, in the wake of it, the world acted in ways that could never have happened without such a catastrophe. I agree that we all wish that it never occurred in the first place, but to see what has come from it is proof that everything is in perfect balance.

If you step back and look at any event in your life that you originally saw as bad, I am certain that you will find that there was an equal amount of good that came from it. I know that I have found this to be true and this is precisely what I do when something happens that I feel is wrong. I look at the situation until I can find as many good things as bad that have come from it.

This is an incredible process called "The Demartini Method" that I learnt from my mentor Dr. John Demartini at his three-day "Breakthrough Experience" event in 2018. I don't have time to explain this intricate process here, but I highly recommend that you attend this event, or at the very least read his book "The breakthrough Experience" to learn more about it.

As a result of the book and seminar, I can now look at any "bad" event and find as many benefits as challenges to that situation. This means that I no longer suffer as a result of something I once perceived as bad; including being charged with murder, or the loss of my beautiful Breeana.

A small example of how everything in life is balanced was when I was new to the travel consulting industry. I sold a client a package including airfares and as a result of my confusion over a ticketing rule with the flights, I made a loss on the booking of $513.00. Due to the pay structure of the company that I was working for, this meant that I was going to earn $513.00 less in commission that month.

Not two minutes after working out my lost commission with my manager, the phone rang, and because I was the only person available, I answered it. The lady on the phone needed to book two business-class flights to Europe and wanted to pay in full on the phone.

WHAT OTHER PEOPLE THINK OF YOU IS NONE OF YOUR BUSINESS

At the end of the call which lasted less than fifteen minutes, I calculated my commission on that booking and it was exactly $513.00.

While this might not be the most spiritual example of what I am trying to explain, it is a perfect example, because it was so obvious to me that this was the world working in perfect balance. I am sure all of us have had a small windfall on the pokies or perhaps a bonus pay, only to receive a bill in the mail, or a flat tyre on the same day. This too is the world demonstrating that it is always in perfect balance.

Society tells us to be good and not bad, but unless we experience one, we can't appreciate the other. On a micro level, I would give anything to have Breeana back and not have to experience the heartbreak of her death, but on a macro level, I can appreciate how this event has benefited me and will hopefully benefit you and many other people by the time anyone forgets the name, Breeana Robinson.

Even my biggest gripe - the media, somehow provides a balance in the world. For several years now I have bitched and moaned about how horrible and negative the media is and how the world would be a better place without them but in fact, they too are ensuring balance in the world.

The more negative and desperate the media get to skew the balance in their negative direction, the more positive and enlightened energy is brought to the world through the ever-growing spiritual consciousness.

Having said that, I urge you to be very sceptical of anything you read or hear in the media because, for the most part, it is factually incorrect and is nothing more than an opinion.

As Buddha said, "Don't believe anything you see, read or hear from others; whether of authority, religious teachers, or of text. Find out for yourself what is truth."

In other words, never accept what is said, just because it seems to come from someone who should know. Most people sprouting their thoughts in the media are doing so in order to push their agenda for their own benefit, whether it be for monetary profit, or simply notoriety.

Similar to what Groucho Marx said when referring to television - I find the news very educational. Every time it comes on, I read a good book. Slowly but surely, people are stepping away from listening to the media (And other authorities) and are making their own decisions, based on fact; not opinion.

We do need these polar opposites in the world though. If the earth only had a north or a south pole, it would spin out of control. For every person spreading hate; someone is sowing love. For every tree that is cut down; someone is planting one. Whenever there is heartache and loss through terrorism or natural disaster; there is always an outpouring of love and compassion.

As Tony Robbins says, "What's wrong is always available, and so is what's right." If you focus on negative things, that is what you will see in life. If you focus on the positives, they are all around for you to see. Personally; I look for both in every situation.

If the world was perfect by the description of most people, there would be no bad or evil in the world. There would be no crime, no death, and no illness. While this may sound nice in theory, it is simply not practical.

When it comes to religion, one of the most common barriers to people believing that there is a God is their questioning about why bad things happen. Their question is, "If there is a God then why does he allow babies to be abused, people to be murdered, or crimes to be committed?" In my opinion, all of this is obvious. I'd like to put what I believe is a logical philosophy on this commonly asked question.

If no one died, the population would explode beyond what the world could sustain, and the world would come to a horrible end all at once; which would defeat the purpose of what we originally wanted. So far as crime and suffering, not only are these both linked to the previous point, but they are essential for the perfect balance of the world. If no one died, no one would experience pain and therefore no one would be able to appreciate joy.

FINDING BOTH SIDES OF EVERYTHING; LEADS TO PEACE IN ANYTHING.

"I can calculate the motions of the heavenly bodies, but not the madness of the people" - Sir Isaac Newton

As I write this sub-chapter, the world is in the grips of the COVID-19 pandemic in 2021. There have been more than two-hundred and forty million cases of the virus and even though we're not there yet, the death toll will no doubt exceed five million in the near future.

By the time this book is published, I am certain that the majority of the world will have moved on and not be paying much thought to this pandemic, but right now, while world leaders are doing their best to get us through this, most people believe that this is the worst time in human history.

I see things a little differently. This pandemic is indeed a tragic loss of life and a huge backward step to the world's economic stability, but just like '9/11' and many other world events that people saw as horrific, there are so many positives that are already emerging and will continue to emerge from this crisis for years to come.

If I was to list them all I'd need a separate book, but some that come to mind even in the mid-stages of the pandemic are as follows:

1. An elevated level of human kindness.

For a few years now "narcissist" has been the go-to buzzword when someone is not able to throw a witty insult at someone else, but instead throws narcissist out there, and rightly so. As a society and with the advent of social media, we have all become very self-centred.

Apart from a select few who got into punch-ups over rolls of toilet paper, since COVID-19 took over the world, I have noticed a huge outpouring of compassion and a willingness to help each other. For the most part, people are also noticing each other more and being much more considerate of each other.

2. An awareness of living within our means.

This may sound terrible given how many people have lost their livelihoods, their businesses, or their elevated level of living, but for far too long millions of people have been living beyond their means. When I was finishing high school the interest rate in Australia was 17% and only two years later the unemployment rate was 11%.

Since then, most of the world has enjoyed a prolonged time of growth and prosperity. In comparison, just prior to COVID-19, interest rates were 0.25% and unemployment stood at 5.1%. This has bred more than a generation that has lived beyond their means.

I know it doesn't help the millions of people around the world who hit rock bottom, but I sincerely hope that they see this for the blessing that it is and that moving forward they always put a safety net under themselves in case something like this happens again.

3. Babies, babies, babies.

Whenever there is death, there is always life. As was the case a few months before COVID-19 in Australia when we were hit by hundreds of bushfires. When a forest burns down, new plants sprout from the ashes. When an animal dies, it returns to the earth and provides new life. When we lose someone, we learn to cherish what we have and share more love. And, when we're forced to stay at home, we fuck like rabbits!!!

What else do we have to do while stuck at home? Go on. I dare you. Go and look up the birth rates in your country for 2019 – 2022 and I bet they go up exponentially.

4. A once in a lifetime opportunity to make a fortune.

No. I haven't lost my mind and yes, I know that many people lost a huge portion of their wealth in the stock market, Superannuation, or 401K (in the USA). Despite this, 2020 will be looked upon as one of the greatest times in our lifetime to invest.

If you're one of the sheep who followed the herd and sold everything in the stock market then yes, it's a bad time, but that's because you stupidly followed the masses and watched too much misleading news.

When the stock market had the biggest crash since 1930, most people sold, but Warren Buffet, myself, and some smart investors bought. I lost a lot of value in the companies I was holding, but instead of selling for a huge loss, I doubled down and bought more of the great companies because they were incredibly cheap.

If you could buy a brand-new Ferrari in perfect condition for 80% off the ticket price, wouldn't you buy it? That's precisely how great companies all around the world were selling; 70-80% off.

Only 1987, 2000, 2008, and now 2020 have been a truly genuine once-in-a-lifetime opportunity to change your life, so what did most people do? They sold everything. They panicked and followed the herd mentality.

As Buffett and his mentor, Benjamin Graham say, "Be fearful when everyone else is being greedy and greedy when everyone else is fearful." If you have the guts to think for yourself and not be swept up with the herd, you will achieve far more success and happiness; not just in finance, but in life itself.

5. The greatest scientific breakthrough of all time.

When I wrote the first four reasons, it was mid-2020. Now, more than three years later, things have moved at light speed. We have a far greater understanding of the pandemic and in particular, the world has had the most incredible breakthroughs in medicine that we have ever seen.

With the entire scientific community working together, science has safely created various vaccines and treatments for COVID-19 in record time. Not by taking shortcuts, but by working together instead of against each other.

In the past, pharmaceutical giants worked alone in developing medicines, but in these unprecedented times, they came together to save the world. From a scientific and global point of view, the sky really is the limit with what is possible in the future as a result of COVID-19 and I for one am excited about seeing what can be achieved.

My point in all of this once again is that in every situation in life, there is both good and bad. When something "bad" happens, find as many good things that came from it and it won't be so painful. Alternatively, when something "good" happens, find all the negative and you will feel more centred and less righteous.

The one thing the virus and economic downturn revealed was people's true personalities. It's a well-known fact that when happy people drink, they get happier and when angry people drink, they become even angrier drunks. The same happened when the virus took hold.

There were so many caring and giving people, but it also exposed the other side of different people's personalities. Even though I am male, I was surprised at how many angry men were abusing people and being complete douchebags during that time.

It's like I said earlier, whatever is inside you comes out when you're squeezed. Without sounding like an old person, it was males aged 20-35 who were the worst offenders.

Dudes on steroids and pot-smoking unemployed monkeys lashing out at the world. Trust me. I lived next to a family of them for a decade. It was for good reason that the government was worried about increased cases of domestic violence during that time. The virus exposed the lack of education in males and their lack of cognitive coping skills.

Once again, this is something that needs to be addressed during schooling. We have children attending school for twelve years and yet if we can't teach them basic cognitive skills, then we have bigger problems than we realise. We spend so much time teaching subjects that are irrelevant to life, yet we neglect teaching kids things that will serve them in later life.

We all know that the education system is antiquated and needs overhauling, but no one is willing to tackle the mammoth task it would require to fix this problem. I would rather see school weeks be overhauled in the following ways.

Start by having fewer subjects each day and more time spent on important subjects. For example; instead of having high school students being tossed between six different subjects in a day, reduce it to three.

They can still have a break every forty minutes, but from the start of the day until morning tea, they focus on one subject; in two forty-minute lessons. This is then repeated twice more during a regular day. It has been proven that we maximise our learning with full immersion; not glossing over things.

Students are overwhelmed with so much information at school and much of it is useless. There should be more time spent on teaching students cognitive skills, coping skills, life skills, and financial fundamentals. If I was taught these things in school then I wouldn't have spent my forties learning them.

Schools spend too much time teaching students to be good little "sheep" instead of teaching them to think for themselves. Society would rather we learn how to navigate Pythagoras' theorem, or dissect a chicken wing, rather than navigate a volatile relationship or dissect a company's balance sheet and manage our own financial future.

FOR A SEASON OR A REASON

For the world to exist there needs to be a natural ebb and flow. Everything that is born eventually dies. Seasons come and go. The stock market goes up and down and things move in natural cycles. Friendships and relationships are no different. People come into our lives for a reason or a season and when we have learnt what it is that God wanted us to learn from that relationship; then the relationship is complete.

The fact that many people turned their backs on me when I was targeted by the media didn't surprise me at all. Most people are uneducated and judgmental (as was I years ago). They don't use common sense (which is not so common) and they think emotionally, rather than logically.

Smart people know that the media is negative but the fact that not one person asked me if any of what was written in the media was true, didn't surprise me either. The fact they simply walked away without a word said, was to be expected as most of them were more "energy vampires" than friends.

The one that did surprise me was my best mate. We'd been best mates since kindergarten and had been through a lot over the years. I was the God Father to his eldest daughter and best (or worst) man at his wedding.

WHAT OTHER PEOPLE THINK OF YOU IS NONE OF YOUR BUSINESS

I'd been there for him through his wife's infidelity, his battle with depression (when he threatened to commit suicide), as well as hiding the secrets of his many marital and pre-marital affairs, as well as his father's infidelity over many years.

I was even the one standing between him and his wife on their front lawn when they were literally pushing each other and being physically abusive to each other; in order to not have one of them dead and the other in jail.

I even carried the guilt of watching his father cheat on his mother and not say a word for years. This occurred on a few occasions when they visited me in Asia on a cruise ship. No matter what happened, I never wavered in my friendship and support.

Even when he launched a tirade of abuse over the phone when his beloved Bulldogs played my Dragons in a footy match. This is what mate-ship is about. You never turn your back on a mate; especially when he is down.

Now, I must say that yes, he was there for me on many occasions and through thick and thin, but when it really counted and when I really needed that one person who knew me completely; he walked away. This was despite me never doing anything to hurt him or doing anything against him.

It surprised me that it was his father who called me and told me never to contact the family again; instead of my friend. A vindictive me would have called the house to tell his mother about his father's blatant infidelity but that was his business to blurt it out during one of their everyday verbal assaults on each other. For all I know if they are reading this, then I'm sure none of this is of any surprise to any of them.

At the time of my best mate turning his back on me, I thought it was a petty reaction to how the media derailed his election campaign when my daughter's mother and her so-called wannabe bikie boyfriend contacted the local paper to advise them that a council candidate was linked to me.

What he didn't realise was that his own sister had a hand in his demise. If this situation was the reason for ending forty years of friendship, then I thought it was quite funny. After all, I'd shagged two of his cousins, two of his wife's best friends, two of his sister's best friends, and even his sister, so surely if he had an issue with me, then it would have come up ten years earlier when all that ended.

* Footnote: In reference to my sexual partners who were somehow connected to my former best mate, I think I listed them all but it's hard to confirm when the police still have my "list" of sexual partners, so if I've left anyone out, I apologise. (Smiley face)

My former best mate knew about all of them, he encouraged most of them and he was even present for some of them, so it had me baffled why the media reporting lies about someone he knew better than anyone else in the world would be an issue worth destroying forty years of friendship. I think it came from his wife and his father, who like I said were both on my "not so popular" lists for their marital indiscretions.

The fact that (in my opinion) a grown man didn't have the balls to stand up to either his wife or father is sad, but that is an individual choice. I don't blame him for it, and it is honourable to stand by two people who have betrayed him as much as his father and wife have over the years, but as they say, "Those who live in glass houses…"

If you're wondering why I would be so cruel as to possibly unearth some dark secrets in a book about people I once called my second family. This book is about how to deal with depression and how to not worry about what other people think of you.

There was always going to be collateral damage when I was coming clean about every aspect of my life and I no longer have a moral obligation to hold onto secrets I carried for decades to protect people who are no longer in my life. Most people reading this book won't have a clue who I am talking about so it's hardly going to have huge ramifications for anyone.

These people judged me despite the many similar or even worse skeletons in their own closets. This is what most people do. They judge others even though they themselves are far from perfect. In fact, the more similar other people are to you, the more likely they are to judge you.

This is because they identify with a trait that they believe you have that they have yet to own or come to terms with themselves. This triggers an emotional response that makes them uncomfortable and hence why they feel the need to judge you, instead of accepting the trait in themselves.

I'm far from perfect, but I'm honest enough to admit it and even put it on paper for the world to know. I do this because unlike most, I've owned my shit and embraced every part of my personality.

If someone is judging you or bullying you, it is very likely that it is because of their own guilt and insecurities over their own lives. We all have shit and most people refuse to own their shit and instead, project it onto other people.

WHAT OTHER PEOPLE THINK OF YOU IS NONE OF YOUR BUSINESS

Take strength from the fact that if they are doing this to you, it usually has absolutely nothing to do with you and everything to do with them. This is exactly what I do when Breeana's family projects their guilt and insecurities onto me by lashing out.

This is why you should never take any notice of what anyone thinks of you. We have this mentality that for someone to win; someone else must lose. It's like the tallest building syndrome and once again I blame the media. No one is born racist. No one is born homophobic and no one is born with hate in their hearts.

The media will moan and bitch and claim that they are simply doing their duty to mankind, but that's a load of crap. They thrive on hatred and division and we all fall for it. People believe that in order to be wealthy, someone else must be poor when there is more than enough wealth in the world for everyone to prosper.

Why do we have to be against someone?

Christians and Muslims. Blacks and whites. Gays and straights. Men and women. Instead of tearing each other down to make ourselves look better, why can't we lift each other up and respectfully embrace each other's diversity?

I get that some groups have been suppressed or treated badly over many years based on race, religion, sexual preference, or gender, but there is no need for us to live in the past and continue fuelling hatred toward each other. Living in the past is not going to fix the issue. The past does not equal the future.

My father was in World War II and as a result, he had a dislike of Japanese people, but that is no reason for me to feel the same as he did. He had his reasons and they may have been justified, but that is no reason for me to carry a similar grudge. Just because something was a certain way in the past, doesn't mean it has to continue on in the future.

Now that I have read four hundred books on religion and spirituality, I have realised that regardless of what people call their faith, they are essentially all the same thing. Sure, there are extremists in any religion or race, but 99% of us are the same and believe the same things; regardless of what we want to call it.

Whether it be Christianity or Hinduism, Buddhism or Islam, the message is essentially the same and despite what the 1% want

CHAPTER 5

you to believe, they are all about peace, love, and grace. Therefore, I find it disturbing that despite the common thread through almost all religious texts being the same, some people will fight vehemently for their religion, race, or sexual preference instead of accepting everyone as one and the same.

I don't give a fuck if you're black, white, Asian, Muslim, gay, straight, or whether you're a doctor, lawyer, cleaner, prostitute, or unemployed. When I look at you, no matter who or what you are or label yourself to be, you are just another human being.

I spent twenty years as an amateur and professional entertainer. From the start of my career, I worked closely with all races, genders, and sexual preferences. I shared dressing rooms with gay, straight, and bisexual people, with Muslims and Christians, and with all races. We shared some wonderful times without ever judging each other based on skin colour, sexual preference, or religious beliefs.

We were all the same. I don't understand why the media or anyone for that matter would need to categorize themselves or other people. We are all human. We all love. We all bleed. We all breathe and we all have similar desires.

I don't give a fuck if your skin is darker than mine, if you pray five times a day, if you want to have sex with the opposite sex, or the same sex; or even both. We need to stop looking at each other as being different and see each other for our similarities; which are far more than our differences.

As I've previously stated, fighting against something doesn't make it go away. Tearing someone down doesn't make you better. I tried that and it didn't work. Even though I did this in my personal life, in my professional life as a singer, I never tore another performer down to make myself look better. If someone was better than me, I learnt from them and became better while encouraging them and lifting them up so we could both share each other's successes.

This is what I am urging everyone (including the media and politicians) to do in every area of their lives. Hate fuels hate, but on the flip side; love breeds love. Lift each other up, and look at each other not as a different race, sex, or religion, but as your fellow human being on a slightly different journey.

I also urge the media and our world leaders to take the lead on this. I get that the mainstream media are struggling to stay afloat and to stay relevant with the internet etc., but it's time they took the moral responsibility of their jobs more seriously.

The same goes for world leaders. The way politicians treat each other is deplorable. The way the media treat people is no better. If the general public acted the way the media and politicians do (hiding behind parliament or "serving the public's interest") then we would all be in jail. The media and politicians are given great powers in the public eye and with that should come a more accountable responsibility.

Sports people and celebrities have come under great fire in recent years. Hardly a day goes by when the media doesn't report that a sportsperson or celebrity has not been "A good role model" in the media's eyes.

What about the media and politicians? They both have more influence over the public than celebrities or sportspeople, so surely they should be more careful with how they act. The public is not well versed in seeing through the media lies and the spin that politicians create.

People believe what they see and read. Therefore, I would like to see both the media and politicians take more of an ethical approach to how they act because young and easily impressionable people learn these behaviours and think that it's ok.

If our parliamentarians spoke to each other and about each other in a more respectful manor then I would bet that the general public would do so too. If a boss swore at their staff, treated them like shit, and belittled them, then that is exactly how the staff would act towards each other.

The problem always starts at the top and filters down. I'll bet the newspapers dissect this book and look for all the things they want to find to discredit me in order to create more hatred, but what's the bet that they read this part and it never gets a mention and never leads to any type of change on their behalf.

I sincerely hope I am wrong and will gladly give the media credit if they do act on the previous paragraphs.

CHAPTER 5

FEED THE MIND, NOURISH THE SOUL

> *"The sole purpose of education is to bring out the best of us"*
> *- Mohandas Karamchand Gandhi*

I read in one book that "Great advances in knowledge do not occur solely through trial and error but await the occurrence of intuition and the readiness of the human mind." I mention this because most of us know how to create abundance, love, success, and happiness in our lives, however very few achieve these things because of their own unwillingness to open their mind to a new paradigm.

As a general rule, humans do what they have always done, and we know that this is the definition of insanity to do the same thing over and over and expect a different result.

Open your mind beyond your usual paradigms and watch how incredible things happen. As I mentioned earlier in the book, we all carry limiting beliefs. These beliefs are what stop us from getting everything that we want in life.

As Tony Robbins and Dr. John Demartini have said on many occasions, "If you are single, it is because you want to be single. If you really wanted a relationship, you would have one." On a conscious level that sounds ridiculous, but if you go a little deeper, it is correct.

If you have a part of your life that you are unhappy with, the reason it is that way is that you have a bigger reason, or limiting belief to be the way you are, than to change it or create the alternative.

The problem is that most people only look at the surface, instead of going deep into their subconscious when trying to solve an issue in their life.

For example; I am not as fit as I used to be, or as fit as I would love to be. On the surface, I could say that I eat well, exercise fairly regularly, and don't smoke at all, or drink much. On a conscious level, I want to be fit, but on a subconscious level, I know that I am predominately lazier than I used to be. I eat crap food now and then and even deeper, I believe that I won't ever reach the goal of having the perfect body, so why bother.

With these limiting beliefs, I would then think, "Why bother" and sit on the couch. At the end of the day, having the perfect body is not a big deal for me these days so therefore I have not made it the highest priority. On the other hand, when I decided that I wanted to become a professional singer and the best in the cruise industry, this was something that I put as such a high priority that it dictated how I spent the majority of my time.

When I first wanted this goal, I was working full-time in hospitality, so I could have easily come home each day and just wanted to relax, instead of practising.

Instead, I would spend hours and hours doing vocal exercises, studying my heroes like John Farnham, breaking down every single note in a song, and repeating that note until it sat perfectly in my voice.

This wasn't just for a week, or a month. This was for several years and this is what it takes to achieve anything in life. If something is not a top priority or your highest value, then you won't make it happen. You will make up excuses, like "That's just the way I am" or "I'm not good enough." These excuses most of the time will be subconscious because after all, who doesn't want a great body, lots of money, and an awesome relationship?

A simpler way of putting it is "The teacher will come when the student is ready." When you are truly ready to make a change in your life, you will see opportunities that will guide you.

I had always wanted to learn and grow beyond "normal" yet for some unknown reason for many years, I was unable to. This was despite having studied personal development for several years at that point. It was only when I was ready and opened my mind to new possibilities that these lessons showed up for me.

For example. In 2004 an older American lady that I was dating onboard the Tahitian Princess gave me a copy of "The Power of Now" by Eckhart Tolle. At the time I wasn't really into reading or spiritual thoughts and teachings. I opened the book and read two or three pages before putting it away and not even looking at it for several years.

In 2008 after having a taste of the law of attraction and more spiritual teachings, an author that I was reading recommended The Power of Now. I remembered that I had the book at home and on returning home from that contract in the U.K., I picked the book up and began reading it.

As I was still a weak reader at the time, I thought that there would be no way I'd get through it, but to my surprise, I finished the book within a few days. This is a simplistic example of the previously mentioned ideas, but I have experienced this type of situation on many occasions in recent years, now that I am ready for my "teachers" to arrive.

As kids, we are always so curious, but as adults, we somehow lose that quality. I encourage you to be like a child and become a student of learning because when you do, learnings happen in the most wonderful places.

I am constantly learning wherever I go these days. Not only do I spend at least three hours a day listening to audiobooks, but I am always looking at things that happen throughout my day that I can learn from.

If you're wondering how I have time to read or listen to books for three to five hours a day, it's a trick I learnt from Tony Robbins called N.E.T (No Extra Time). I discuss it in detail in my book "The No B.S Approach to Create the Life You Want" in the chapter on learning and growing.

These types of learnings that I have throughout the day can come through a painful experience, a challenging situation, or even a chance encounter or occurrence that opens your eyes and mind to a different way of thinking.

The key is to develop the same curiosity as that of a child. This curiosity led me to read books on topics that I would never have imagined just a few years earlier. I'm talking about books on business, religion, finance, and even physics.

For example; I saw a program on TV that talked about a famous person from hundreds of years ago (I can't recall exactly who it was) and instead of glossing over the story, I Googled them and learnt a lot more about this important person in history than I ever would if I paid no mind to it other than to hear what the documentary said.

I also found two audiobooks on them which I listened to. My point is, take the time to be curious about everything instead of glossing over life and I promise you, your life will take on a different meaning altogether.

When reading a couple of books by the late, great Stephen Hawking, I instantly realised how much information there was in the world and how much pure potential we have as humans. I don't mean to put myself down, but after reading Stephen's books, I also realised how dumb I may potentially be compared to him.

As Einstein once said, "The more I learn, the more I realise how little I know and the more I realise how little I know; the more I want to learn."

I too found that as I gained momentum on my quest to read 280 books in one year (2016), I couldn't devour the books fast enough to satisfy my insatiable curiosity for answers to so many questions about my life, life in general, and the universe and everything else.

CHAPTER SIX

THE "HERO'S JOURNEY" (FROM WRITING IT TO LIVING IT)

"Where you stumble, is where your treasure lies" – Joseph Campbell

While almost all teachers make great sacrifices for their students, there are a few teachers who leave a lasting impression on their students for the rest of their lives. In the show Glee, it was Will Schuester. In my case, that teacher was Mr. Eddie Leeon.

Not only was Eddie one of the coolest teachers at the school, but in my opinion, he was also a brilliant mind and visionary. A slim Chinese Australian man, but if you closed your eyes you would swear, he was a honky-tonk white boy.

Eddie taught film and television in the state's first-ever school that taught the subject. Eddie had a vision for the 1990 rock eisteddfod and no detractors were going to sway him from that vision. Many doubted what he was doing, but at the end of months of planning, rehearsals, and performances, his vision became a reality.

I remember the feeling when the compere called out "Miami State High School" as the state rock eisteddfod champions in front of ten thousand people at the Brisbane Entertainment Centre in May 1990.

That win began a decade of dominance by Miami High. The school won eight of nine years they entered the competition in the '90s. The other year, they took a break from competing to tour their show in the U.S.A.

Despite having left school more than thirty years ago, Eddie is still a constant source of inspiration and learning for me. Like all great teachers, Eddie has not only influenced me in formal subjects but also in how to conduct myself and be a man.

Eddie's first great lesson for me was a few weeks after I had landed the role of Danny Zuko in the school musical. Eddie wasn't my teacher for any subjects, but he brought me in three days before the Rock Eisteddfod finals as a replacement for a guy with a punctured lung. Up until that point, I was just another student, but suddenly, my role in Grease and filling in for an important position for the Rock Eisteddfod finals meant that everyone knew who I was.

With that sudden notoriety came my own misguided attitude and self-inflated ego. I must have thought that I was hot shit because even though Eddie never taught me in any subjects, he pulled me aside one day near the tuckshop and told me to pull my head in.

The thing about Eddie's advice was that it wasn't a teacher yelling at a student or being strict. It was like a big brother looking after his little bro. I could tell that while Eddie was being totally blunt, his advice came from a place of genuine compassion.

Of all the teachers I had, only Eddie and Miss (Eleesa) Zlatic who was my Speech and Drama teacher had that influence on me. Both Eddie and Eleesa saw my potential, but at the same time, they wanted to keep me focused.

When I began writing screenplays in 2001, I had absolutely no clue how such a story was supposed to come together in order for it to be turned into a successful movie. Besides the "Hollywood standard formatting" that must be adhered to in order for anyone to even look at your screenplay, there are certain elements that need to be written into the story for it to be a successful film.

Hollywood has a formula that almost every film follows. Thankfully, Eddie has been an incredible mentor for almost two decades as I learnt this intricate craft.

One of the biggest challenges I faced while learning the art of writing screenplays was to do with genre. Eddie was always asking me if our first movie (C.R.U.I.S.E) was a romantic comedy, straight comedy, thriller, or even a soft-core porn movie. In movies, there needs to be a clear genre throughout the film, but in my opinion in real life, there can be many different genres to our stories.

Society wants to label us as one thing when in fact we are all things. Kind of like the movie "Love Actually" where there are many different subplots that all somehow intertwine to create the brilliant storyline that drives the movie forward.

My life has many parts and in the movie of my life, I play many different roles. I play the villain, the hero, the saviour, the troubled one, the father, the son, the lover, and according to some people; the stalker.

WHAT OTHER PEOPLE THINK OF YOU IS NONE OF YOUR BUSINESS

Your life doesn't have to be confined to a single genre. Others will try to make you be that way but it is all those different attributes that when combined, that make you unique and your own hero in your movie.

In every good story, there must be a protagonist (Hero), an antagonist (Villain), and a mirror character (friend/ally of the hero) along with many subtle plot elements that drive the story forward.

While there are varied opinions throughout Hollywood as to what the most important element of a successful screenplay is for it to become a box office blockbuster, the consensus is that your lead character (Hero) must be flawed.

We all think of a hero as someone who is perfect, but in fact, a hero is not really a hero unless he is flawed. It is those flaws that drive the hero to greatness, and it is his greatest challenges that take the most courage but offer the most satisfaction too.

Look at any Hollywood hero and there are flaws. Pete "Maverick" Mitchell played by Tom Cruise in Top Gun has major insecurities about whether he was good enough to be a top gun pilot after his father's death. He had to overcome those insecurities in the highest-pressure situation to gain the respect of his peers.

Charlie Babbitt, also played by Tom Cruise in "Rain Man" had to look beyond his own self-centred, ruthless lifestyle to connect with his long-lost brother. In movies, these examples are known as "inner motivations". As an audience, we often don't see them taking place parallel to the more obvious "outer motivation" that drives the story forward, but in every good screenplay, they are more important than the outer desire of the hero.

One of the biggest things that makes us as an audience connect with the lead character/hero is if we can relate to him or her. The thing that makes us trust the hero, is when we realise that they are just like us. We all have flaws and if we read a book or watch a movie where we can relate to the character, we are more likely to get emotionally involved in the story.

Take Rebel Wilson's character "Fat Amy" in the Pitch Perfect movies. She is the most obvious example of what would be considered a flawed character. She is uncouth, overweight and so down to earth that everyone can relate to her. We may not be overweight, swear, or be anything like Fat Amy, but who wouldn't want to be like her where you live your life not giving a flying fuck about what anyone else thinks of you?

Probably the least obvious, yet the most profound example of the hero's journey is in the 1939 movie "The Wizard of Oz". To most, the story of Dorothy's journey to get back home to Kansas is simply a cute, colourful, and incredibly imaginative story that has been adored by almost everyone born over the last century. While this is certainly the case, as Oprah writes in her book "The path made clear" this movie is one of the greatest spiritual journeys of all time.

I too think the movie has all the elements of the perfect hero's journey. Despite being nearly a century ago, no movie since has come close to the journey in The Wizard of Oz; with the exception of the Harry Potter franchise, which I will touch on shortly.

To paraphrase Oprah; "The yellow brick road represented the path for Dorothy to find her true self. Along the yellow brick road, Dorothy was confronted with the disempowered parts of her personality, or to put another way, the parts she had yet to accept."

When you look deeper, Dorothy is not happy with the life she has and goes searching for a better place (life). Along the way, she was shown traits that she believed she lacked in the form of her friends that she met along the way.

The scarecrow searching for wisdom (a brain), the lion who is cowardly and scared (wanting courage), and the tin-man who desired something to be his compass throughout life and allow him to feel love (a heart). These were all traits that the young Dorothy (and most of us) was searching for.

The wicked witch symbolised Dorothy's inner demons trying to keep her held back from her true self. (You know, that little voice that tells you that you're not good enough). The witch kept popping up just when Dorothy seemed to be getting on top of things.

It took Dorothy to face (her greatest fears) and defeat the witch in order to find her true self. In order to find her way, she needed to follow the path (yellow brick road) to find her way home (back to her true self).

Dorothy having to kill the wicked witch of the west in order to realise her dream is brilliantly symbolic of how we must kill the part of our mind that constantly tells us that we're not good enough. It is only when we achieve this that we are able to realise our true potential.

The yellow brick road is a metaphor for our true calling, our God-given purpose, or our destiny. We often get pushed off track by distractions in life, but if we stick to the path (yellow brick road) then we will reach our destin-(y)-ation.

Just like Dorothy, we often search for some sort of super force outside of us (The Wizard of Oz) to show us the way home. What

Dorothy discovered when explained to her by Glinda, was that Dorothy already had those traits. She just needed to find them for herself. No one (including the Wizard) could show her what her true calling was; only she could.

This was beautifully tied together at the end of the movie when Dorothy says, "If I ever go looking for my heart's desire, I won't look any further than my own back yard, because if it isn't there, then I never really lost it to begin with."

This is the classic full circle of the hero's journey where the hero realises that what they searched for externally, was always there on the inside. This was captured perfectly with the line "There's no place like home".

No one outside of you can show you what your path is; only you can. As Tony Robbins chanted in one of his most famous affirmations, "All I need is within me now". All Dorothy needed was already inside her and all you need is also within you; right now.

A LITTLE HARRY POTTER IN ALL OF US

Harry Potter; the boy who lived, believe it or not, is the poster child, or better still holds the blueprint for achieving your deepest desires in life. You see. Even though Harry had many people around him who were willing to sacrifice themselves and even die for him, Harry was the only person who could conquer his mortal enemy; Lord Voldemort.

This was not because Harry was the world's greatest wizard. That accolade belonged to his mentor, Professor Albus Dumbledore. Nor was it because he was the best student at Hogwarts. That honour stood squarely with his best friend, Hermione Granger.

The reason Harry Potter was the chosen one to defeat Tom Riddle's evil alter-ego Voldemort, was because, like all of us, our greatest, most evil of enemies are in our own minds.

Even though we, along with all of the characters in the Harry Potter movies saw Lord Voldemort, the subtle reality was that the entire series of movies was seen through the eyes of just one person; Harry Potter. Just like there are many "cast members" in our life, everything we experience is through our eyes, and not theirs.

In order for him to defeat Lord Voldemort, Harry needed to conquer his greatest fear. The fear of succumbing to the same fate as his parents. The only way he could achieve this was to embrace his dark side, not suppress it.

CHAPTER 6

Throughout the movies, Harry grappled with the fact that he had a dark side. From his first day at Hogwarts when the sorting hat tried to put him into the evil Slytherin house, to Harry learning that he was a parselmouth (someone who can talk to snakes), like Voldemort.

Harry got himself tied up in knots with the confronting thoughts that he might have a dark side, and was therefore an evil person, like that of the orphan boy Tom Riddle, who went on to become the evilest dark wizard ever.

It wasn't until Harry's godfather Sirius Black said to Harry in The Order of the Phoenix, "The world isn't split into good people and death eaters. We've all got both light and dark inside of us. What matters is the part we choose to act on. That's who we really are."

It is from that point on that Harry discovers (first subconsciously and then on a more conscious level) that the way to conquer the evil of Voldemort is through its opposite; love. Once Harry accepted death and faced it, he had the one power (love) that Voldemort didn't possess, and this became Voldemort's weakness.

Once you embrace your dark side instead of trying to suppress it, you overcome your greatest fears. Combine this with the "Deathly Hallows" and we have the secret recipe for creating our deepest desires.

The Deathly Hallows are three possessions that when combined, give us the ultimate power to achieve anything. While these may be mythical objects in the world of Harry Potter, when applied to the "muggle" world, they give us great power.

"The elder wand" is our heart that thrusts us towards our greatest desires. Once we cast our hearts in any given direction, with the same certainty that Harry had when pointing his wand, anything is possible.

When Harry pointed his wand with the most determined of intentions, he could do anything. It is this same power that we all possess when we point our hearts in the direction of our most heartfelt desire.

The "Resurrection stone" is the moral compass that guides us, drawing on our past (including loved ones lost) to keep us on the right path in times we get disoriented along the way.

Harry achieved his greatest success when all of those he treasured most came back to protect him. When we draw on our moral compass, we too are protected from the type of evil that only we can bring on ourselves.

The "Invisibility cloak" is the protective shield that allows us to see the world around us without allowing anyone else to see, or more importantly penetrate our desires, or our mind, which would in turn bring us down.

WHAT OTHER PEOPLE THINK OF YOU IS NONE OF YOUR BUSINESS

When inside our own invisibility cloak we block out the outside voices that can potentially harm us and we focus on what comes from within. Put simply, as Mark Manson said; "The subtle art of not giving a fuck", or in my own words, "What other people think of you is none of your business".

I too had to confront and eventually embrace my dark side in order to overcome my greatest fears. Until I did that, I was not able to defeat my own Voldemort, in the form of Breeana's Aunt. Once I embraced the dark side that we all have, Breeana's Aunt was no longer able to control or manipulate me in the same way that Voldemort penetrated Harry's mind and infiltrated his thoughts.

"Those who are best suited to power, are the ones who have never sort it"
– Albus Dumbledore

While we're on the topic of Harry Potter, I wonder if J.K Rowling was referring to mainstream media when she created the group of evil entities in her Harry Potter books called "Dementors". I mean, after all, dementors exist only to (as stated on several occasions in the eight movies) "drain hope and happiness out of people".

A group entity spreading fear and hopelessness among people sounds a lot like the media don't you think? They certainly are not spreading joy and giving away puppies now, are they? Just like the dementors, our pain becomes their power, so my suggestion is to suffocate them by denying them what they desire most.

Back to the hero's journey.

In the context of this book, the word hero is not meant to be as most people think a hero is – an all-conquering, god-like human. A hero is a person who is just like you. The true definition of a hero is someone who overcomes insurmountable obstacles, putting themselves and their safety secondary to the needs and well-being of others. This is what I had previously done in all my relationships and it is what I am doing by sharing this story now.

I could easily go back to my quiet life with my dogs and not worry at all about other people, but that's not me. When I published "The Blame Game" in 2016, I thought that my job was done, but as it turned out God had bigger plans and was determined to have me stay in the spotlight so I could be his messenger.

CHAPTER 6

The interesting thing about how God uses us in life is that God only uses us in areas where we have the expertise and real passion. God didn't call on me to raise awareness for human trafficking in Africa. That is what he called people like Angelina Jolie or Amal Clooney to do. My strengths are in communication, story-telling, and writing screenplays, so that is what I now feel compelled to do to get that message across.

Like any hero, I too was reluctant and refused "the call" on several occasions. ("Refusing the "call" is always a part of a hero's journey in movies) I wanted the quiet life but when God made it so obvious that I was meant to continue on this journey; I had to accept.

Again, I have to be very clear about the context in that I am using the word hero here. This is not about calling myself a hero, or thinking I am a hero in any way shape, or form.

I am simply someone who was chosen to embark on this journey and l am being of service to God and to anyone who may benefit from my story. As I said in the introduction, If I can help one person to overcome depression, find a way to not be consumed by bullies, or to move from a volatile relationship to a loving one, then my journey has been worthwhile.

Along with several other elements of a movie that are not relevant in this book, the most important element, other than a flawed hero; is a strong villain. There aren't too many successful movies that don't have a villain; and a strong one at that.

Forest Gump, 50 First Dates, and Finding Nemo are the exceptions to the rule. The success of the James Bond franchise over several decades is testament to the strength of their villains.

Whether it be a comedy or drama, the villain is crucial to driving the plot forward and leaving us with that warm and fuzzy feeling when we leave the cinema. Without the villain, the movie would be so boring and predictable. The villain is also incredibly important for the hero to realise their potential, through the endless challenges that the villain presents.

Mr. Chow in the Hangover, Principal Rooney in Ferris Bueller's day off, or Darth Vader in Star Wars. Without a strong nemesis, our hero can't grow. Life is exactly the same. We all want a simple, uneventful life with very few dramas, but let's be honest, if we didn't have these challenges, we would go looking for them to keep life interesting.

While "certainty" is the number one human need, number two is its polar opposite; "uncertainty". We need challenges to grow. Just like a tree needs wind to force it to strengthen its roots so it can grow stronger, humans need challenges to help us grow stronger.

The other thing that makes a great villain is the same as what makes us love a hero; they need to be flawed. Of course, most nemeses are flawed, that is why they are the nemesis. What I mean in particular is that almost every great movie villain thinks that they are acting for the greater good of the world, their family, or an organisation.

Take for example Shooter McGavin in the movie Happy Gilmore. He believes in his heart that he is protecting the integrity of the golfing fraternity by stopping Happy Gilmore from being successful. All of his actions are driven by this belief and it is this that allows us to empathise with him, despite how horribly he is conducting himself.

Another example of this is Robert De Niro's character in "Meet the Fockers". The guy is a complete arse to Gaylord Focker and makes his life hell throughout the movie, but we know deep down, he is simply trying to protect his family.

I know I have highlighted two comedy movies, but the same applies to almost every great villain. Deep down, they believe they are doing the right thing. Even in the screenplay I wrote called "The Paternity Test", the villain who is an international drug lord truly believed that he was doing the crew a favour by doing what inevitably led to harm for many on board the ship.

Breeana's Aunty is no different from these villains and believe it or not, I respect the fact that she believes that what she is doing is for the greater good. It is my opinion though that she is majorly misguided in this belief and this has led her to act in a less than honourable way on many occasions over the past nine years.

If what Bree's aunty has alleged was even close to correct, it would be honourable in the way that she had steadfastly pursued her goal. Unfortunately for her, her family, and myself, her efforts have been well wide of the mark.

Having said that, I am very thankful to have faced such a nemesis. Her actions and behaviour have forced me to take stock of my life, of what I do, how I act, and how I protect myself and my loved ones, and it has allowed me to grow beyond anything I dreamt possible a few short years ago.

I spent the first forty years of my life thinking that people were sent into my life to piss me off and make life hard for me. I knew from working out at the gym that the only way to build muscle was to tear the muscle so it could reform bigger, yet I somehow didn't think that was the case with growing my mind.

It finally dawned on me that the people who I previously thought were a hindrance, were actually helping me. I don't necessarily mean that they were good people and that I had them all wrong. I mean that even though the things they were doing were shit, by going through these things I was benefiting from them; not being hindered.

Just like in the movies, the tougher the villain, the stronger the hero becomes. The more obstacles the nemesis puts in front of the hero, the more muscle the hero builds and the better person the hero becomes.

In each of the Rocky movies, Rocky's opponents get tougher and tougher. As a result, Rocky had to dig deeper and work harder, but ultimately, he became an even better fighter than he was in the previous film.

As much as it pains me to be too complimentary about a woman who has acted in what is quite a disturbing way in trying to ruin my life, I am thankful for having a nemesis with as much conviction as Breeana's aunty. While most of what she has done, alleged, or sought was way off the mark and downright ill-informed, her tenacity and determination are to be applauded.

Because of the circumstances of this entire situation, I am much stronger, wiser, content, and most of all; happier than I have ever been. It sounds absurd that going through such a horrific situation over several years could produce such outcomes, but that is how life and God work.

We all go through trials and at the time they seem insurmountable. If we have faith and realise that at some point in the future, this too shall pass, then we can all find a positive outcome from any challenge that life throws at us.

Even my screenwriting mentor has taught me this lesson. A few years ago, upon leaving the twentieth-plus draft of our movie script on his doorstep, he called and let rip at the quality of what I had written.

Despite this man being my former teacher at school and a long-time friend, his words which culminated in him calling me a C.U Next Tuesday (I'm sure you can figure that one out) and questioning why I was wasting his time, upon reflection, were the best thing that could have happened to me.

Despite the fact that his verbal tirade had me, a forty-five-year-old man in tears, what occurred only a few short days later was a screenplay that had changed so significantly that he not only gave me my first positive feedback in twenty years, but it left us both believing that we finally had the makings of a story that could get to Hollywood.

God only ever gives us challenges that we can handle. I know that I have questioned this myself recently, but when I took a moment to think about it, I realised that it was true. I knew that if I hung in there just a little longer that the current challenge would also make way for better times.

Life moves in seasons, just like the earth does. It's not always summer, nor is it always winter either. When the stock market goes down, you don't sell; you buy. Instead of running on the wheel like a hamster and getting nowhere, ride the wheel to the top, then all the way to the bottom and back to the top again.

If you're wondering why I've spent a substantial portion of this book telling stories of seemingly obscure things that I've observed, along with adding song lyrics, the answer is simple. Go deep! That's the key message here.

Most of us live a "surface life" and therefore only have "surface happiness". We also relate better to stories than being told what to do. I love telling stories and intertwining the message in more of a subconscious way, than blatantly preaching about something.

Treasure is always buried well below the surface and so are the keys to happiness in life. Back when I used to tolerate talent shows that largely manipulated its contestants such as Pop Stars, Australian Idol & The Voice, the most common note judges would give to contestants was the same note that all good singing teachers give.

That message was to connect with the lyrics; don't just sing them. Any great singer will understand the meaning behind the lyrics and the feel that the original artist was wanting to portray in the song. Music is the most powerful way to elicit emotion, but most amateur singers fail to connect with the song and therefore their audience.

In all aspects of life, the same message applies. Most of us are living a "surface life" but the real juice of life is found by going deep. That's why throughout the book I've relayed stories of how I've looked deeper at things.

I'm not suggesting that you dive deep into Quantum Physics or even Metaphysics, just look beyond the surface of things. This is why I bag the media so much. Mainstream media report on the surface for the sake of clicks and hits on websites. If you go deeper into every story they portray, the truth is much different than what they suggest.

Even with mine and Breeana's story, this is the case. I'm not suggesting you believe everything I say. You should not blindly believe anything you read. You should go deeper and find out the truth for yourself. That's when you will gain a deeper understanding of any topic and life itself, and that's where you will find happiness.

Don't let other people or organisations dictate what you believe. Without being cynical, question everything. People and organisations are always pushing their own agenda and unless you are armed with your own knowledge, you will be easily swayed. As they say "he who believes in everything, believes in nothing."

You are in control of how you feel and that begins with your convictions and beliefs. As Incubus' 2000 hit song 'Drive' begins "Sometimes I feel the fear of uncertainty stinging clear. And I can't help but ask myself how much I let the fear take the wheel and steer."

If you don't take control of your mind and your life, they will control you. As the song continues "It's driven me before and it seems to have a vague, haunting mass appeal." Why follow the masses? Most people aren't happy, so why strive to be like everyone else?

And then comes the answer as the song approaches the chorus, "Lately I am beginning to find that I should be the one behind the wheel." This is your life, so live it as you want to: not how others want you to.

SUNDAY NIGHT INTERVIEW

> *"I am willing to be the villain in someone else's story in order to be the hero in my own"*

When I agreed to a sit-down interview with Denim Hitchcock for the Sunday Night program in 2018, my motivation for doing so was the same as it is today, which was to shed some light on these topics and hopefully inspire others to move beyond their dark moments.

Up until then, I had barely said a dozen words to the media because of the way they manipulate things and misguide the public. Watch any news bulletin and any smart person can see right through their lies.

I reluctantly agreed to the interview because Melissa Doyle and the show's producer Rebecca Cox had flown up from Sydney to have lunch with myself and my lawyer. They had hounded me by phone for weeks beforehand and this continued for months after as well. During that time, they told me that they wanted to shed light on suicide and wanted the public to know my side of the story.

Having dealt with media prior, I knew that they would not just want the truth without Breeana's family's lies because the truth doesn't sell advertising spaces on television; only scandal does.

After much reassurance that Breeana's family had not been contacted, I agreed to shoot some footage at mine and Breeana's old unit, some footage of me driving my speed boat around the Broadwater, as well as a sit-down interview.

What most viewers don't know is that when I was filmed entering my old unit as part of the story, I had been there chatting with the crew for ten minutes before we started filming. I had also lived in the unit for ten months after Breeana killed herself so when the camera rolled and I entered the unit, it was hardly an Oscar-winning performance.

Rebecca said it would make a great shot if they filmed me entering for what was supposed to look like my first time in the unit since Breeana committed suicide.

One thing about being an entertainer is that you need to know your strengths. I was a world-class singer, once upon a time an award-winning professional dancer, but at no point would I classify myself as an actor. Apart from an extra role (As a cop) in the Lindy Chamberlin story and a speaking role as a detective (go figure) in Forensic Investigators, I have never professed to be an actor.

I have friends that are incredible actors who have been in Hollywood blockbusters and in 2001 and 2002 I even worked for the man who voiced the 1980's kid's cartoon "He-Man", but I knew my limitations.

Incidentally, when I worked with Blain Fairman who was He-Man, and also the doctor in the movie Aliens, I got him to do the He-Man voice for me which was a fucking blast and took me back to my childhood.

Like most things, I could have trained myself to be a decent actor, but I preferred to focus on becoming the best dancer, then singer possible. My acting was sufficient for musicals, but not for movies, television, or lying to audiences by trying to fake emotion walking into my old unit.

The truth of it was that I had walked in that front door hundreds of times after Breeana killed herself and pretty much every time, I had that same feeling of my breath being taken away as was the case when I turned and saw her jump to her death.

CHAPTER 6

For several weeks after Breeana's death, I would come home from work, open the door, stare at the spot on the balcony rail where she jumped, and expect her to come bounding out of the bedroom with that gorgeous big smile she used to always have for me when I came home to her.

As was the case every time I opened that front door for the rest of my lease, the night I walked in during filming, Breeana wasn't there so the mere sight that was in front of me felt more like a "clinical reaction" for me as I had spent months adapting to that situation and view, so as to not lose my shit every time the realisation of Breeana's absence in our apartment hit me.

Two nights before my interview for the program, I received a call from my friend with who I did support act for Vanilla Ice. He was my manager when I was eighteen and we have remained friends since. He does quite a lot of extra work and was called to a job in the same building that Breeana and I lived. He was told he was to play the part of a security guard and was given some brief details of how filming was going to go.

Because we have known each other for so long, he knew my story, so he questioned the producer if this was in relation to Breeana Robinson's death. When she advised him that it was, he said he was not going to be a part of it because he was a close friend of mine. (Small world hey). As soon as he left, he rang me to let me know. At that point, I knew that the entire situation was going to be a stitch-up.

Despite the apparent stitch-up, I rocked up to the hotel I used to be concierge at in Surfers years earlier for the interview. From the moment myself, Denham, and my Lawyer Chris Hannay sat in the room, Channel Seven were on the back foot.

Unexpectedly Chris piped up before the interview started by asking "How do you want me to interject if you get too heavy with the questioning?" Everyone including myself was stunned at Chris' boldness, but while I remained calm on the surface, underneath I was pissing myself laughing.

"Don't fuck with us" was the clear message Chris sent by saying those words. I had agreed that no question was off-limits and I knew of my own ability to handle idiot reporters, so I wasn't too worried, but this was a good start for us and it set the tone for the rest of the two hours.

Throughout the interview, Denham tried to set me up and corner me with either stupid or irrelevant questions. On each occasion, I was articulate, direct, and snuffed out each attempt he made to make me look bad.

At the end of the two hours, Chris said that it was awesome to watch how I controlled the interview and put Denham in his place on several occasions. "You handed him his own arse on a platter," Chris said.

Unfortunately, as smart people know, the media may not always control interviews, or get the dirt they want, but when they don't, they still find a way to cut and edit questions and answers to make even the best-trained interviewee look bad.

The version that the show aired a few weeks later was vastly different from the copy I have of the two-hour interview. The show also included blatant lies by so-called "eyewitnesses" claiming to have heard screams and moving furniture on the night of Breeana's death.

Even though Breeana and I had a disagreement on the night she killed herself, at no point was there any screaming. Breeana was not the type of girl to scream and even though I have had arguments with other girlfriends, I found it impossible to yell at Breeana. She was the most beautiful soul and even when I was upset at her, our argument would be no more than a robust discussion.

To the alleged point of "moving furniture" I have laughed a few times when hearing or reading about this comment. While Breeana and I lived there and even after she died, I often heard what sounded like someone moving furniture over the floor.

Given the concrete floors and walls in each unit, it was hard to decipher where the noises came from but I thought it was either the unit directly above us or one on either side of that unit that was making those noises.

It seems that someone in a unit near us had the same troubles working out who was moving furniture but of course when people were harassed by Police following Breeana's suicide, the topic was brought up and the Police thought it would help their desperate attempt to pin something on me.

This was then relayed by the tenants to Channel Seven during their interviews, despite no evidence that we were the ones moving furniture.

We never did find out where the noises came from but on a few occasions throughout my year-long lease, security came to my apartment to say that they had received a complaint about me moving furniture. On one such occasion, I was in bed when security knocked, so even they were baffled at where the noise came from.

CHAPTER 6

I'm pretty sure that during my interview with Channel 7 Denham asked about this. Apparently, the noises that were heard by others were like metal scrapping on tiles. I explained that not only was it not true but simply not possible that the noises could come from our unit.

You see, the lounges I had at the time had metal legs, but because my previous lounge room was carpet, I bought plastic casters for each of the legs to sit on so they could glide and not tear the carpet. In order to protect the tiles in our new unit, I left the casters on each leg as well. This meant that if anyone was to slide the lounges then it would be effortless and very quiet.

Having said that, two of the three chairs were against the wall so there was no reason for Breeana or myself to move them. The only time they were moved was well after Breeana's death when the dust had built up on the wall behind the lounges as a result of them never being moved.

Even after several years of contemplating this, the only thought I could add, was if Breeana moved one of the chairs closer to the TV so she could see better, because of her eyesight.

Even that doesn't seem plausible, because I never saw her do that when I was home, so it doesn't make sense that she might do it any other time. Either way, the chairs would certainly not sound like a "scrapping noise" as was alleged.

In the interview with Channel 7, I was asked the blunt question, "How many women have you slept with?" I don't think I have heard a more inappropriate question come out of a journalist's mouth.

We all know that smart questions are not journalists' strong point, but this one was just ridiculous. The question itself was invasive and is none of anyone's business, but for a journalist to ask it shows how desperate he was to claw his way back after being figuratively knocked down so many times to that point of the interview.

Imagine the feminists screaming and the uproar if a woman was asked the same question.

At the time, I side-stepped the question because like I said, it was inappropriate and also because I didn't want to be disrespectful to any past partners; regardless of how I felt about them.

Denham was alluding to the fact that there was a "list" that I had supposedly kept with the names of all the women I had slept with. Yes, there is a list, but at that point, it wasn't anyone's business. (It still isn't anyone's business)

Having said that, I guess I should address that topic, as it is somewhat unsavoury. There has been much talk about the alleged "number of victims" that I supposedly have and that the Police have a list that they were going through.

There is a list and while I am not too proud to admit it, there is quite a substantial number of names on it. Okay, so there are over two hundred names on the list. There. I said it! There is no specific reason for having this list, other than the fact that there are far too many women who I have dated (more specifically slept with) for me to remember all of them.

I started keeping the list when I was in my late twenties. My best mate and our other friends were all married and were constantly complaining about how they were envious of my lifestyle. It's funny how we all want what we don't have. Back then, I wanted the wife and kids and they wanted the bachelor life that I lived.

The boys hit me up at one of their buck's nights and asked how many girls I had slept with. Having downed a few drinks before the question being asked, I tried to recall the girls' names in chronological order. Throughout the night I kept remembering new names and this led me to sit down a few days later to try to accurately account for all of them so I could give the guys a definitive answer.

Even after having spent a good amount of time compiling the names, I found myself remembering other names over the next week. This led me to keeping the list until I was certain I had accounted for every girl I had slept with.

Now that I had the list, I didn't see the harm in keeping it. At no point was it intentional, or an egotistical thing so I could boast to anyone. The list was and still is for my eyes only. No one has ever seen it; except the Police now.

I keep a list of the 400+ destinations that I have visited. I have a list of the 1,500+ books that I have read. I keep a list of the 1 million miles I have sailed, and I keep a list of how many kilometres I travel each year totalling 484,624 km as of 2019.

Keeping these lists doesn't mean that I'm going to stalk my destinations, nor does it show any intent, so why would a list of women I've had sex with suggest this? This is how ridiculous that claim by Police was when they hit me with nine stalking charges.

CHAPTER 6

An interesting thing is that quite a few female friends who were on the list have told me that the police have called and harassed them; even though some have been married for a decade. In all instances, they said that the detective was aggressive and pushy. They also said that the detective was trying to lure them to say bad things about me.

One friend told Police that I was a gentleman and very respectful, to which the detective said, "Well you must be the lucky one." This is an example of how even highly trained officers are human and can be dictated by their emotions, ego, and the pressure of getting answers to something that may always remain unanswered.

With the advances in technology, I keep very little day-to-day information in my head these days. I'd rather save my grey matter for absorbing new information through books.

I have notepads on my phone, each one with crucial information that I may need throughout the day. This information may be in relation to business or simply facts and figures that I want to refer to, but don't want to have to try to recall them.

The notepads ensure accuracy of what I need to refer to without me having to clog my mind up with things that are not always required. By keeping so many notes, I never have to worry about remembering something and this frees my mind to focus on things that I want to, rather than constantly having to think about what I need to do or remember.

I recommend this approach for anyone because it really does free up your mind for important things. Just like a hard drive on a computer, if you fill your brain with too much shit, it runs slower and is less effective.

I know we only really use 5% of our brain's capacity but unless you're one of the few who is accessing the other 95% then I recommend offloading non-urgent information into what is really a part of us anyway (your phone).

The list of my sexual partners was never shown to anyone (not even my best mate of forty years) and I had never disclosed the actual number of partners to anyone, other than when I had a fight with a girlfriend years later.

During the fight, she made some comment about me not being able to get laid, so I shot back with "That's not what 200 women said." Stupid, childish, and well, she laughed and didn't believe me anyway, so who cared, right?

I really didn't think anyone would see it or know of its existence. If I wanted to boast about the number of women I had slept with, I would have told Denham Hitchcock that it was over two hundred.

A part of me wanted to tell him because at the time the media were claiming that there were "more than ten victims". Doing the math, that's less than 0.5%. Most businesses or escorts would be happy with a complaint's ratio that low.

I AM FUCKING KIDDING.!!!

I know I am making light of what is offensive to some people and sensitive to others, but you have to admit, the fact that this list is even being discussed by media is not worth taking seriously.

My point is that while compiling, having, and keeping the list is one of the dumbest things I've done, there was no other reason for it, other than because I have a pretty shit memory. Ask anyone I've met and they will tell you that I am terrible with remembering even one name, so how could I be expected to remember over two hundred? In hindsight, it's also a great reminder of the other 200+ mistakes I have made in my life.

All jokes aside, I don't consider any of my partners as mistakes per se. In some strange way, they have all been a part of the journey and I have learnt something from every one of them.

NEVER TRUST THE MAINSTREAM MEDIA

Anyone who saw what aired that Sunday night would have been forgiven for thinking that I was some sort of monster. Someone who is a predator, a misogynist, and someone who always treats women like shit. That's precisely what Channel 7, the producer Rebecca Cox and Denham Hitchcock set out to achieve, regardless of what the truth was.

Close friends called me the following day and were filthy at how wrongly the show portrayed me. My close friends were furious. The interesting thing was that my screenwriting partner mentioned that his wife, who I had known for several years seemed to think what she saw was true.

This caused huge issues at the time for the relationship because he could see exactly how Channel 7 manipulated the story, yet somehow, she was blind to the network's behaviour.

He had taught film and television and media studies at high school for thirty years so he knew exactly what the program had done. She,

CHAPTER 6

on the other hand, was too ignorant to find out the truth and had already made her mind up.

I wasn't too bothered about the hatchet job Channel 7 did that night. The issue for me was that once the media publish something like that, it's out there and can't be taken back. The media are very quick to defame someone but extremely slow to apologise or make amends. They did the exact same thing to Lindy Chamberlain in the early '80s and it wasn't until recently that it was even remotely corrected.

The man who did most of the damage to Lindy Chamberlain's reputation was actually Denham Hitchcock's father, Kevin Hitchcock. It took Kevin Hitchcock more than three decades to apologise to Lindy Chamberlain for the way he portrayed her during his time as a journalist.

Let's see how long it takes his son Denham to realise that he too was wrong in the way he tried to portray me as a murderer in his misleading Sunday Night story in 2018.

Whether that apology shows up or not, one thing is for certain; the Hitchcock name has a long history in Australia of misleading the public for the sake of a headline. They have shown that they will happily attempt to destroy people's lives in order to further their careers.

Unfortunately for them, in both cases, their targets (Lindy and myself) have benefited by becoming stronger people as a result of the Hitchcock slander. The clues of both Kevin and Denham's deceit actually sit in their surname; "Hitch-cock".

"Hitch" means to "move something to a different position with a jerk". In other words, to manipulate something (such as a person's opinion) to a different place than where it originally was. And "Cock" ... Well; 'nuff said.

After her convictions were overturned, Lindy was asked in an interview if she had learnt anything from the saga that she had endured, to which she replied, "don't trust the police." While I agree in part with this statement, I believe that there are many good police officers that are doing a great job; often under trying circumstances.

I have four cousins who were police officers and three friends who are also retired cops, so I know not all police are tard with the same brush as the detective who chased notoriety at any cost by charging me with murder.

In both Lindy's case and mine, it is clear that there are dishonest detectives, but I'd like to believe that they are the exception, rather than the norm. The media on the other hand are almost all dishonest.

So while I do hesitate to trust Police, I would trust far more police officers than I would trust journalists.

The police may overlook evidence, or choose to ignore things that might make them look bad, but the media just make shit up. The media have a flagrant disregard for the consequences that their actions cause those who they are slandering. The one thing both industries have in common though is that both are rarely held to account for their mistakes; regardless of how monumental they are.

MY REAL MESSAGE; THAT YOU NEVER SAW

As I mentioned earlier, when Channel 7 approached me and throughout their begging to get "my side", they constantly said that they wanted to bring light to suicide and to start the conversation about suicide and cyberbullying.

These were the only reasons I was willing to do any sort of interview. This is also the only reason I will agree to do any interview in the future as well. I was not interested in defending myself or continuing down the same path of what the media had pursued for the previous few years.

At the end of the interview, Denham asked, "So what would you say to anyone struggling with depression or going through what Breeana went through?" Now, keep in mind, when you see the interview that aired, this question and several other questions about this topic were never aired.

If you saw the program that aired this question might seem out of place. In the context of where Channel 7 led me to believe the program was headed, this question was all part of the theme.

Unfortunately, this part of the interview was never going to be used and was a ploy by the producer Rebecca Cox to make me think it would be a "balanced" story; which it certainly was not.

When asked the above question, I said that many years ago I had read a book by Paul Hanna, and in the book, Paul said that he wakes up every day and says to himself, "Nothing will happen today that I can't handle."

I went on to say that I started saying the same thing to myself every morning and sure enough, each day when I went to bed, I looked back at the day and realised that nothing had happened that I wasn't able to handle.

I told Denham that this had been my mantra for over twenty years, and I recommend it for everyone. I then mentioned that I wished that

Breeana could see how much she had grown in the months before her death after her mother kicked her out of home.

I said that if she had just held on for one more day, perhaps things would have been different. I quoted the lyrics from the 1990 song "Hold On" by Wilson Phillips that are "Don't you know things'll change, if you hold on for one more day" and that was how the interview ended.

The song itself was one that I wasn't a big fan of in 1990, but for some reason, it came to mind at that moment when I was asked to think of something inspiring for anyone going through depression or a tough time.

I always thought the song was about a break-up, but it is actually about personal inner strength. I thought I'd share the lyrics below in the hope that they inspire you if you're ever struggling to put one foot in front of the other.

The lyrics of the song are more relevant these days than they were in 1990 with the amount of pressure on people of all ages as a result of social media. Besides the chorus that I quoted in my interview with Sunday Night, a couple of lines that really stand out are, "No one can change your life except for you. Don't ever let anyone step all over you."

Hold on – by Wilson Phillips

I know there's pain
Why do you lock yourself up in these chains?
No one can change your life except for you
Don't ever let anyone step all over you
Just open your heart and your mind
Is it really fair to feel this way inside?

Someday somebody's gonna make you want to turn around and say goodbye
Until then baby are you going to let them hold you down and make you cry
Don't you know? Don't you know things'll change
Things'll go your way, if you hold on for one more day
Can you hold on for one more day. Things'll go your way
Hold on for one more day

WHAT OTHER PEOPLE THINK OF YOU IS NONE OF YOUR BUSINESS

You could sustain
Or are you comfortable with the pain?
You've got no one to blame for your unhappiness
You got yourself into your own mess
Lettin' your worries pass you by
Don't you think it's worth your time
To change your mind?

Repeat Chorus

I know that there is pain
But you hold on for one more day and
Break free the chains
Yeah I know that there is pain
But you hold on for one more day and you
Break free, break from the chains

Repeat Chorus

Don't you know things can change, Things'll go your way
If you hold on for one more day. Can you hold on?
Can you hold on?

Incidentally. Another thing that viewers of the Sunday Night Show did not see, and might think is quite alarming and somewhat distasteful, was how the interviewer Denham Hitchcock conducted himself when he perhaps thought the cameras were not rolling.

As part of my committal hearing, my barrister gained access to all of Channel Seven's footage from the program. While some of it was used to illustrate to the court how Denham Hitchcock coerced some interviewees to say certain things, what I found interesting was irrelevant to my committal hearing, but showed me what sort of a man Denham is; or more precisely how much of a man he isn't.

In some of the footage, Denham and the producer are seen telling a couple who lived in the same building as Breeana and I exactly how to say certain things and even what they should say.

CHAPTER 6

Over several takes the couple either didn't say things the way Denham wanted them to, or they simply didn't want to. It was clear to the court when shown this footage that Channel Seven was trying to mislead the public. This is precisely why the media should not have any influence on our legal system.

The media have an agenda and are biased in their approach to stories. This is a dangerous thing, but thankfully for us, our judicial system in Australia is far more robust and ethical than the media.

What was even more disturbing though, was how sleazy Denham was towards Breeana's cousin Bianca during out-takes of her interview. The fact that Bianca was an attractive woman, should not have been an excuse for Denham's behaviour.

Not only were Denham's sleazy advances towards a stranger inappropriate and totally unprofessional but at the time, Denham was engaged to his now-wife. Of course, as you know by this point of the book, I am no angel, however, I think it is important for people to understand the double standards that some journalists live by.

WHO IS THE REAL STALKER?

After my interview was recorded, the usually annoying and pestering Rebecca Cox from Channel Seven suddenly disappeared and was not contactable by myself or my lawyer Chris. We contemplated getting an injunction to stop Sunday Night from airing the story, but we decided to let them hang themselves. We figured that the amount of publicity that this story was gaining would help us in the long run.

As I mentioned in "The No B.S. Approach to Create the Life You Want" journalists are like prostitutes. Once they've screwed you to make money, they don't want to talk to you.

This was the case with Sunday Night and was also what happened with Channel Nine's Brittany Klein. Brittany had my lawyers on speed dial for months and used to pester them relentlessly asking them if I would give a comment or interview.

On one occasion I did give a brief interview and like all media, they manipulated it to suit their biased and negative agenda. The funny thing was, that Britany literally stalked me for months in a way that would have seen her jailed if she wasn't hiding under the disguise of a journalist.

In contrast, when I sent her TWO text messages several months later to inform her of my real story "The Blame Game" coming out and to see if she then wanted to do an interview, she called my lawyer and said she was going to make a stalking complaint to police if I didn't stop. I know right. I pissed myself laughing at the irony.

Why am I even bothering typing this? Well, there are still some people who truly believe that the media accurately reports the facts of stories we hear and read. This leads to much ill-informed anger, which in turn leads to online bullying and violence.

While I am not blaming the media completely for this, if they showed a responsible duty of care, the problem would be significantly reduced, and fewer people would be suffering from depression and cyberbullying.

MORE ABOUT "THE LIST"

When news first broke about how police had a list of over two hundred women that I had slept with, I felt a little embarrassed, but also relieved. For the several years that I had kept this list, I had not shown a single soul.

The only way anyone else could have seen it prior to the police getting it was if my only live-in girlfriend since having the list found the excel sheet labelled "data files" while snooping through my external hard drive and took a look.

Given that my old phone that I had when Breeana was alive also went missing when Casey lived with me, I wouldn't be surprised if she found the file and gave them both to her other lover who was a cop, or gave them to someone he knew to gain revenge on me.

Even though I am a very honest person, one lie I did tell on a few occasions, was the number of partners I had been with. Most men brag about their numbers or embellish the number and most women lie by subtracting a few.

I on the other hand would be very vague when asked by girls what my number was because I know how judgemental, yet hypocritical some women can be. Now that the truth is out, it is what it is and I and any potential partner need to accept it.

The list was not to boast or brag. Even my best friend of forty years, who knew everything about me, only knew of its existence and not its contents as he had never seen it either.

In hindsight, the list was a way for me to accurately remember some of the most important moments in my life. When people ask me about whether or not I had been to a certain place, I usually answer

"Yes" but when they ask for specific details about the destination, I am often stumped because I've been to so many.

The list of partners is something that jogs my memory of times of my life that are long gone, but that were important in the overall journey. Each woman that I've dated was unique and each one of them (despite some issues) provided me with fond memories, regardless of the final outcome.

For example; I don't look at the list and see Dolores' name and think of how she physically attacked me to the point where Canadian police were going to arrest her for domestic violence, or how she jumped out of my moving car as we travelled at 30kph along Surf Parade in Broadbeach.

I see her name and think about how many fun times we had like the night she ran from her cabin to mine completely naked on the Tahitian Princess ship. She knocked on my door and I knew she was naked, so I waited a while before letting her in. Our cabins were in passenger areas so the chance of an elderly passenger walking past and seeing a hot, busty Canadian girl standing in the corridor, was high.

When I see Charlotte's name on the list, I don't think of how she faked a pregnancy or threatened to tell my girlfriend that we kissed in order to have sex with me before costing me a six-figure job as Cruise Director.

Instead, I laugh and think of the threesomes with her and another female cast member or the nudie runs around the ship with her and a soon-to-be star of London's West End.

Even though I discredit many of my romantic partners for the sake of a good story, I have been very blessed to have shared intimate times with all of them. Despite our differences and incompatible personalities, each and every one of them has had at least one very special quality that I adored.

Even though most were stunning, one was a multi-millionaire and a few were quite famous overseas, I was always more attracted to special qualities that ran much deeper than superficial attraction.

My life is one that many people find hard to believe has occurred, but somehow it has. I have been so fortunate to have done so much in the first half of my life that some people question if it is all true. I have travelled the world and experienced things that so many dream of, but never get to do.

Aside from my former best friend of forty years and my family, the women who make up the list, have been the biggest part of my life. I have shared good and bad times with all of them. I have shared things physically and emotionally and in some small way, each and every one of them has made me who I am today.

Regardless of what they think of me, when I look at the list, I remember the good and choose to forget the bad. I wouldn't take any of them back and the feeling would be mutual, but I don't see the point in holding onto bad thoughts of someone who once meant enough to me that I was intimate with them.

Don't get me wrong, the majority of the list's "participants" were not relationships. Most were fleeting encounters, one-night stands, women I met at swinger's clubs and swinger's parties, and girls I met at the nudist beach or on Tinder.

Regardless of who they were or how it happened, I am glad that we shared that time together. I mean, even I shake my head sometimes when I see the names on the list and think of the circumstances.

Having married men wanting to watch me bang their wife while they watch horse racing in the next room, or while they watch on with five other guys.

I look back and think "why on earth did I do that?" Some of these things might be considered by some as immoral, or distasteful, but I can be certain that when I'm on my death bed, I will be laughing to myself while making the nurses gag while taking care of me, as I recount my tales. At the end of the day, it was always consensual and respectful, so where's the harm in it?

I agree that giving a female waitress at Coco's nightclub $5 for a taxifare so she could get a cab to my place when she finished at 3 am to shag me might be slightly distasteful, but she didn't seem to mind that I left my front door open for her so she could sneak in and wake me and she was happy to leave when she was finished.

Shagging a hot Thai wife while her husband played poker in the same room might not be everyone's description of wholesome fun, but I'd rather do that than take drugs for fun.

These women were empowered and were able to explore their own sexuality as much as I was. Isn't that what we're all about these days? Some of them were older, some were married, and some were just wanting casual intimacy so no harm, no foul.

Yes, I concede that having sex with a different married woman at a swinger's club while her husband and five other guys watched is not the norm for most people, but hey, I'm a performer so I saw it as just another stage, and "the show must go on". Once again, I am having a

CHAPTER 6

laugh and making light of the bizarre situation that unfolded, so make a note that I don't care if it offends you.

My other point to all of this is that life is to be enjoyed. As previously stated, no one was hurt, and at no point would any of them have felt unsafe in these situations. The world applauded sexual minorities for exploring boundaries, and we are accepting of women finally opening up sexually, so why can't men be the same? After all, unless the women are exploring their sexuality with other women, then some man has to be the one to benefit; right?

As much as I have no desire to revisit any of these situations, I found it interesting to share myself with two women, married women (with their hubby's consent), have women use me purely for sex, or sleep with older women.

I even dated a couple of "professionals" as part of the journey. By that, I mean we dated. It wasn't a business transaction; although there was also a "business transaction" in Thailand from memory.

All of this coincided with an old school buddy's buck's night where I found out some very useful information about his new career. His twin brother, myself, and my best mate had all met in grade one, but by this point, we didn't see each other that regularly. Two of the group had started families and I was travelling the world so having the four of us catch up in one place was pretty rare.

The groom-to-be had been a paramedic for many years so when I asked how that was going, I was pleasantly surprised when he informed me that he had moved into the pharmaceutical industry. There were about six of us standing around when he explained that he was now selling the direct competition for Viagra.

As you can imagine, everyone's eyes lit up; including mine. He laughed and said he often thought of me and my bachelor lifestyle and thought I'd be a perfect candidate to "test" any new products so he could give firsthand results to doctors to whom he was trying to recommend the products.

My immediate response to this was "Well that would stop me from rolling out of bed on a rough night on the cruise ship." This drew much laugher from the slightly inebriated men in the group.

I asked him why he couldn't test it on his fiancée to which he laughed, "You are so naive if you think married men get sex." He said he had a boot load of stock and that he'd pop over on Monday morning to give me some; if I wanted. "Sure," I said and thought nothing more of it.

At six o'clock on Monday morning, my phone rang, and it was Darren. He informed me that he was out the front, so I jumped up and headed downstairs. As I walked out the front door and around to the open boot of his company car, I realised that even though he was drunk the Saturday night before, he was not kidding about having a boot load of this stuff.

I'm not sure how a woman would feel walking into Tiffany's and knowing she could have not just some, but all of the contents of the store, but I would guess that it would be a similar feeling to that moment for me. My eyes must have been as wide as a deer in a car's headlights on a remote road because Darren started laughing at my reaction.

He began reaching into the boot and grabbing various boxes of Cialis. Apparently, there were all different types and he wanted me to give them all a run and give him some feedback on how they all went.

I've never taken part in an official drug trial or been anyone's guineapig, but I was up for this challenge; so sorry for the pun. Darren loaded me up and as I stood there with my arms fully grasping more boner pills than a worldwide swinger's convention, my best mate's dad came out of the house.

At this time, I was between six-month contracts at sea and was only home for a few months, so my mate's parents were kind enough to let me stay with them instead of having to rent a place for a short period.

As my "second dad" came out and saw what was going on, he asked Darren if he could try a sample. Darren happily loaded him up with an armful of supplies. Just as we were both ready to take our stock inside, my mate's mum came out to see what was going on.

When we told her what we had, she immediately told her husband to put his stock back in the boot and to go inside. Thankfully she just laughed as she saw the amount I had and said while smiling knowingly, "I hope you don't come back with ten children," before going back inside.

I admit that over the next few months, I became slightly obsessed with finding willing participants to test these products and how far I could push this whole "having fun" thing. I recall a few times when I actually couldn't focus on work at all as I was too busy communicating with several women in order to not knock back an opportunity when it presented itself.

Once back home from ships again, this led to a two-hour drive to Noosa to meet a smoking hot wife who wanted to shag me on their couch while her millionaire husband watched. It also led to another occasion with a six-hour round trip from the Gold Coast to North Brisbane and back where I went to bed with two women, (in different suburbs) in one night. I even met a nudist woman who invited me to a nude dinner at her place, before the inevitable took place later in the night.

Now. Here is the most important part of this story of debauchery. It would come as no surprise to you to hear that none of this made me truly happy. I had a wonderful time and some amazing sex, but it will be no surprise to you to discover that I was not fulfilled.

Yeah, my superficial ego was bursting, and hearing my best mate howl with laughter as I relayed some of the stories to him was priceless but other than sowing my wild oats, there wasn't much more to gain from all of it.

The reason for the lack of real satisfaction had nothing to do with my performance or the performance of my sexual partners. It came from the fact that I was either living this lifestyle as a way of punishing all women for past hurt, or I was trying to fill a void in a completely inappropriate way.

Women do this a lot when a relationship ends. I have met many girls who have ended a long-term relationship and then go out and sleep with dozens of men in the space of a year; or even a month. I am not judging them and most of my "list" comprises of these types of women, so I have benefited greatly from their attitude. My point is that in the long run, this only hurts the person involved.

I share these stories not to boast of sexual conquest or of unsavoury exploits, but rather as a way of saying "This is me, and no matter what, that's okay". I share them so that you can look at things you may have done and know that if I can be ok with my past; then you can too.

While some of these stories may seem distasteful, they have in some way been a part of what molded me into who I am. In the context of storytelling in social settings, these yarns have brought much joy and hysterics to my friends as I recount them with much vigour.

Unlike many people, I have never done drugs, never smoked and I rarely drink. Okay, so I used to pull out a cigarette and start "bum-puffing" on rare occasions in nightclubs as a way to freak friends out because they knew I hated smoking and it used to make them laugh.

I also pretended to be stoned when on tour with the "Australian Backstreet Boys" and "Spiced Girls" in order to make the rest of the crew roll around in hysterics when they thought I was off my tree.

My point is that most people look for vices outside of themselves as a way of compensating for their ability to cope with their own insecurities. My vice was to have casual sex in many different settings and situations.

When we go searching for something outside of ourselves, or inside someone else, (pardon the bad sexual pun) it never ends well. From the age of seventeen when my second girlfriend dumped my ass, I always seemed to be searching for happiness in someone else.

Perhaps this stems back to my disjointed relationship with my biological mother, or perhaps that is merely an excuse that I have held onto for so long that it seems to be the best logic I can conjure up to validate my behaviour.

Either way, I have finally discovered that true love can only be found within. The love we share with others is like the notes on a piece of sheet music for the sweetest love song, but it is the love that we find inside ourselves that are the spaces between the notes, that is what makes the beautiful song come to life. Without the spaces; all we have is noise.

DOES GOD LAUGH AT YOU TOO?

> *"If you want to make God laugh; tell him your plans"*
> – Woody Allen

Have you ever had grandiose plans in life, only to have them be obliterated? That's God's way of reminding you that he is in charge. I had everything planned as to how life was going to work out when I left cruise ships in 2008. And. Well. Let's just say that none of what I envisaged has eventuated.

Having said that, I don't mind God's version; even if it is far more challenging than the one I had planned. My plan had the marriage, mortgage, kids, etc, but more than ten years later, not one of them is part of my life. I must say that I'm glad they aren't.

There is no way in the world I would have chosen to go through what I have been through, but I can tell you now that I am much happier and a better person for having been pushed in this direction.

The old me was looking for a simple life, but that's nowhere near as rewarding as the growth that I have experienced by being thrust into such tumultuous circumstances over the past decade.

Back then as I plodded along post-ship life, I was insecure, fearful, reactive, abrasive, and self-righteous. Now, as a result of God's vision for me, I am much stronger, empathetic, giving, loving, purpose-driven (Outside of myself), and forgiving.

These are all traits that I had inside me, but which I had not let out. It took for my life to be shaken to its core for me to discover them. It was only when I had no other option but to look beyond my usual thought processes in order to survive that I discovered a new way of thinking, a new way of living, and an entirely new set of traits that I never knew existed in me. It was only when I had no other option that I surrendered to God and let Him guide me in a different direction in all areas of my life.

As a result, I now see each and every area of my life in a different light. The way I earn money, spend money, interact on a daily basis, and how I see myself have all changed dramatically.

I mean, there is no way I would have dreamed that I would have gained two diplomas, two advanced diplomas, and read 280 books all in one year, but I did. That year (2016) set me on a path that I would never have thought possible for me. 280 books grew to over fifteen hundred books and from each book came so many lessons about all areas of life.

Back when Breeana died, I had dreams of working with charities on a grand scale to help others overcome suicide. After several of my attempts were shot down by Breeana's family and ill-informed media, I realised that to contribute on a grand scale, you don't have to do grand things.

Now I look for ways to help others every day in a small way. This in time adds up to a grander scale than I could have ever done in one go.

When travelling to Bali in 2017 and to the USA and Caribbean later that year, I found myself looking for opportunities to share. They say, "If you won't give a dollar out of one hundred, then you won't give ten thousand out of one million."

There is no point saying you will donate once you have money because we never usually do. Now is the time to start, regardless of what you have.

When visiting Bali, I contacted a local orphanage that I knew was doing great work and I convinced Virgin Australia to give me an additional 30kg in baggage allowance. I then asked all of my friends to donate kid's clothes and I purchased some essentials that the orphanage needed.

I literally travelled to Bali with the clothes on my back and two suitcases and my carry-on bag full of stuff for the kids. Instead of dropping the clothes off at Kuta, I trekked up into the mountains and delivered the stuff in person. Wow! Am I glad I did?

When I arrived at the orphanage, a group of kids rushed me and started chatting and showing me their toys. The staff took my bags while I went and hung out with the kids. I had the opportunity to walk around the place and see all of the great work the doctors and staff were doing for these kids who were all suffering from debilitating diseases. I left the orphanage and was so touched by the experience that I vowed to do something every time I travelled.

In December of that year when I arrived in Las Vegas after my Caribbean cruise, I was at a loss how I could replicate my experience in Bali. I was in Vegas just before heading up to the mountains nearby for a white Christmas, so it was extremely cold at night.

As I wandered down the strip, I noticed a lot of homeless people begging for change. On more than one occasion, the homeless person had a dog or young puppy with them.

This brought tears to my eyes. It was only a few years earlier when the shit hit the fan that I lost everything except for the roof over my head and my two dogs.

During that time, I grew even closer to my pups and fully understood what it meant to have "Man's best friend" by my side. I realised that if I had my dogs, then everything else would be fine.

As I continued down the street, I thought to myself, "These people may or may not have a choice to be there, but their dogs don't." Their dogs were doing what all dogs do; they were loyal no matter what.

I headed to the ski resort a few nights later and on Christmas Eve, I decided that instead of sitting by the fireplace with Santa, eating homemade cookies, and drinking, I would drive down to Vegas and spread some cheer. I headed off on the forty-five-minute drive and along the way, I stopped at a grocery store.

I loaded up with water, chips, snacks, fruit, and small tins of dog food. All up it only cost me USD$50. I then stopped at the nearby cinema to watch "Pitch Perfect III" which was released that day, but not yet in Australia. I know – It's an entertainer thing. I love those movies.

As I waited for the movie to start, I threw a few dollars in a pokie machine. Two spins in, I won $50. Now if that's not the law of attraction and the law of equality working, then I don't know what is.

I watched the movie and continued into the strip. I grabbed dinner at Hooters Casino (Yes, they used to have a casino) then grabbed two shopping bags in each hand and headed down the strip.

CHAPTER 6

As I walked along, I saw homeless people, but I kept walking. For some reason, I was suddenly too shy to stop. What if they abused me? What if they robbed me? "Are you fucking kidding," I thought to myself. "Stop thinking about yourself and do what you set out to do."

I headed over one of the overpasses and saw a young guy with his dog, both curled up, trying to keep warm. I slowly approached and when I was within earshot, I said "Hey, mind if I join you?" The young guy looked up and said, "Sure."

I sat down and patted his gorgeous little staffy pup. I said, "Are you guys hungry?" He nodded, so I pulled a bottle of water, some muesli bars, and chips from the bag and placed them in front of him.

He smiled as I reached in for a can of dog food. I opened the ring pull on the can and put it in front of the puppy. I thought my two dogs ate fast, but this little fella inhaled the contents of the tin in seconds. The poor pup must have been so hungry and petrified that if he didn't eat it fast, then someone might steal it from him.

I sat for a few moments and chatted with the guy as people walked past, oblivious that we were there. As we chatted a young lady walked up and handed him two bottles of water.

I looked up at her and we smiled at each other before she continued. It was nice to see that there were people in the world who had a similar thought to me. I said goodbye to the guy and his dog and continued down the strip.

Over the next hour, I found nearly ten guys and girls who were all sleeping rough. I didn't just want to hand out food. I wanted to share some love and show that even though they were out on the streets, they weren't totally alone. They all had a unique story and it was so humbling to hear their stories and realise how easy it can be for any of us to end up in a similar situation.

When it came time for the following Christmas, I wanted to do something similar in my own backyard. I was home for Christmas and given that I no longer spend Christmas' with family, I wanted to make this sacred day a little better for someone else.

A week before Christmas I went to Big-W and bought 20 x $5 gifts and wrapped them all up. I found out that "Rosies" (A local charity for the homeless) did their nightly coffee/meal van at the local church in Surfers Paradise.

I packed my presents into a huge Santa sack and lobbed at the church for a cup of coffee. I sat quietly in one corner and as the homeless people arrived, I dragged my Santa sack over and handed them each a present. The shock on their face was worth the small effort I had gone to. Once again, I sat and listened to their stories.

One lady told me how she had just given birth a week ago to twins who were six weeks premature. The babies were still too sick to leave, but she was released from the hospital.

She had lost her home and was on the streets. This was heartbreaking to hear, but it was good for me to hear it, as it made me realise that even with everything that I had been through, I was lucky.

The reason I am sharing these stories of me sharing with others is two-fold. No matter what happens to us, there is always someone worse off and no matter how bad we have it, there is always something we can do to make life a little brighter for someone else.

I can tell you from my own experience that the little money I spent in Bali, USA, and at home and the little time and effort it cost me, is nothing compared to the incredible warmth and life lessons that I got in return. My gifts may have helped in a small way for these people, but what I got back was tenfold.

For Christmas 2020, I thought I'd do something different. I still bought a few hundred dollars worth of gifts, but instead of finding homeless people to give them to, I thought I'd give them to some heroes who have kept the world safe during the COVID-19 pandemic; the nurses. The shock on all of the nurse's faces when I handed our gifts in the wards of the University Hospital on Christmas morning was so humbling and heart-warming.

The nurses were genuinely surprised that someone understood what a thankless job they do every day. The biggest kick for me was as I handed out gifts and quickly walked away, I heard one nurse read the card that I attached out loud which read "To: A Hero. From: The world".

I thought it was a nice little touch and the nurses all seemed to appreciate it. The nurse yelled as I disappeared, "You're the hero", to which I turned and smiled while saying, "No. You are." I honestly admire people who so thanklessly put the needs of others before their own as nurses and carers do.

Depression, anxiety, and stress can all be greatly relieved by having a purpose greater than yourself. For the most part, we live in a way that is totally self-centred. As I have previously said, you're the only one who is going to take care of you, but the kicker is that we need to be careful not to get too caught up in "us".

By having a focus and purpose bigger than yourself you will find that you don't stay in a place of stress or suffering for long. It is true that what we focus on, we bring more of into our lives, so focus on sharing love and that is what will come back to you.

THE BIGGER THE OPPONENT, THE GREATER THE HERO

> *"Whatever the mind can conceive and believe, it can achieve"*
> *- Napoleon Hill*

Every single one of us is on a hero's journey; whether you realise it or not. I want you to think of each event that happens in your life just like a hero in a movie would. The hero we love the most is the one who overcomes insurmountable odds to reach their goal. Just when we think they've conquered the antagonist, something else happens that seemingly puts them back to square one.

Throughout life, you're going to get knocked down. The key is (As Sylvester Stallone famously said) "It isn't about how hard you can hit. It's about how hard you can get hit and still get back up again."

Get knocked down seven times; get back up eight. That's the key. The hero never gives up. The hero is usually never reactive either. From time to time, they react to events around them, but for the most part, they take charge of the situation, stand tall, and face their greatest fears.

At first, when I was all over the front page of several papers at home and around the world, I wished that all the haters and abusers would leave me alone. Over time, I realised that they were doing me a favour by making me much stronger than I ever dreamed possible.

If you want to know how to become a better person; embrace challenges and opponents. They are brought into your life to help you become your own hero and achieve the dreams you have in life.

To become a better fighter or athlete, you need to fight better fighters or compete against faster and better athletes. If something comes easy, you won't appreciate it, but if you have to fight and struggle to achieve it, it will mean so much more to you when you achieve it.

WHAT OTHER PEOPLE THINK OF YOU IS NONE OF YOUR BUSINESS

THE GREATEST OF LESSONS ARE FOUND IN THE SIMPLEST OF PLACES

> *"To live, is to suffer. To survive is to find some meaning in the suffering". – Frederick Nietzche*

In my book "The No B.S Approach to Create the Life You Want; I recalled a great story that I heard by one of my favourite authors; Dr. Wayne Dyer. It's his interpretation of how one of the world's most famous nursery rhymes has in fact some of the most incredible lessons for living a happy life.

At the time, the media tried to put a negative spin on the story, so I'll repeat it here in the hope that I can educate them while enlightening you.

The story Dr. Dyer tells involves the nursery rhyme "Row, row, row your boat". I'm not sure if this is something that he came up with himself (highly possible), or if he himself was relaying the story. Either way, I want to share this story again with you. I am paraphrasing, but I am sure you will get the gist of it.

The first verse of the song, which we all know so well, goes like this: "Row, row, row your boat, gently down the stream. Merrily, merrily, merrily, merrily, life is but a dream" If we take the lyrics and break them down, there are some clues, as to how to live a happy life.

"Row, row, row your boat" – The song doesn't say row someone else's boat. It says row your boat. Stop trying to live your life on someone else's terms or the way that they live theirs. Do what you want to do and live how you were meant to live.

"Gently" – There is no mention in the song, of rowing your boat forcefully or aggressively. Row your boat gently and peacefully. There is no rush. There is no finish line in life. We are all living on different time frames, so if someone gets a pay rise before you, buys a house that's bigger than yours, or gets a better body faster; that's ok.

There is no need to compete with people who are running different races. It's like having a scientist and a bodybuilder compare themselves to each other. You are rowing your boat, at your own pace.

"Down the stream" – I personally couldn't think of anything more stupid, than trying to row upstream and wondering why I am getting nowhere. As Tony Robbins says, "It's like running east, looking for a sunset. No matter how fast you run, it is not going to happen."

Life is not meant to be so hard. If you believe that it is, then that is why it is that way. Let the river of life take you to where you are meant to go. Yes, you can negotiate obstacles along the way, but stop trying to battle against the currents. Go with the flow.

"Merrily, merrily, merrily, merrily" – Most importantly, enjoy the ride. Embrace every moment. Be grateful for everything that you experience. The more grateful you are, the more things to be grateful for that will show up. When you're happy, happy things, events, and people present themselves to you.

Finally; "Life is but a dream" – Everything that is in your external world began in your internal world. Everything that you have in your life, is a result of what was once just a dream. Dream big and dream often. Dream of everything that you desire, then watch those dreams manifest into reality.

BEING CHOSEN IS A GIFT

Throughout my life, I have always known that I was adopted, and I have always known that it was my grandparents who adopted me. I have seen my biological mother marry and have two more children with her husband who she is still with more than forty years later.

We have shared a special bond as brother-sister/mother-son, and for the most part, this has been hassle-free, yet on occasions in my own head, I have had many unanswered questions about the situation.

While my adopted mother and father were alive, the topic was almost taboo. By that, I mean that Sue was so petrified to bring the subject up for fear of Dad scolding her, that it really wasn't talked about.

The downside of this was that even though I felt that there were no issues with the situation, subconsciously I was holding onto feelings that were perhaps unhealthy. The topic of why Sue gave me up for adoption, or how she could do that was never discussed and this left me feeling somewhat lost.

As an adult, I can see logically the reasons why she made that decision, but that has not always been the case. Like most adopted people, the feeling of abandonment was front and centre and in hindsight, this somewhat dictated how I approached romantic relationships up until recently.

Like anything in life, these feelings of abandonment were driven solely by my own perception of the events that had occurred decades earlier. Perception is what dictates almost everything we do and how we feel on a daily basis.

WHAT OTHER PEOPLE THINK OF YOU IS NONE OF YOUR BUSINESS

Some people wake up and see rain and think, "What a miserable day" while others see the exact same situation and think "Awesome. My grass will get some much-needed water." Rain is a good thing if you're a farmer, but maybe not so much on your wedding day.

Speaking of rain on your wedding day. On the day that Sue got married in 1982, it absolutely pissed down. Even though I was only eight, myself and everyone who was there that day can remember how torrential the rain was all day. I guess it is true that it is good luck for it to rain on your wedding day. It all comes down to your perception.

There is a well-known story of two identical twins who grew up with an abusive, controlling, alcoholic father who used to beat their mother, as well as them. They were interviewed many years later in their thirties and what was discovered was remarkable.

The first son was a drunk, unemployed, and abusive to his wife himself. When asked if his upbringing had anything to do with how his life turned out, he said, "How else could my life have turned out with a father like that?"

The other twin was happily married with a great job and a long list of achievements helping his local community. He too was asked the same question, but what was surprising was that he gave the exact same answer; "How else could my life have turned out with a father like that?"

Everything in life is a matter of perception. My situation was no different. I went through life wondering if I was truly loved. My parents weren't really my parents, so how did I know that they truly loved me? This was something that simmered on an unconscious level until May 2016.

I have been a huge fan of the life coach/performance coach, Tony Robbins since he first flooded our late-night TV screens with his infomercial for his "Personal Power" tapes in the late 1990s. In 2001 I bought his "Get the Edge" CD set and got a lot out of them but somehow, I still had the same unanswered questions and a mostly unfulfilled life.

In 2016 I was contemplating what to do with my last $7,000 that I had in my bank one Saturday afternoon. My original thought was to buy a quadbike, but thankfully a different thought took over.

I remembered that Tony Robbins held his signature six-day event "Date with Destiny" on the Gold Coast each year so I checked out when the next event would be. As luck would have it, the event was only a month away.

CHAPTER 6

I called the company taking care of tickets for the event and found out that the price was $6,995 per person. Now normally you can get the event for a lot less, but with only a month to go, I was paying full price.

I had always wanted to go to the event but could never justify the cost of doing so. People always said that this was a limiting belief and that the event would more than justify my investment, but until I actually did it, I just couldn't see how. FYI: I now see how and I am so glad I took the leap. I literally spent my last $7,000 to attend this event, but it has paid off tenfold in the last seven years.

I don't have time to explain the many ways that this event changed my life, but let's just say that almost every area of my life has benefited from spending more than eighty hours with this incredible human being. The part I want to talk about in particular was in relation to my before-mentioned thoughts about my adoption.

It was on the first evening, about nine hours into the day's proceedings when a lady in her forties stood and Tony began interacting with her regarding her mental roadblocks in life. The lady explained that she was adopted and that she blamed her biological mother for her life.

Tony explained that her blockage was a result of her not blaming correctly. He suggested that if she was going to blame her mother for all the bad shit, that she must blame her for all the good stuff too.

For me, this hit home. I blamed Sue for many things, but I didn't blame her for the wonderful life that her parents gave me which was a direct result of the choice that Sue had made all those years earlier.

You see, if you're going to blame, you need to blame properly. I used to blame Breeana's family for her death and for so many bad things, but now I blame them for being the reason Breeana was such an incredible young lady.

If they were more loving and supportive, Breeana would never have been as incredible as she was. I now blame them for this wonderful opportunity that I have to help others and hopefully save lives. I blame them for pushing Breeana right into my arms so that we could have such a beautiful love, even if it was for only a short time.

Even though this realisation at Tony's event was a huge breakthrough for me, what came next was even better. Tony explained to the lady that her adopted parents did not have to love her. He reminded her that her adoptive parents chose to love her.

A biological mother has to love her child; even if it looks like a monkey. That is how humans are wired. But a complete stranger has no chemical ties to a child, like a biological mother does, so for a stranger to love a child is even more special.

God knows my grandparents could have put their feet up and enjoyed retirement, but instead, they chose to love me and raise me as their own. Apart from the spiritual debate that we choose our parents before we are born into this world, we can't choose our children.

We must just love them. However, any person who adopts, or fosters a child chooses to love that child, and that evening with Tony Robbins, made me realise that the love that I had been given was a greater gift than most children receive.

This is not to lessen a mother's love for her own child. I am merely suggesting to anyone who has been adopted and perhaps felt less loved, that in fact they are more loved (or at least equally as loved) because they were chosen and not just born into a family.

To understand that I was not abandoned, but rather I was chosen was life-altering. Not only did I discover this incredible fact, but in doing so, I realised the power of one's perception in life.

These days, no matter what happens to me (including being charged with murder) I look at the situation and make sure I am perceiving it in the best way possible. Everything in life is a gift and every single thing that happens to you is an example of life happening for you; not to you.

CONCLUSION

DON'T STOP BELIEVING

I've always been someone who spends more time outdoors than indoors. That's probably why I felt so at home on the water and at sea. As I mentioned in my most recent book "C.R.U.I.S.E" there is no better feeling than sailing along with the sea breeze in your face as your cares just wash away.

Apart from watching cartoons as a kid, I've never really been a big watcher of television. Throughout the years the most memorable shows for me were the "slightly off-centre" shows that didn't appeal to everyone.

In the seventies, it was Welcome Back Kotter, then The Love Boat into the eighties, before The A-Team took over. In the nineties, I pretty much skipped TV, and then in the "noughties", I was at sea so I missed the start of what became my two favourite shows in recent times; Two and a Half Men & Glee.

While you regain your composure from laughing at a late-forties guy rating Glee in his top two shows, let me make it clear that I was not a fan of Glee while it was on TV. It wasn't until 2019 when I was on bail that I watched my first episode.

As a professional entertainer, I kind of thought that the show was all fluff and not a true indication of the "entertainer's journey". I now know that this assumption was way off.

You can actually sum up my life by looking at my favourite TV shows of all time. These five shows give you an insight into my life and personality. A rebellious (Welcome Back Kotter) playboy bachelor (Two & a Half Men) entertainer (Glee) obsessed with cruising (The Love Boat) with a non-confirmative desire for justice (The A-Team).

The funny thing about that analogy is that the more I look at it, the more precisely it fits. I was always the class clown; like Arnold Horshack. Just like Charlie Harper, I performed on several radio jingles throughout Australia and New Zealand. I didn't fit into one category in school. Like Finn Hudson, I was the captain of a sporting team who also became the leading man musically. I spent ten years at sea and fell in love on every cruise; like the people on The Love Boat. And finally, my friends often called me "Murdock" because I was the crazy kid who did the things that no one else had the guts to do.

Besides being a "singing/dancing" show, what I failed to realise about Glee was that the show not only captured the essence of what it was like to have that dream of being an entertainer, but it perfectly embodied the secret to living a truly authentic life.

Throughout the one-hundred and twenty-one episodes over six seasons, Glee's creators left us with some memorable moments with all the sparkle and sequins that you would expect from a group of wannabee entertainers with stars in their eyes.

Even with that being the case, by far the most pivotal point in the entire show's history was created in the final moments of the pilot episode. Will Schuester (Glee club teacher played by Matthew Morrison) was grappling with a heart-wrenching choice between becoming the man his family, wife, and society wanted him to be, or following his lifelong dream of performing.

I too faced that same choice at the age of twenty-three when my then-girlfriend gave birth to our beautiful daughter. I had to choose between my dream of being a performer or being a responsible father and partner etc. It took a few years for me to realise that as much as I wanted to be the best father I could be, I would never be happy unless I pursued my true calling.

When you start rehearsing a new show, it is hard to see the finish line when everything seems so foreign and nothing gels the way everyone hoped it would. I have lost count of how many shows I have been in where it is the day of opening night and even though everything should be perfect, the dress run / technical run is a complete fucking dog's breakfast.

Everyone has lost faith; no one believes the old adage that "She'll be right on the night". You even start to wonder if this is the beginning of the end of your career. Just then, by some sort of divine intervention, everything clicks, harmonies blend perfectly, choreography hits that sweet spot and you feel like you are precisely where the universe intended you to be.

In the Glee scene, Emma (Guidance councillor) gets Will to watch an old video of him performing on stage when he was a student. On reflection, Will smiled and said, "That was the greatest moment of my life."

CONCLUSION

Emma looked up from the laptop screen and simply asked, "Why?" Right then Will's whole demeanour changed as he replied, "Coz I was doing what I loved. Being a part of that, in that moment, I knew who I was in the world."

Will then brought himself back to reality with a thud by saying that he had to provide for his family, at which point Emma suggested that the only life worth living is one that you're truly passionate about.

That is that pivotal moment that appears seemingly out of nowhere, but in reality, it is a result of you following your passion and knowing in your soul that it is where you are meant to be. In Glee, Will Schuester realised the same thing as he left the school's guidance counsellor's office and headed down the school corridor to quit teaching. As Will pauses, he hears the culmination of passion and dedication echoing through the halls.

In that moment, Will realised that he was about to give up on his dreams and settle for the life that other people wanted of him and not the one that was embedded in his heart.

It took his thrown-together group of musical misfits to show him that the journey of following your passion is the only thing that will make you truly happy and that no matter what, you should never stop believing in that.

The real kicker was the perfect song choice that the glee club was singing at that very moment. A song by the band "Journey" called "Don't stop believing". As Will stood at the back of the school's auditorium, with his eyes welling up, the teacher became the student.

He realised that his greatest legacy in life was the impact he could have on his students. This beautiful synergy goes full circle in season five when all of his many Glee club members return from their own lives, (that Will Schuester inspired), to perform the same song as a tribute to him and his soon-to-be-born child.

The greatest lesson that I have learnt is that in order to live a truly authentic life and one that will make you blissfully happy, you have to follow your dreams. Not the dreams of your parents, your partner, your peers, or society, but those that are weaved into the fabric of your very existence.

The dreams that you were born to live. The ones that make you bound out of bed and inspire you all day. Whatever your passion, follow it, enjoy the journey, but whatever you do; "don't (ever) stop believing".

On a side note, Glee tackled more controversial topics of its time than any other show in history. These include Gay sexuality, Lesbian relationships, transgender, bullying, suicide, inclusiveness, racism, teen pregnancy, slut-shaming, disabilities, obesity, domestic violence, religion, STD's, mental illness, body shaming, gender identification, and several other more discreet ones that I missed while watching the entire series.

These are all the topics that make people uncomfortable, but ones that needed to be addressed. As I mentioned earlier, before watching Glee, I thought my former friend was crazy for not letting his teenage daughters watch it. Then as I starting watching it, I realised that maybe he was protecting his girls from all the hidden (And not so hidden) sexual references that the show threw up.

As I approached the end of the sixth and final season, I realised that more than likely the real reason he refused to let his girls watch Glee was because the show tackled all of the things that made him (and most people) feel uncomfortable.

The things that are not discussed openly or honestly; but should be. We often do what is easy or what feels comfortable in life, while putting off, or avoiding what is uncomfortable. This is another reason why domestic violence, suicide, bullying, and other issues in the world continue to be a problem.

So let's get uncomfortable and make a difference. Doing what is comfortable may feel better in the short term, but it is doing what is uncomfortable that feels better in the long run. Above all else, Glee endeavoured to share with its audience that feeling that only entertainers understand when they sing, dance, or act. The feeling of giving such happiness to those with who we share our God-given ability.

That feeling is the one that is summed up in one of the simplest TV show names ever created; Glee! Some of us entertain for the adoration, some for the money, and some for the prestige of the title, but all of us do it for the love of seeing the way that we can make people feel with what other people call "talent".

While Mark Twain famously said that we should "Dance like nobody's watching, love like we've never been hurt and sing like nobody's listening", I instead encourage you to "Dance because the world is watching, love until it hurts, and sing so that the entire world can share in your joy."

CONCLUSION

LOVING THYSELF

> *"Mastering others takes force. Mastering thyself takes strength."*
> *- Lao Tsu (in Tao Te Ching)*

After being released on bail in 2019, I reclined on my super comfy couch and watched old episodes of Two and a Half Men (The better versions with Charlie Sheen) on my monster flatscreen TV. As I chuckled every few minutes at Charlie's antics, I realised that my life wasn't too dissimilar to Charlie's.

Sure; the closest I got to that type of luxury was the before-mentioned couch and TV and I'm not a millionaire living in Malibu but hear me out. I don't drink, smoke, or gamble and I don't live with my dysfunctional brother and nephew, but there are still many parallels in my life compared to that of both Charlie the character on Two and a Half Men, and Charlie Sheen the actor.

On the surface, we both appear to be afraid of getting close to women for fear of getting hurt. We both love sex and are open to trying lots of interesting things with women and even though I am not paid as well as Charlie, our love of sarcasm and witty comedic timing are second to none.

Oh, and we both have stalkers who just won't go away. His is named Rose and mine calls herself Amanda and has been stalking me for over a decade now.

The thing that makes Charlie so relatable to me and many people is that while he seemingly lives every man's dream, just like the hero I mentioned earlier, he is flawed; as are all of us.

For many years, I too lived the dream and was blessed to be paid well to do what I loved and to travel the world. The position that I had also came with the added perk of being thrust into the fantasies of many women on board.

By that, I don't mean that I was some sort of God or sex symbol. I mean that for most of us when we watch a movie or see a theatre show, for the duration of the performance, we see the lead character and become somewhat swept up or besotted by them. If the performer does their job well, then it's natural that we drift off into some sort of idyllic fantasy.

When the movie ends, quite often this feeling lingers. In the case of a cruise ship singer, more often than not passengers would see me around the ship throughout the rest of their cruise.

WHAT OTHER PEOPLE THINK OF YOU IS NONE OF YOUR BUSINESS

Fellow crew members would see me in the bars and crew areas too. This often led to me interacting with them and subsequently that "fantasy" going further than it otherwise may have.

It's not that I had many more offers than most guys; alright, I had quite a few more. It was more a case that because of my desire to find love outside of me, rather than realise it from within, I rarely said no; even if I should have.

I think we can all relate to searching for something outside of us; just like Dorothy in the Wizard of OZ. We want wealth, love, possessions; all in the hope that it will bring us eternal happiness. In my opinion, none of that will bring lasting happiness or fulfillment.

The only true happiness that can be found comes from within. Sure. We can achieve things in life that make us happy for a moment or a short time, but if we try to use that as our way of discovering real happiness, then we will always be chasing something instead of discovering what happiness really is.

Love is the same. I thought that someone else was the reason for my happiness or sadness. My love or hatred. My peace or chaos in my life. When these people (usually partners) didn't live up to my idyllic expectations, I was left disappointed, frustrated, angry, and feeling betrayed.

What I now realise is that while another person can enhance your life, that won't occur unless you are the driver of the "happiness/love vehicle". In every area of our lives, most people try to control external forces such as people, circumstances, organisations, and even nations in order to discover their ideal feelings and situation.

I learnt long ago that I cannot control a person, the weather, politicians, media, or in fact anything in life; other than my own feelings, how I perceive things, and how I act or react to those situations.

As psychiatrist and holocaust survivor Viktor Frankl once said, "When we are unable to change a situation, we are challenged to change ourselves."

For more than a decade Breeana's Aunty has tried to control me, my life, whether I was in jail, if I had a job, who I dated and how my quality of life was. She was constantly on the phone to the media and even my employers and current girlfriends when she managed to find out who they were.

While this may have seemed honourable to her, she failed to realise that her pain, her hurt, and how to overcome that, would only come from within. It was never going to happen by controlling me or the legal system.

She may gain some superficial satisfaction from trying to make my life hell or seeing me in jail, but it will never truly bring her the level of peace that she would find by looking within for the answers she desired.

I too tried to change the outer landscape to find that peace of mind. I wanted to stop the media from defaming me and harassing me the way they did. I tried to stop Bree's aunty from stalking me and spreading such horrific lies and I continued to look outside of me for the love I had always longed for. In the end, I realised that none of these things were moveable and more so, none of them would bring me what I eventually found inside myself.

On my journey of devouring over fifteen hundred books in eight years, I found answers to many questions, but it was by chance that I stumbled upon true love. During my time of long stretches of being single, I found that I had to make myself happy instead of relying on others to do so.

Slowly but surely, I grew more comfortable with being single, spending nights alone, and enjoying my own company, instead of trying to find happiness and love in other people.

As a person who used to always bounce from one girl to another in either relationships or casual flings, this was a huge change of approach. I won't lie. At first, I spent much time thinking about how I could meet someone and who I could date/spend time with to fill the void that I perceived existed in my heart.

As time went on and as I began giving myself the things that I had relied on others to give back then, I realised what has been said many times in the most clichéd of ways. "True love comes from within; not from the outside".

We've all heard it and most of us laugh when we do, but having found that myself, I now know it to be true. It is only once you find that inside yourself that you can receive it and give it to someone else.

Try filling up someone else's cup with water from your cup when your cup is empty. You can't. If you have nothing yourself, how can you give it to someone else? If you have no money in your wallet, you can't give it to another person, can you? Love is the same. If you don't give it to yourself, you can't give it or receive it from others.

On top of this, if you go looking for it in others, it will never be good enough. This is precisely why I was never satisfied with any relationships I was in. Even though I should have avoided some of the girls I was with, there really wasn't too much wrong with them. The only thing wrong with them was the same thing that was wrong with me at the time.

We both lacked self-love and were looking for it in each other. Whether or not any of them would admit it, I saw it in them, but at the time I didn't see it in myself. We were both looking for it in each other and because neither of us had it, things turned pear-shaped quickly.

Before my adopted Mother died, my Dad used to love pottering in the yard on his own, or just sitting and reading. When Mum died, he sold their house, bought a campervan, and began travelling up and down the east coast, migrating as the weather fluctuated.

He mostly spent his days alone and appeared to prefer it that way. I used to feel sorry for him and wonder how lonely he might be, but what I didn't realise was that he had actually discovered one of the mysteries of true happiness; being comfortable in your own company.

Yes, the purpose of relationships indeed is to magnify experiences, but if you're not happy alone, then you will never be happy with someone else. Now that I too have discovered this, I am certain that when I meet that right person, they will compliment me not just "complete me", as so many people desire their partner to do. I don't need completing.

I am whole just the way I am, so why would I need someone who "completes" me? I'd rather have someone who compliments me. The ying to my yang. The salt to my pepper, or the coke to my Southern Comfort. Someone who is already whole so when combined with me, as another whole person, creates something special.

If you take two incomplete objects like a banana peel and a mango skin and put them together, it ain't gonna end well. On the other hand, if you take a complete banana and a whole mango and blend them together, you get one hell of a smoothie.

If you're looking for someone who completes you then you're not whole and won't make any relationship work. If on the flip side, you are whole and find someone who compliments you then it will be pure bliss.

Having wanted to get married once, but having never been married, I now wonder if this is the best way to be. I am by no means discouraging marriage, but as I said, many married friends envy that I never took the plunge.

The way I figure it, I am either the smartest man in the world or the dumbest for not ever getting married. The thing is, that I won't really know the answer to that question until I am much too old to care what the -truth is.

That said, after sitting through the cross-examination of several of my ex-girlfriends, and what they made up, distorted, and outright lied about during my committal hearing, I am starting to lean toward the first conclusion; that I may be the smartest man in the world!

Either way, at this point in my life, I am still very content with the way things are. I get to do what I want, when I want. I travel where and how I want and I have a lot less stress in my life than when I was in a serious relationship.

Yes, the downside is that I don't have that person by my side along the journey, but as we've discussed, there are always an equal number of positives and negatives to every situation in life.

There is a beautiful quote in the book "The fight to flourish" by Jennie Lusko that read, "If I had my life to live over again, I would find you sooner, so that I could love you longer."

Jennie and her husband Levi are a Christian couple who lost their five-year-old daughter Lenya a week before Christmas in 2012.

When I read this quote, I first thought that I wished that I had met Breeana sooner, so that I could have loved her longer. Although, if I had have met her much sooner, I may have gone to jail for a different reason. In all seriousness, my immediate thought after that was that of an inward reflection.

While the fact that I have now found myself is a wonderful gift, I truly wish that I had found myself sooner, so that I could have loved myself longer. It's a subtle spin on this beautiful quote, but one I hope resonates with you. My wish for anyone reading this book is that you find yourself sooner, so that you can love yourself longer.

LESSONS FROM ED SHEARIN (NOT SHEERAN)

"If it floats, flies, feeds or fucks - it's not a good investment"
- my Dad

Okay, so I added the "fucks" part because Dad would never have said that. Regardless, the rest was great advice from a man who knew the difference between a good and bad investment. My adopted Dad (Biological grandfather) spent his life taking care of at least half of the Gold Coast business owner's investments in the 1970s and 1980s.

When the G.C was a small town, Dad was everyone's accountant. I've lost count of how many times older people have seen my name

WHAT OTHER PEOPLE THINK OF YOU IS NONE OF YOUR BUSINESS

and said, "You must be Ed Shearin's son." Yes, that's right. My Dad was Ed Shearin. It usually gets a laugh when I say I'm related to Ed Shearin.

Growing up, I never knew how good Dad was when it came to investments. We lived in a gorgeous house overlooking Palm Beach and Burleigh, perched high up on the exclusive Skyline Terrace at West Burleigh, but even so, everything else about Dad was low-key.

It wasn't until after his death that I became qualified in the financial industry and to be honest one huge regret of mine was that I didn't discover my love for investing before his passing.

These days I often look at companies and investments and wish I could pick his brains about them or how to better evaluate them because he really did know everything I wanted to know about the industry. We all want to have more money at the end of our life, than more life at the end of our money and he achieved this, despite living until the age of ninety-one.

Apart from financial advice, Dad imparted very little advice about other things unless asked. He was a man of very few words, but when he did speak; you listened. Despite this, you could learn a lot from him by his actions rather than his words.

He read and exercised every day without fail, he spoke only when asked, and only if he had something to add to a conversation, and he rarely spoke ill of anyone. These are all lessons that I haven't always been great at, but of which I want to emphasise are important to a truly happy life.

Jim Rohn, who was Tony Robbins' teacher and mentor said, "Formal education will make you a living, but self-education will make you a life." As I've stated previously, I read at least three hours a day and spend an additional hour or two looking over company financials or listening to podcasts. I also read a lot of movie scripts, which is an essential part of developing as a screenwriter in Hollywood.

In a world where everyone thinks they should be voicing their opinion to the entire world, I myself try to refrain from doing so unless I have something that can help others. Having been subjected to such abuse and harassment, I try not to speak badly of others as I know how it feels to have this happen to me.

So, in summary, nourish your mind and body daily. Speak only when you need to and not when you think you have to and don't say anything to someone else that you wouldn't say to yourself.

If you follow these simple tips, you too could live a long and happy life like my Dad did. Oh, and as for the quote at the beginning of this story, don't invest in boats, animals (horses/greyhounds), or airlines. They are endless money pits.

THE PATH TO FORGIVENESS STARTS WITH YOU

The term "forgiveness" is one that I wasn't comfortable with until recently. Up until my forties, if someone hurt me, or did wrong by me, forgiveness was the last thing I was going to give them. I would never have caused them harm, but I certainly wasn't going to let them think that I was weak by tolerating their behaviour. I began to have a shift in mindset once I stopped being angry at Breeana for committing suicide.

As much as I loved Breeana, as I moved through the various stages of grief, I seemed to stall at the angry/resentful stage. I was angry at Breeana for doing this and putting me through this pain.

I was angry at her mother for treating Breeana so badly in the months leading up to her suicide, but most of all I was angry at myself. While the resentment towards Breeana and her mother faded, the same feelings that I aimed at myself lingered for much longer.

I was angry at myself for not seeing the signs of depression, or taking Breeana's threat to "throw herself off the balcony" more seriously a few weeks earlier. I was angry at myself for not being able to save her and yes, I was angry for that stupid text message that I sent to her when she was in the spare bedroom only minutes before she ended her life.

It's crazy to think that so much love that Breeana and I had and so many wonderful times and yes, text messages, could all be undone by one throw-away text. I know that neither that text message nor the tiny amount of "not so perfect" texts that I sent on rare occasions compare to the thousands of loving ones that we exchanged.

I also know that they were not in any way responsible for her decision that night, but that is one moment in time that I do wish I could relive. It's true when they say that "It takes years to build a reputation, but only a second to destroy it."

As I said a couple of stories ago, I wish that I could have loved myself more so that Breeana's "emotional distance" that night didn't upset me. I wish that instead of being upset with her that I wrapped my arms around her and reminded her that no matter what; I loved her.

Most of all I wish that instead of going to bed to defuse the situation, I went into the spare room and worked through things with her so that she didn't feel the need to give up on me, her mum, her friends, and life itself.

WHAT OTHER PEOPLE THINK OF YOU IS NONE OF YOUR BUSINESS

Any of my exes will tell you that I am not one to walk away from an argument. I would always stand there and slug it out verbally until we resolved it. I was not one to walk away to calm down or defuse the situation. So why did I choose that night to do things differently? Because I truly loved Breeana and I did not want to hurt her anymore by saying something stupid in the heat of a disagreement.

Breeana and I had never argued. If either of us was upset, the other would always play the calming influence. This is a part of our relationship that hardly anyone ever saw. Despite the age difference and different stages of our individual lives, we really did have a special bond and love.

On the evening Breeana committed suicide, I had already sent the stupid text about her having her priorities all fucked up, so I didn't want to make things worse. I honestly thought I was doing the right thing by going to bed. I thought I knew her and thought she would eventually come to bed once both of us were no longer upset with each other.

At that point, I was certain things would have been fine. I don't blame her for not coming to bed. I just wish that she believed in me, herself, and us to at least stop and think about things for a few more minutes. If she did that, she would have been in the spare bedroom when I got out of bed.

At that point, I was already in a better frame of mind. I would have given her a huge hug, reminded her of how much I loved and adored her. We would have talked and she would be alive today.

In hindsight, if I had any clue of what was about to occur, I would have never let her out of sight. No matter how upset we were, or how hard it may have been to resolve what was a petty issue, I would have done whatever I could to have fixed it.

Unfortunately, I didn't and by the time I did surface from our bedroom, she was already on the other side of the balcony railing, and there was nothing I could do to stop her. That said, there had to come a time when I forgave myself for not making the best choice that may have avoided the horrible outcome that was her suicide.

Even though I thought that going to bed was the best thing for us at that moment, in hindsight, perhaps Breeana interpreted my actions as turning my back on her, not just physically, but emotionally too.

For a young woman who had recently experienced her mother turning her back on her, her father turning his back on her years earlier, and then the only person she had in her life doing the same, may have been the straw that broke the camel's back.

CONCLUSION

I certainly know what it is like to feel all alone, but for a young woman who already had many obstacles in her path, this feeling would have only been amplified.

Despite the vicious misleading stories about Breeana and I, we were very happy. At no point did I ever think Breeana was going to leave me, but if she did, or even if she just wanted to go home to her mother, I would have never stood in her way.

I would much rather that Breeana left me and moved back in with her mum than commit suicide. I know that she wouldn't have left me because she loved me too much, but my point is that I would have done anything to save her life if I knew it was about to end.

That's the part that is the hardest to fathom. We rarely fought and when we did, it was as a result of the pressure that we allowed her mother to put on our relationship.

By that, I am not blaming Elaine. She did what she felt was best at the time and Breeana and I reacted how many people would. I just wish that we could have found a way to deal with it so it didn't affect our relationship and Breeana's mental health the way it did.

There is no doubt that her mother kicking her out of home, refusing to give Breeana any of her belongings, and then not calling on her 21st birthday or Christmas truly devastated Breeana.

I always wanted Breeana and her mother to reconcile and I tried so hard for Breeana not to move out of her mother's house months earlier, but for all the gentleness that Breeana possessed, she was a surprisingly strong-willed young woman.

All of these things were why I stalled in the anger stage of my grief and why learning to forgive others, but more importantly, myself, has now been the greatest gift I have gained from this experience.

I thought to myself that if Nelson Mandela could walk from prison after spending almost half his life locked up and still have forgiveness in his heart, then surely, I too could find it in my heart to forgive the Police, the coroner, the media, and Breeana's family for all that they have done to me.

I mean, the entire situation was one series of unbelievable events that had to happen in order for me to be put through what I had endured.

For years I searched for the strength to forgive these people for how they had either not completed simple tasks (Police and Coroner), which should have cleared my name, or how they had misled the public in one way or another for their own benefit or agender.

WHAT OTHER PEOPLE THINK OF YOU IS NONE OF YOUR BUSINESS

While I would like to think that I had forgiven them all by early 2019, to be honest, it wasn't until the shit really hit the fan when I was charged with murder (You have no idea how hard it is to type those words when they refer to me), that I was able to understand why I could forgive them properly.

It was while I sat in the watch house that I realised that I wasn't a victim; I was a messenger. It was once I discovered this fact, that I was able to forgive them fully. As the bible states in "Luke 23:24", as Jesus lay dying on the cross. "Forgive them Father, for they know not what they do."

Somehow the people who have defamed me, accused me, ridiculed me, abused me, or showed anger towards me were doing what they believed was right. Whether misguided or misjudged, they were acting in the best way they knew how. It is for that reason that I can forgive them. Forgiveness of others is good, but forgiveness of ourselves is the only way to true freedom.

I didn't become free when I walked from the watch house, or when I was acquitted of murder. I became free when I forgave myself and Breeana and all those who had done wrong by me.

Some people have all of the physical freedom that the world offers, yet they are prisoners in more ways than any person who is in custody. They say that the truth will set you free, but I have learnt beyond a shadow of a doubt that even more than the truth, it is forgiveness that sets you free. Forgiveness and the truth together will also uncover your true purpose.

God will continue to guide you to your purpose by way of roadblocks, challenges, and blindingly obvious events to show you if you are not on the right path.

Just like in the movie "Field of Dreams" when Moonlight Graham said, "If I'd only been a doctor for five minutes; that would have been a tragedy," he realised that if he became a pro baseball player then he would not have had the rewarding life he had as a doctor.

Moonlight Graham wanted that dream of being a pro player, but in hindsight, his life would never have been as rewarding as it became by being a doctor.

Tony Robbins reiterates this point in his Get the Edge audio program by saying, "Sometimes when you don't get what you want; you get what you need." It's great to have dreams and to do whatever it takes to achieve them, but sometimes by the grace of God, we don't get what we want because God wants us to get what we truly need. Sometimes the thing that we get is even better than what we originally wanted.

Since I wrote my first story in grade nine, "The Ultimate Muso's Party" of which I got an A+, I've always had a passion for telling stories. I've never made a huge amount of money from my books, but I've loved the process of bringing those stories to life.

In one of my screenplays, there is a line where the female love interest says to the protagonist, "The only thing worse than having a lack of sight, is having sight - with a lack of vision." The line is a quote by Helen Keller but fits perfectly in the context of the movie; perhaps one you might recognise the story if it ever makes it to the cinemas.

Besides the fact that it is extremely cathartic to put your life onto paper, it is an eye-opening experience to look at it and realise how blessed I have been to live the life I have thus far. I never dreamed that I'd have to go through so much heartbreak, so much pain and so many hard times, but more to the point, I never realised that it was these things that have brought me the story that I am most proud of.

Not proud of the way I had acted on occasions or the things that I've said or done, but proud that I could rise above them, accept them, and learn from them. Proud to forgive myself for all of them and to be able to come out the other side and share this story.

We are all sinners and saints and we are all here for a purpose. We all make mistakes and while it's one thing to not make them, or to learn from them, it is equally important to forgive ourselves for them. As Dr. John Demartini says, "No matter what you have done or haven't done; you are worthy of love."

I'M SORRY! | PLEASE FORGIVE ME! | THANK YOU! | I LOVE YOU!

These ten words are the centrepiece of the ancient Hawaiian practice of forgiveness, called "Ho'opnopono". I urge you to remember and recite them in your mind throughout your day whenever you have something that you need to cleanse in your life, or perhaps someone (including yourself) that you feel you want or need to forgive.

I first heard these words used in this way on the final night of Tony Robbins' Date with Destiny seminar in 2016, but it was explained in more detail in Joe Vitale's book "Zero Limits".

I strongly recommend this book, as it goes into detail, about how the ancient tradition came about and how it can work in healing your life. The mantra is a great way to let go of resentment and forgive others; or yourself.

WHAT OTHER PEOPLE THINK OF YOU IS NONE OF YOUR BUSINESS

In a nutshell, the mantra recognises that we are all one and are spiritually connected, so if someone has done wrong by us, or has done something that may require forgiveness, then it is ourselves that also requires this forgiveness because we are all interconnected. Even though we may not think about it too often, everything we do affects other people in some way; whether great or small.

It's kind of like taking in second-hand smoke at a restaurant in the old days. It makes as much sense to have a smoking section in a restaurant as it does to have a peeing section in a swimming pool.

Everything we do in life affects other people so my mission these days is to do as much as possible that positively affects others; not in a negative way.

Anyone who has spent time in prison will tell you that the number one rule is to "not do anything that will affect anyone else's time." In other words, don't do things that impact other inmates. If you can adhere to that, then you won't have too many issues in there.

That should be how we live our lives in the outside world too. Everyone has done something that has had a knock-on effect on others. If so, remember the following phrase. "I'm sorry, please forgive me, thank you, I love you."

A MILLION DREAMS

As 2018 came to a close, I was preparing for what I hoped would be a triumphant 2019. I was listening to the radio when Pink's "A million dreams" came on. I'd heard the song before but hadn't taken too much notice of the lyrics. Like I said earlier, the teacher will come when the student is ready and, on this occasion, I was ready to hear these lyrics on a deeper level.

I bought both the Pink version and the version from The Greatest Showman and over the next week, both versions were playing non-stop in my car. Every time I listened to the lyrics, I felt like it was me singing them. Throughout my life, I have had so many dreams. Some have come true, while others remained dreams. I know I am not alone in these feelings, but at that point in my life, the lyrics really struck a chord.

I was still struggling to find the purpose of why I had to experience what happened with Breeana and my subsequent trials and challenges as a result of her committing suicide. It was almost New Year's Eve and I wanted to make 2019 count. As I set myself many goals, one jumped out of particular importance.

CONCLUSION

That goal was to have complete closure in relation to Breeana's death. At the time, an inquest was unlikely to happen because the Coroner was too incompetent to rule Breeana's death as suicide despite overwhelming evidence suggesting that no one else was involved.

There was no way known I thought I would ever have been charged with murder, so I really wasn't sure how the closure would come about. I knew that closure was something that I had to give myself, but I somehow thought that what I envisaged was far greater than just me.

If I am honest, I was hoping that the entire situation would just go away, but as I now know, God works in mysterious ways and he was ready to see me have my wish, but only if he could find a way for me to grow exponentially through the process while being his messenger.

Less than a month later when I was arrested and charged with murder, I sat in the watch house cell beginning to understand how this closure was going to happen. On the previous two occasions that I had spent in the watch house, I had never heard any music played in the cells. There was an intercom in each cell and a button that said "Music" but despite this, I had never heard music there.

To pass the time I had been trying to remember lyrics to songs and one that I was focussed on the most was "A Million Dreams." I could remember the second verse and chorus, but I couldn't recall the lyrics to the first verse of the song.

A few days into my stint in the cell, one of the officers said that a technician was working on the music system and that we'd have the radio to listen to later that day. An hour or so later music started playing in the cell. It was nice to have music but what happened next gave me the clarity that I had been searching for over the previous six years.

The second song to come on once the system began working was "A Million Dreams." I looked up at the speaker where the sound was coming from and smiled. From that moment on, literally a million ideas of what I was supposed to do and how I was supposed to use my situation to benefit others came flooding into my mind. The unfortunate thing was that I had no paper or phone to capture these thoughts, so it wasn't until I was released a week later that I was able to capture them.

Among those thoughts was the idea for this book, and how with the help of authorities I could educate people and help others who were going through tough times through face-to-face and online education.

I also had an idea of how I could take this story and Breeana's story all the way to Hollywood, by way of a screenplay. Over the following week in the watchhouse, this song was on repeat all day and night in my mind and served as my inspiration and my strength until I was released.

These ideas have become my purpose and why I had to experience everything that I have been through. Everything in life does happen for a reason and it is to guide you to your unique purpose that the universe has set out for you. You can deny it all you like, but life will continue to push you in that direction until you wake up and accept the purpose that God wants you to fulfill.

As a singer and storyteller, I love to combine the power of music and lyrics to my storytelling. In the screenplays that I have written, I have broken many rules of screenwriting by doing so, but that is what life is about; pushing boundaries. That's how all the greatest breakthroughs in the world have come about.

Music is such a powerful instrument and can transform our emotions in an instant. I want to share these lyrics below because they remind me that it doesn't matter what other people think about your dreams or aspirations. Your journey belongs to you and only you and no matter how crazy people think you are, never let anyone or anything deter you from turning your dreams into reality.

"A Million Dreams"
by Pink / Ziv Zaifman, Hugh Jackman & Michelle Williams

I close my eyes and I can see
A world that's waiting up for me
That I call my own
Through the dark, through the door
Through where no one's been before
But it feels like home

They can say, they can say it all sounds crazy
They can say, they can say I've lost my mind
I don't care, I don't care, so call me crazy
We can live in a world that we design

CONCLUSION

'Cause every night I lie in bed
The brightest colours fill my head
A million dreams are keeping me awake
I think of what the world could be
A vision of the one I see
A million dreams is all its gonna take
A million dreams for the world we're gonna make

There's a house we can build
Every room inside is filled
With things from far away
The special things I compile
Each one there to make you smile
On a rainy day

They can say, they can say it all sounds crazy
They can say, they can say we've lost our minds
I don't care, I don't care if they call us crazy
Run away to a world that we design

Every night I lie in bed
The brightest colours fill my head
A million dreams are keeping me awake
I think of what the world could be
A vision of the one I see
A million dreams is all its gonna take
A million dreams for the world we're gonna make

However big, however small
Let me be part of it all
Share your dreams with me
You may be right, you may be wrong
But say that you'll bring me along
To the world you see
To the world I close my eyes to see
I close my eyes to see

WHAT OTHER PEOPLE THINK OF YOU IS NONE OF YOUR BUSINESS

Every night I lie in bed
The brightest colours fill my head
A million dreams are keeping me awake
A million dreams, a million dreams
I think of what the world could be
A vision of the one I see
A million dreams is all its gonna take
A million dreams for the world we're gonna make

For the world we're gonna make

LIFE IS ALWAYS HAPPENING FOR YOU; NOT TO YOU

"Knowledge is knowing that a tomato is a fruit, but wisdom is knowing not to put it in a fruit salad" – unknown

We are all going to have pain in our lives. It's your choice to play the victim and allow yourself to sit in that suffering state, or to become the enlightened one who not only lives in a beautiful state, but uses your pain for your own benefit while helping others.

In 2015 and again in 2019 the police took away my music, my camera gear, and my computer equipment, all of which made it near impossible to earn a living doing what I loved doing.

They tried to take away my dignity and for a short time in 2019, they even succeeded in taking away my freedom. The one thing they could never take away was my innocence in relation to Breeana's death.

My story and this book are living proof that no matter what people do to you and no matter what hand life dishes out, you have a choice as to how you act and how you feel. You can roll over and give up, or you can make something good out of it.

The way I see it, life is like running a race. If you want to win a sprint, you might have to endure a little pain, but if you want to finish a marathon, you're going to have to go to hell and back.

The difference though is that the amount of growth and personal satisfaction that you get from the sprint is insignificant compared to what you feel after finishing the marathon. If you want to do something extraordinary in your life, then start praying for some serious shit to go down.

CONCLUSION

You don't build muscle in the gym by lifting the same weight every day. You build muscle from tearing the muscle and having it regrown bigger. Let life tear you to pieces, go through the pain, then watch how much stronger you become as a result.

Most people will never go through half of the things I have endured in recent years, yet they will bitch and moan, or just give up on life because it all seems too hard. They would rather take the "simple life" than build muscle.

I'm not saying this to make me out to be special or to make anyone feel inferior. I simply want to make a point that if I can endure the suicide of my partner, the abuse and public scrutiny over several years, being completely unemployable, and then move beyond being wrongly accused of murdering the woman I loved, then surely everyone can overcome the challenges they face; no matter how insurmountable they seem.

As I stated in the opening pages of my book "The No Bullshit Approach to Create the Life You Want," the greatest people of our lifetime and those who achieved great success, all had one thing in common; they went through adversity and overcame it.

Stevie Wonder, Oprah Winfrey, Tony Robbins, Nelson Mandela. The list goes on and on. None of these people let adversity get the better of them and neither should you.

Remember: If you want to achieve greatness or change the world; start praying for some serious shit to go down in your life!

A NEW REASON WHY

At the start of this book, I listed a few reasons for writing yet another book about Breeana's tragic death and my subsequent battle over the following years. While those reasons remain valid, as I went along this path, I discovered another one.

As Holocaust survivor Viktor Frankl said when referring to our journey through life, "Pain is inevitable, but suffering is optional." We're all going to endure pain in life, but if we can find a purpose to our lives that is beyond ourselves, then our suffering will surely decrease.

When I started writing my very first proper book in 2010, I wasn't sure I would finish it, or if it would serve any meaningful purpose in my life. I could never have imagined writing eight books, but more so, I could not have envisaged how important they have become to me and hopefully others.

WHAT OTHER PEOPLE THINK OF YOU IS NONE OF YOUR BUSINESS

Beyond what these books have done for other people, the economy, or anything else, these books have proved to me that we all have a story. More so, everyone's story is unique, just like we all have a unique fingerprint.

As humans we tend to only share the parts of us that we feel are good, or that other people will love and accept. Therefore, while those close to us may know a lot about us, the only person who really knows who we truly are, is ourselves.

While baring your all the way I always have in my books may make us as vulnerable as entering a nudist colony for the first time, it is equally as liberating.

Speaking of which, no one in the world knew that Breeana and I went to the nudist beach in northern New South Wales while we were dating. Kind of funny because while people could see Breeana's beautiful body, she could only see silhouettes of people.

For anyone who has been to a nudist spot, Breeana's lack of eyesight gave her the advantage of not having to see some of the "not so sexy" bodies that were unfortunately burnt into the back of my fully functioning eyeballs.

When my daughter was born in 1996 it began a chapter in my life that brought more pain over a prolonged period than anything else; other than Breeana's death. For more than twenty years my daughter's mother has been everything you would imagine a woman could be so far as how any estranged parent should not act.

From emotional and physical violence to harassment then defamation and taunting in recent years, she is the prototype that Hollywood screenwriters use when creating the worst type of character in bad break up movies.

All that being said, apart from the previous paragraph and a few small mentions in my other books, I have refused to act in the same way she has acted, either in front of my daughter or otherwise. Unfortunately, the same can't be said about her mother. It is for this reason that I have been denied the opportunity to have a healthy relationship with my daughter over the past two decades.

I know that I have preached throughout this book that we are all responsible for the lives we have, but over many years, the constant torment by my daughter's mother became so painful that even though not seeing my daughter was hard, it was best for my own mental health.

I am not sure what type of person my daughter thinks her father is, but as I near the end of this my eighth book, I know that if and when

CONCLUSION

she wishes to open the pages of any of my books, she will learn who I really am and not what her mother or others may portray me to be.

Apart from a brief meeting with my biological father when my daughter was only a few months old, I never got the chance to know who my father really was. Whether he was an arsehole or a great guy doesn't matter.

What matters, is that like many children from broken families, foster homes, or adopted families, I have always had a piece of my personality that seemed to be missing.

I know that in the grand scheme of things, it probably doesn't matter, but still, I have had so many questions throughout my life that this missing piece may have helped solve. I know that I am not alone in feeling this way. I am certain that any child from a similar situation would feel the same way at some point in their life.

Unlike most areas of life where I profess to have the answers to solve such a conundrum, this is one area where I don't. They say that the simplest ideas are the best, so it may be as straightforward as ensuring that the lines of communication between estranged parents remain open, or that foster children and adopted children are always able to connect with their biological parents in order to fill the aforementioned missing pieces.

I know that my proposed ideas are far more complicated than that, but if we can put a man on the moon and cure COVID-19, then surely, we can solve this mystery too. For my part, I have learnt that my books will ensure that my daughter, and one day her children will be able to flick through the pages and discover the real me.

Not the me that Google searches throw up (Or whatever form we use in decades to come). Not the me that her mother wants to suggest she fell pregnant to, or the me that the media have fabricated.

In my books, she will discover the me that has expressed myself openly and honestly throughout more than seven hundred thousand words throughout my books. That me is the real me. The me that lived life with very few regrets.

The me who will probably make her smile, make her cry, and make her think "what the fuck was my Dad thinking." Either way, good or bad, that's the me who I have grown to love and who I hope she will respect for being exactly who I am.

My other hope is that anyone who has had the patience and or questionable sanity to plough through my disjointed stories and creative use of grammar will realise that true happiness is when you can look at how wonderful you are and how divinely fucked up you are and still love yourself for everything that you are.

BREEANA'S LEGACY

People are often asked what they want their legacy to be at the end of their life and of course, their responses are as varied as their actual lives themselves. To be honest, I've not given too much thought to what I want my own legacy to be, but on several occasions over the past decade, I have wondered what Breeana's legacy might be. I'm certain that Breeana's family might have a different opinion about this, but my thought is that her legacy is as follows.

It has been widely documented that Breeana was legally blind. She struggled with mundane tasks every day that most of us also struggle with for different reasons. For example; She hated cleaning because she couldn't see dirt on the floor or surfaces. We hate the same task but for lazy or self-centred reasons.

Breeana disliked putting on makeup because she simply couldn't see what she was doing in the mirror, whereas most women begrudge this task for its time-consuming nature. I'm certain that if Breeana was given the chance to be able to physically do either of these things later in her life, she would have done them with the joy of a child opening presents on Christmas Day.

All Breeana wanted to do was to see more clearly, yet most of us go through life with the same lack of vision that she had; despite being able to see better than she could. Breeana hid her natural eyes because she was ashamed of them, while we often divert our eyes because we are ashamed of who we are.

Despite what a person might think about themselves, everyone is special and has a unique gift to offer the world. It doesn't matter who you are, what you look like, or what you have done, you are perfect.

As I've said before, I loved Breeana for so many reasons, but it was the one thing that she saw as her biggest flaw, that I saw as her greatest gift and most adorable asset.

When Breeana opened her eyes, she saw very little and what she did see was often a blur. Quite often, despite our perfect eyesight, we suffer from the same problem. Unlike Breeana, it's because we don't take the time to open our eyes to all that is around us.

Despite Breeana's many challenges, she went about life with an incredible appreciation for the things she could do, rather than bitching

CONCLUSION

about the many things she couldn't do. I honestly cannot recall a single time that Breeana complained about not having perfect vision. Like many people with a disability. She just got on with life.

Even though I would do anything to have Breeana back on this earth, if I had just one more day with her, I would swap my vision with hers so that she could experience all the things she missed out on and so she also knew that someone in the world actually understood the challenges that she faced every day.

Perhaps if we all had that understanding of how she and others with disabilities felt, then not only would we be more compassionate, giving, patient, accepting, and understanding, but they too might not feel so helpless, alone, or a burden on others. These are the simple, yet profound lessons that I hope we can all learn from Breeana Elaine Stewart Robinson.

Next time you feel like you're about to judge anyone in life (whether they have a disability or not), take a moment to think about life from their perspective and how you might like people to treat you if you were where they are.

I'm sure that this is all Breeana would have wanted. For people to understand her and the obstacles that she faced and for people to realise that while life can be challenging, it is still an incredible gift to have the things that we do have.

Isn't it true that when we feel most sad or frustrated in life, it is often simply because we don't feel understood by others?

I'd like to think that part of Breeana's legacy is to turn me into the person that I have become and hopefully, someone who has been able to learn and share what I believe can make a big difference in the lives of anyone who is either in a volatile relationship or struggling with mental health issues.

There is no way known that I could have become the person I am today and subsequently written about the topics in this book, without having gone through what Breeana's life and her death have allowed me to experience. Perhaps by way of her life and death being so prominent over recent years, Breeana has also touched many others in an equally profound way.

WHAT OTHER PEOPLE THINK OF YOU IS NONE OF YOUR BUSINESS

THE FINAL WORD

"What people think of me reveals more about themselves, than it does about me" – J.D Moórea

When writing a book, a speech, a screenplay, or a song the most important parts are the beginning and the ending. What goes in the middle is mostly noise. If you can nail the start and the end, most people won't remember what filled in the remainder.

I think life is similar on many levels. We celebrate our birth and death, but those many years in between are largely forgotten. As has been said so many times, "People won't remember what you said or did, but they will remember how you made them feel".

Even though it was more than a decade ago that I retired from professional singing, when I think back on those times it seems like yesterday that I was travelling the world and living my dream.

Of all the hundreds of songs I was fortunate enough to sing, one resonated with me then and haunts me now. On the Pacific Sky, in a show called "Tribute", we had a Beatles section, where I stood front and centre on stage singing the song "Yesterday".

Everyone knows the song, but when I think back now and look at my life in recent years, those lyrics have a deafening meaning.

Yesterday, all my troubles seemed so far away.
Now it looks as though they're here to stay.
Oh I believe in yesterday.

Suddenly, I'm not half the man I used to be.
There's a shadow hanging over me.
Oh yesterday came suddenly.

Why, she, had to go.
I don't know, she wouldn't say.
I, said, something wrong
Now I long for yesterday

CONCLUSION

The entire song has significant meaning, but the last verse hits the hardest. There comes a time in everyone's life when they are faced with their own mortality. It is a given that as we age the things that we once took for granted are now not only a struggle but a distant memory.

What is important though is that just because we can't run, jump, build, create, or do things like we used to, doesn't mean we should shut up shop and wait for the inevitable.

It was recently that I read a brilliant quote that I want to share with you which goes, "Your looks may be gone and your hair may be thin, but there are plenty of good tunes in an old violin."

Just like the book, song, speech, or movie, it doesn't matter what was in the middle, but how we end that really counts. No one remembers which team was on top halfway through the season, or which runner led at the start of the one-hundred-metre Olympic final. They only remember how it finished.

As I draw to a close on this long-winded tale, bringing all of it together is my utmost priority. Have you ever watched a movie and many things don't make sense, then all of a sudden something happens towards the end and you get it?

That's precisely how a good screenwriter should write their story. Big and little things throughout the script seem to be throw-away moments or lines, but then all of a sudden, it all comes together.

Sometimes you get so lost in a cause that you lose track of its original purpose. Like REO Speedwagon wrote when he sang the line "I've forgotten what I started fighting for", I too have forgotten on occasions what I was doing this for. Then I remembered that Breeana no longer had a voice and that she couldn't tell people how she felt, what she was thinking, or what she did on that fateful night in 2013.

People can speculate on how she felt or what she was thinking and that is fine by me. I too have my own opinions on that, but at the end of the day, none of it matters. We will never know exactly what she was thinking or how she felt and no one in the world knows what happened in her final moments on earth; except for me.

Just like Lindy Chamberlain and Schapelle Corby and their individual cases, I am the only person in the world who absolutely knows about what happened to Breeana Robinson on the 29th of January 2013 and that is why I have continued to push to have the truth about her death made public.

As I stated in "The Blame Game" in 2016, despite my thoughts on her mother, aunty, family, or friends, the only thing I cared about was to ensure that they all knew the truth. As her partner and the last person to see her alive, I felt that it was my duty to make sure that the truth did not get manipulated or distorted like so many other things pertaining to her last few months.

Sometimes the truth hurts, and I know that some people don't want to hear it. I know the truth is so very hard for Breeana's family to accept and I promise you, it has fucking hurt like hell for me too, despite knowing the truth all along.

Having lost both parents, I know that death is hard to accept at the best of times. But when it's someone so young and with so much to live for, it is all the harder to get your head around it.

There will always be many unanswered questions surrounding Breeana's suicide. I've tried my best to answer some of them in my books, but even for me, some questions will forever remain a mystery.

Beyond all the loss, despair, anger, and grief that followed her death, Breeana gave me the greatest gift anyone has ever given me. You see, once you witness someone take their last breath and take their own life in the way that I saw, any other challenge that life presents after that pales in significance.

Once you deal with something like that, you know with every fibre of your body that you can overcome anything. I now look at things that once upon a time would have upset me, pissed me off, or caused me gut-wrenching pain, and I simply brush them aside like a fly annoying a dog.

This is not to say things don't happen. I just see them as minor disruptions, rather than life-altering events like most people do. I've found that not getting wound up or emotional about challenges also allows me to keep a clear mind and therefore formulate a plan to deal with a challenge as it arises.

Breeana's suicide has taught me how wonderful perspective is in life and while I may not have wanted this lesson prior to that night in 2013, I am eternally grateful to my beautiful girl Breeana Elaine Stewart Robinson for it now.

As my amazing lawyer Chris Hannay said to the media outside court when I was first charged with murder, "There are no winners in this situation." Breeana's family has lost a beautiful daughter, sister, and niece. Her friends have lost the sweetest friend, and I have lost the most wonderful partner any man could hope for. Nothing any of us do can bring her back. In my opinion, the best thing to do is to remember her as the wonderful soul she was; and still is - now in heaven.

CONCLUSION

At the end of the day, nothing has changed from the night Breeana committed suicide. I have always been innocent in relation to Breeana's death. I didn't need a jury, a judge, police, DNA, a coroner, or anyone else to tell me this fact. This hasn't changed over the past decade and it won't over the next five decades either.

> "Don't bet against me. You can't defeat someone who knows exactly who they are" – Oprah Winfrey

When you know something is true in your heart, no one can ever take that away; no matter how hard they try. If you believe in yourself and believe in who you are, that can never be stolen from you. That, along with your dignity.

Despite the relentless abuse and low tactics by Breeana's aunty, the police, and the media, I have maintained my dignity and acted in a way that allowed me to rise above all of the challenges that I faced.

At my adopted father's funeral in 2015, my biological mother watched on as I held my head high in front of my daughter's mother and grandmother, as they tried their best to bait me; as they had done for twenty years.

Sue left a voicemail the following day and said how proud she was of me and how well I had handled myself on what was already a challenging occasion. This was heart-warming to know that someone noticed that I had been determined to act in a way that Breeana would have wanted in honouring her and not turning her death into a circus.

If you are true to yourself, hold steadfast to your truest beliefs, and act with dignity, these qualities will shine through in the end. Forgive yourself for your mistakes and forgive those who you believe have done wrong by you.

I have no idea whether Breeana's family will ever let go of their resentment, or if they will ever stop hating me and forgive me as I have forgiven them. One thing I do know though is that it doesn't matter what they say or think because…..

> **"What other people think of me; is none of my business."**

God Bless
J.D Mo'orea
(The author)

WHAT OTHER PEOPLE THINK OF YOU IS NONE OF YOUR BUSINESS

RECOMMENDED READING

Below is a list of some of the books and authors I have quoted throughout this book. They are a small portion of the 1,500+ books I have read over the last six years. As a part of your journey, I highly recommend all of these wonderful authors and their books as a part of your quest for a greater life.

If you wish to view my entire reading list, it is available at http://jdmoorea.com/reading-list/

Conversations with God – Neale Donald Walsch

The monk who sold his Ferrari – Robin Sharma

Teo Te Ching – Lao Tzu

Man's search for meaning – Viktor E Frankl

The Alchemist – Paulo Coelho

The power of now – Eckhart Tolle

The law of attraction – Esther & Jerry Hicks

Ask and it is given – Esther & Jerry Hicks

Money master the game – Tony Robbins

Think and grow rich – Napoleon Hill

As a man thinketh – James Allen

RECOMMENDED AUTHORS

The authors listed below are all world leaders in their fields of expertise. I urge you to tap into their incredible wealth of knowledge by reading any of their books.

Dr. Wayne Dyer, Tony Robbins, Deepak Chopra, Dr. John Demartini, Bob Proctor, Joe Vitale, Joyce Meyer, Napoleon Hill, Esther & Jerry Hicks, Paul Hanna, Sir Richard Branson, Marianne Williamson, Gary Vaynerchuk, Ram Das, Dalai Lama, Joel Osteen, Paul Clitheroe, Rhonda Byrne, Michael Bernard Beckwith, Jim Rohn, Brian Tracey, Robin Sharma.

CONCLUSION

For more information regarding my other books, "C.R.U.I.S.E", "The No B.S Approach to Create the life you want", "The Ultimate Musician's Party", Blogs, or My C.R.U.I.S.E Apparel, head to www.jdmoorea.com

Oh. And keep your eyes open for a little movie called
"Through the Eyes of Love."